Pope Clement XIV

Interesting letters of the late Pope Clement XIV. (Ganganelli.)

Pope Clement XIV

Interesting letters of the late Pope Clement XIV. (Ganganelli.)

ISBN/EAN: 9783741129100

Manufactured in Europe, USA, Canada, Australia, Japa

Cover: Foto ©Andreas Hilbeck / pixelio.de

Manufactured and distributed by brebook publishing software (www.brebook.com)

Pope Clement XIV

Interesting letters of the late Pope Clement XIV. (Ganganelli.)

Permansura tibi quæ sacrat marmora Virtus,
Tempus edax, Clemens, sternere falce nequit.

INTERESTING LETTERS

OF the Late

POPE CLEMENT XIV.

Giovanni Vincenzo Antonio

(GANGANELLI.)

Translated from the ONLY GENUINE EDITION of LOTTIN, jun. Bookseller, in PARIS.

Exactly REVISED, CORRECTED, and ENLARGED,

WITH

A TRANSLATION of the LATIN PASSAGES,

AND

A COPIOUS INDEX to the Whole.

NEWCASTLE:

Printed by T. SAINT, for W. CHARNLEY.

MDCCLXXVII.

AN EXPLANATION

OF THE

FRONTISPIECE.

THE FRONTISPIECE reprefents TIME, aftonifhed to fee his Scythe broken againft the bafe of a Pyramid, erected in honour of CLEMENT XIV, which he in vain attempts to deftroy, and reduce to the ftate of the mouldering monuments behind him.

It is accompanied with a LAUREL, a Symbol of the glory this Great Pope acquired during his Pontificate; and is adorned with the attributes, which characterize Science and Immortality.

The Lines at the bottom may be thus tranflated.

*This Pyle, to CLEMENT rais'd by virtue's hand,
In spite of all-devouring Time shall stand.*

The Editor's Preface.

THE fale of thefe Letters, which may be called an *Explofion*, is, beyond contradiction, their greateft Elogium. The Authenticity of them could never be contefted, if people would fimply judge of them from the ftriking conformity they bear to the learning, genius and conduct of CLEMENT XIV.

Befides the honourable teftimonies borne by ftrangers and the learned to GANGANELLI before his Pontificate, as to a perfonage the moft affable, the moft impartial, the moft pacific and the moft enlightened; the fuppreffion of the Bull *In Cænâ Domini*, a perfect harmony re-eftablifhed between the Court of ROME and the Monarchs, who were offended at it, teach the whole world, that this IMMORTAL PONTIFF was influenced neither by opinions nor prejudices; and that he really thought too much deference could not be fhewn to thofe Potentates, who were ever the Protectors of the Holy See; and that the Popes will never be more powerful than when fupported by the houfe of BOURBON.

Thus the Letters of CLEMENT XIV are fully juftified by his conduct and fentiments. There are found in them the fame principles with refpect to Religion, which he always publickly taught; the fame maxims which he followed during the courfe of his life; the fame good fenfe which ever kept him clear of whatever favoured of Fanaticifm and Superftition.

But what evidently proves that thefe Letters are not fuppofitious, is, that having myfelf copied a certain number of them at FLORENCE in the year 1758, from Originals communicated to me by the Prelate CERATI, and Abbè LAMI, I was defirous of publifhing them in the year 1762; and I received the following anfwer from F. GANGANELLI, then become Cardinal, whofe

a   confen

consent I had desired: an answer, which I now have before me, and which I can shew to any one, who is willing to see it.

ILLMO SIGRE

LE lettre che hanno communicate a Fiorenze, a V. S. Illma sono state scritte con precipitazione, e non meritano affatto l'onore ch'ella vuol compiacersi di far loro, dandole alla luce; motivo per cui prego istantemente V. S. Illma a non divulgarle. Quel c'ho scritto non ha per merito che la verita, e la Schietezza. Nulla di meno le no sono molto tenuto, e saro sempre riconoscente al di lei zelo, che in qualunque sia si rincontro, le ne testificaro la mia gratitudine, & con tutta la stima mi ratifico di V. S. Illma servid. vero,

F. LORO Card. GANGANELLI.

Roma, 19 di Sett. 1762.

SIR,

THE letters communicated to you at Florence, were written in haste, and no way deserve the honour you are desirous to do them by making them public. Therefore I earnestly beg you would not publish them. What I have written hath no other merit than truth and sincerity. My obligations are no less to you, and shall always be so grateful for the affection you testify for me, that I will seek every occasion to shew you my gratitude, and to give proofs of the esteem with which I profess myself your humble servant,

F. LAWRENCE, Cardinal GANGANELLI.

Rome, Sept. 19, 1762.

It is therefore manifest that, so early as 1762, I had some genuine Letters of GANGANELLI; and it is not less evident, that those which have been sent me in the course of the last year, are so like the others, that no body can be deceived in them. Hence the Author of the *Journal of the Sciences and the fine Arts*, has reason to say, that whoever will allow only three of the Letters to have been written by CLEMENT XIV, must allow all to be so; because the same soul and the same genius dictated them all: the Connoisseurs cannot be deceived in this point.

Whoever

The EDITOR's PREFACE.

Whoever has any practice or taste, will easily distinguish in letters, as well as in painting, an original from a copy. CLEMENT XIV, every where shews his soul, and that is the only thing, which cannot be copied. Moreover it is a thing so extraordinary, that GANGANELLI, raised by his merit to the dignity of Cardinal and Pope, celebrated by the famous F. BERTI, an Augustinian Friar, in a public act as a personage in whom ROME had a right to glory; boasted of by several Cities in ITALY, as one of the most eloquent Panegyrists; taken notice of by LAMBERTINI (BENEDICT XIV) as a most promising young man: lastly cited as a most rare man by the Authors, who have written on ITALY; is it, I say a thing so extraordinary, that he should write ingenious and learned letters? Had it not been for a party-spirit, which would have GANGANELLI pass for a man of only indifferent parts, no person would ever think of disputing their authenticity.

If CLEMENT XIV had left behind him a powerful family; if a spirit of party had discovered itself in his Letters; if the work in itself had been only of the middling kind, and had stood in need of a respectable name to make it pass, there might be some reason to suspect interest or passion: but here a man is forced to acknowledge the truth.

The ITALIANS are wrongfully accused of being acquainted with only a superstitious devotion: the most excellent book we have on enlightened piety comes from MURATORI; and no one is ignorant, that BENEDICT XIV proved by his Discourses, as well as by his Writings, his sovereign contempt for trifling practices of devotion; and that the Sacred College at all times has had men truly bright.

It is no less certain, that there are found in the Cloisters, and especially in ITALY, Religious men of knowledge, principles, and views; and who want nothing, in order to become great men, but an opportunity of shewing their talents. Put, for instance, in some eminent place, F. GERDIL, a Barnabite, Preceptor to the Prince of PIEDMONT, and you would, no doubt,

see

see genius, learning, and a piety difengaged from every thing that is Pharifaical, and a party-fpirit, fhine forth in his perfon. A man muft not know the ITALIANS, to difpute their being able to write fuch ingenious and fenfible letters.

The objection ftarted againft this work, and induftriouſly circulated, drawn from hence, viz. that there are people even in ROME itfelf, who have no knowledge of them, is undeferving of a refutation. When a perfon writes a letter, he doth not call in his neighbour or friend to witnefs it; and it every day happens, that even thofe we live with, do not know our correfpondence.

But it will be faid, that it would be the fhorteft way to let people know how the letters in queftion were procured: but as it is an affair of confidence, and thofe from whom we had them, are unwilling to be known, it is impoffible to betray their fecret. It requires no great effort of fenfe to guefs what the motives of their fecrefy may be: thefe will be made known one day or other, and they will be found well grounded.*

The reafon why the SUPPLEMENT,† which the public waits for with fo much impatience, hath not yet appeared is, that the productions of GANGANELLI are not manufactured in FRANCE, as fome give it out, but that authentic pieces are wanted to fill it. Thofe which I already have, with others which I am promifed, will enable me hereafter to publifh another volume abfolutely diftinct from the *Letters*, but not lefs interefting: therein will be found fome curious Anecdotes, and pieces of extraordinary Eloquence. The Abbé FABRI, Nephew to CLEMENT XIV, will take on himfelf the trouble of publifhing the Theological Treatifes of the late Pope, and which are immenfely efteemed. It is thus he wrote to me concerning them, from *Rome*, the 6th of February

---

* The Tranflator has here omitted above two pages in the Original, as they regard only the faults which had crept into the firft Edition, but which are corrected in this.

† This *Supplement* is defigned to be given the public in the fame fize and type with the letters.

laft:

The EDITOR's PREFACE. vi

laſt: *Li quali di qui a non molto io ſteſſo mandero alla luce.*

I have only to add, that poſthumous works are generally ſuſpected; and that notwithſtanding the Arret of Parliament, which Monſ. BOSSUET, Biſhop of TROYES, formerly obtained to aſſure the Public, that the productions he publiſhed under his Uncle's name, were really the works of that great Prelate, many people ſtill obſtinately refuſe to believe it. But it may be obſerved, that it is always prejudice, or ſome ſpirit of party, or ſome perſonal intereſt, which engages people to contradict and deny what they do not know.

Theſe Letters will ſubſiſt in ſpite of whatever can be ſaid about them; and the older they grow, the more honour they will do to GANGANELLI, his age and country, becauſe the *remembrance of the righteous man ſhall be eternal*,* and he hath nothing to fear from people's prepoſſeſſions or prejudices.

The Counterfeits, which are multiplied on all ſides, and ſwarm with faults, oblige me to repeat here again, that the only Edition, which is accurate and genuine, is that ſold by *Lottin*, Junior, Bookſeller at *Paris*, ſigned and marked by him.

The perſons guilty of the counterfeits I have mentioned, when they printed the LIFE OF CLEMENT XIV, took it from the firſt Edition, which was very imperfect in compariſon of the laſt: and having prefixed it to the two volumes of his Letters, they ſold and publiſhed them every where, as an Edition enlarged more than one-third.

* Pſ. cxi. *Vulg.*

INTERESTING LETTERS

OF

POPE CLEMENT XIV.

LETTER I.

To Monsieur DE CABANE, *a Knight of Malta.*

SIR,

THE SOLITUDE you have formed for yourself in the bottom of your own heart renders it unnecessary for you to seek any other. Cloisters are of no value, but in proportion to the recollection of mind enjoyed in them: The walls do not constitute the merit of a Monastery.

The house of la TRAPPE which we have in Italy, and to which you wish to retire, is no less regular than that in France. But why should

should a man quit the world, while he edifies it?—It will forever be perverse, if all good Men abandon it.

Is not moreover the Order of MALTA in which you live, a religious State, and capable of sanctifying you, if you comply with the Duties of it?

A person ought to think seriously, before he overcharge himself with obligations. The GOSPEL is the true Rule of a Christian; and the vocation is to be well tried, before a man bury himself in solitude.

Whatever withdraws us from the common mode of life is an extraordinary way; and a person ought to be apprehensive of illusion, when he embraces a Cenobitic life. I have the greatest regard for the solitaries, who follow the Institute of the CHARTREUSE and la TRAPPE; but they ought to be few. Besides the difficulty of finding a great number of fervent Religious; the impoverishment of the state is to be apprehended, by rendering ourselves useless to society. We are not born *Monks;* we are born *Citizens* The world stands in need of subjects to promote its harmony, and to make Empires flourish by their talents, labours and manners.—Those profound solitudes, where people give no exterior signs of life, are real tombs.

SAINT

SAINT ANTHONY, who lived so long in the desert, had not made a vow to remain there for ever. He quitted his retreat, and came into the heart of ALEXANDRIA to attack Arianism, and to disperse the Arians; being convinced that we are obliged to serve Religion and the State, more by our actions. than by our prayers. When he had therefore fulfilled his mission, he returned to his solitude, mortified to carry back thither the small quantity of blood, which old age had left in his veins, and that he had not suffered Martyrdom.

When you go to la TRAPPE, it is true, you will pray night and day; but cannot you continually raise your heart to God, though in the midst of the world? Vocal prayers constitute not the merit of praying. The divine Legislator hath himself informed us, that a multiplicity of words will not procure us the assistance of heaven.

Several respectable writers scruple not to say, that the relaxation introduced into Monasteries, partly proceeded from the multiplication of the offices. They judged very truly, that the attention could not be kept up in prayers of too great a length; and that manual labour was of more advantage, than the continual chanting of Psalms.

The world would not have cried out so much against Monks, had it seen them employed in useful labours. The memory of those is still blessed, who first cleared the fields, and enriched the towns with learned productions, respecting both historical facts, and the date of events.

The BENEDICTINE Monks of the learned Congregation of St MAUR in France, whom we commonly call *Maurini*, have gained themselves a reputation, which will last a long time, by publishing a multitude of works, equally curious and useful. The famous F. MOUNTFAUCON, who is not one of their least ornaments, filled all Italy with his erudition, when he gave himself entirely up to the study of Antiquity.

SAINT BERNARD, the reformer of so many Monasteries, which still follow his rule, did great service to Religion and his country, not by preaching up the Croisades (which nothing can justify but the intention of them) but by giving solid advice to Popes and Kings, and composing immortal works—He never would have been a Father of the Church, had he done nothing but pray.

F. MABILLON, in his famous *Treatise on Monastic Studies*, appears to me to have much the advantage of the *Abbé de Rancé*, who

pretends

pretends that Monks ought to apply themfelves folely to Contemplation and Pfalmody. The deftination of man is to labour. " There " is only one ftep from a contemplative to an " idle life," faid Cardinal PALEOTTI; and nothing is more eafy than to pafs from one to the other.

You will do more good by aiding the poor, and confoling them by your difcourfe, than by burying yourfelf in a defert. JOHN THE BAPTIST, who was the greateft among the fons of men, quitted it to preach the kingdom of God, and to baptize on the banks of the *Jordan.*

Do not imagine, my Dear Sir, that while I fpeak of an ufeful life, my defign is to make an apology for the Mendicant Orders to the difparagement of the folitaries. Each Religious Order hath its own practices; and here it is we may fay: *Let not he that eats not flefh, defpife him who eats it.* But I own that I have the greateft efteem for the ftate of the FRIARS-MINORS, in as much as they join the active life of MARTHA with the contemplative life of MARY: and whatever fome fpiritualifts may pretend, I think this kind of life more meritorious.

SAINT BENEDICT was fenfible of the obligation of being ufeful to one's country; and therefore

therefore built seminaries for young Gentlemen at *Monte-Caſſino.*—He underſtood the rules dictated by the love of our neighbour.

If, notwithſtanding what I have alledged, you ſtill find a ſecret inſpiration, which calls you to a Cenobitic life, act therein as you like; for I ſhould be afraid of oppoſing the will of God, who leads his ſervants, as he pleaſes, and often by ſingular ways.

I wiſh I could be with you at Tivoli, to contemplate there that famous Caſcade, which dividing itſelf into a thouſand different ſtreams, and falling down with the greateſt impetuoſity, repreſents, in the moſt expreſſive manner, the world with all its agitation, and hurry.

I wiſh you joy on the approaching feſtival, and am more, than all the Eloquence of Cicero could expreſs, ſir, your moſt humble ſervant, &c.

  Brother Lawrence Ganganelli,
  Of the Convent of the Holy Apoſtles.
      Oct. 29, 1747.

My moſt humble reſpects to the very worthy Biſhop.

LETTER II.

To the Abbè FERGHEN.

YOU can do nothing better, Abbè, towards diffipating your pains and troubles, than to vifit Italy. Every man of underftanding owes homage to this country fo much boafted of, and fo deferving of it. It will be an inexpreffible fatisfaction for me to fee you there.

You will firft of all difcover the bulwarks which nature hath given it in the *Apennins,* and the *Alpes,* which feparate us from the *French,* and from which circumftance we have obtained from them the name of *Ultramontanes.* They are majeftic mountains, made to ferve as a frame to the magnificent picture they furround.

Torrents, ftreams, rivers (to fay nothing of the feas) are other objects which prefent to the travellers and painters the moft curious and moft interefting profpects.

Nothing can be more wonderful than the richeft foil, every where interfected with ftreams of frefh water; every where peopled with villages; every where embellifhed with fuperb cities:—And fuch is *Italy.*

If Agriculture was here held in as much esteem as Architecture; if the country was not divided under so many Governments, all of a different form, and most of them weak and of small extent, one would not there find misery close to magnificence, and industry without activity.—But unhappily people are there more taken up with the embellishment of the towns, than the culture of the grounds; and on every side uncultivated lands reproach the inhabitants with their sloth.

If you enter by Venice, you will see a city, which, for its situation, is the only one of its kind. It is exactly an immense ship, lying still on the water, and on which you cannot go aboard without boats.

But this is not the only thing which will surprize you by its singularity. Inhabitants masked during four or five months of the year; the laws of a Despotic Government, which however allow the greatest liberties in the public diversions; the rights of a Sovereign, who hath no authority; the customs of a people afraid of their own shadow, and who enjoy at the same time the most perfect tranquillity, form so many contrasts, which must be particularly interesting to a traveller. There is scarce a single Venetian, who is not eloquent, and Collections have been made of

sallies

fallies of wit from the very *Gondoliers*, replete with the moſt poignant ſalt.

FERRARA will ſhew you within its encloſure a beautiful and vaſt ſolitude, almoſt as ſilent as the tomb of ARIOSTO, who is buried there.

BOLOGNA will preſent you with another picture. You will there find even the fair ſex intimately acquainted with the Sciences, and appearing, with dignity, in the Schools and Academies, where every day trophies are erected to them. A thouſand paintings will gratify your ſoul and eyes, and the converſation of the Inhabitants will charm your mind.

You will afterwards, in the ſpace of about a hundred leagues, paſs through a multitude of ſmall towns, each of which hath its Theatre, its *Caſino* (or Rendezvous for the Gentry) ſome man of learning, or Poet, who employs himſelf according to his taſte and leiſure.

You will viſit LORETTO, a pilgrimage famous for the concourſe of ſtrangers, and the treaſures which enrich its ſuperb temple.

You will at length come within ſight of ROME, which may be ſeen for a thouſand years together, and always with new pleaſure. This city, placed on ſeven hills, which the Ancients called the Seven Miſtreſſes of the world, ſeems from thence to rule the univerſe,

verse, and haughtily to tell all nations, that she is their Queen and their Capital.

You will call to mind the ancient Romans (whose memory will never be blotted out) when you cast your eyes on the TIBER, of which they have so often spoken, and which hath been so often swollen with their blood, and that of their enemies.

You will be in an extasy at the sight of the BASILIC of St. PETER, which the Connoisseurs call the wonder of the world, as being infinitely superior to Saint SOPHIA's at CONSTANTINOPLE, Saint PAUL's at LONDON, or the temple of SOLOMON itself.

It is a building which grows larger and larger, as you go through it; where every thing is Colossal, and yet every thing appears of an ordinary size. The Paintings are enravishing: the Mausoleums alive: and a person imagines he sees the new Jerusalem coming down from heaven, described by *St. John* in the Revelation.

You will find in the whole, and in every particular part of the VATICAN (raised on the ruins of the false Oracles) beauties of every kind, which will at once tire and charm your eyes. It is there where RAPHAEL and MICHAEL ANGELO have displayed, sometimes in the terrible, sometimes in the tender way, the
master-

master-pieces of their genius, by expressing, in the most lively manner, the full energy of their own souls. It is there that the learning and wit of all the writers in the world are deposited in a multitude of works, which compose the richest and most immense Library.

Churches, Palaces, Squares, Pyramids, Obelisks, Columns, Galleries, Facades, Theatres, Fountains, Gardens, Landscapes, every thing will tell you, that you are at ROME, and every thing attach you to it, as to the City, which hath been ever universally admired in preference to all others. You will not indeed meet there with that French elegance, which prefers what is pretty to what is majestic; but that loss will be compensated by the objects you will find every instant to excite your admiration.

In a word, you will see a new world in all the pieces of painting and of sculpture both of the ancients and moderns, and you will imagine this world animated. The Academy of Painting, occupied by the *French*, will shew you pupils destined one day to become great masters, and who do honour to ITALY by coming thither to receive lessons.

You will admire the Grandeur and Simplicity of the HEAD of the Church, the servant of the servants of God in the order of hu-

milit y

mility, and the first of men in the eyes of faith. The CARDINALS, with whom he is surrounded, will reprefent to you the four and twenty Elders, who ftand round the Throne of the Lamb; for you will find them as modeft in their deportment, as edifying in their manners.

The misfortune is, that this magnificent view will terminate in a group of beggars, which ROME, by pouring forth ill-judged charities, injudicioufly fupports in idlenefs, inftead of fetting them to fome ufeful employment.—Thus the thorn fhews itfelf with the rofe; and vice is too often found clofe by virtue.

But if you have a mind to fee ROME in its fplendour, endeavour to be here by the feaft of St. PETER.

The illumination of the Church begins with a mild light, which one would willingly take for the reflection of the fetting fun. It caufes the moft beautiful pieces of Architecture to ftart forth, and then ends in undulating flames, which form a moving picture, and which laft till day-break. This is accompanied with the playing off two pieces of fireworks, the brightnefs of which is fo great, that one would imagine the ftars had detached

tached themselves from the heavens, and were falling down with a noise.

I shall say nothing to you of the strange metamorphosis, which hath placed, even in the Capitol, Friars of the order of St. Francis, and hath made a new ROME come out from the very ruins of the ancient ROME; to teach the whole world, that Christianity is truly the work of God, and that it hath subjugated the Conquerors of the world, to settle itself in the centre of their possessions.

If the new Romans do not appear to you of a warlike disposition, it is owing to their present form of Government not inspiring them with valour; for they have in themselves the germ or bud of every virtue, and make as good soldiers as any others, when they bear arms in the service of a foreign power. It is certain, they are very ingenious and have a singular aptitude for the sciences: and one would imagine they were born Pantomimes, so expressive are they in their gestures from their very infancy.

You will go from hence to NAPLES by the famous APPIAN way, which, unhappily, its great antiquity renders at this day very inconvenient; and you will come to that PARTHENOPE, where rest the ashes of VIRGIL, on

whose

whose tomb is seen to grow a laurel, that could be no where better placed.

On one side Mount Vesuvius, on another the Elysian Fields will present you with objects, the only ones of their kind; and when you are satisfied with them, you will find yourself surrounded by a multitude of Neapolitans, full of life and wit, but too much abandoned to pleasure and sloth to be what they might be. Naples would be an inchanting city, did we not there meet with a croud of plebeians, who have all the air of beggars and thieves, often without being either the one or the other.

The Churches are richly ornamented, but with an Architecture of a bad taste, no way corresponding to that of Rome. You will take a singular pleasure in going through the Environs of this city, delightful for its fruits, its prospects, its situation: and you will penetrate those famous subterraneous passages, where the city of Herculaneum was formerly swallowed up by an eruption of Mount Vesuvius. If perchance it should be in a passion, when you are there, you would see torrents of fire coming from its bosom, majestically spread themselves over the country. Portici will present to you a collection of what hath been gathered from the ruins
of

of HERCULANEUM, and the neighbourhood of PUZZUOLI, celebrated by the prince of Poets, will infpire you with a tafte for Poetry.

You muft go thither with the *Eneid* in your hand, and confront what VIRGIL fays with the Cave of the CUMEAN SYBIL and with the ACHERON.

You will return by CASERTA, which for its decorations, its marbles, its extent, its aqueducts, worthy of ancient ROME, will be the fineft CHATEAU in Europe; and you will pay a vifit to MONTE CASSINO, where the fpirit of St. BENEDICT ftill fubfifts, for near twelve centuries paft, without any interruption, notwithftanding the immenfe riches of that fuperb monaftery.

FLORENCE, where the fine arts firft fprung up, and where the moft magnificent mafterpieces are depofited, will prefent you with other objects. You will there admire a city, which is fo handfome and prettily decorated, that it ought not to be fhewn, but on Sundays; according to the remark of a Portuguefe.

There are every where feen traces of the fplendour and elegance of the MEDICIS, who are infcribed in the annals of tafte, as the Reftorers of the fine arts.

LEGHORN,

Leghorn, a Sea-port, as populous, as it is profitable to Tuscany. Pisa, which hath always continued to have fchools, and learned men of every kind: Sienna, famous for the purity of its air and language will entertain you, one after another, in a very particular manner. Parma, fituated in the midft of the moft fertile paftures, will fhew you a Theatre, which holds fourteen thoufand people, and where each one hears what ever is faid, though only in a whifper: and Placentia will appear worthy of the name it bears, as an abode which, for its agreeable fituation, particularly pleafes travellers.

You will not forget Modena, as being the native country of the Illuftrious Muratori, and as a city famous for the name it hath given its fovereigns.

At Milan you will find the fecond Church in Italy for grandeur and beauty. Above ten thoufand marble ftatues decorate the outfide of it; and had it but a Front, it would be a mafter-piece of workmanfhip. The converfation of the inhabitants is perfectly agreeable fince the French befieged it. People live there as they do at Paris; and every thing, even to the Hofpital, hath an air of fplendour. The Ambrosian Library is interefting to the curious, and the Ambrosian Rite

is

is no lefs so, particularly to an Ecclefiaftic, who is fond of knowing the practices of the Church, as well as their antiquity.

From the account you will receive of the BORROMEAN ISLANDS, they will invite you to go to fee them. Placed in the middle of a moſt delightful lake, they prefent to your fight whatever is moſt magnificent and pleaſing in Gardens.

GENOA will prove that ſhe is truly the STATELY, by her Churches and Palaces. It is remarkable for its Port, famed for its commerce, and refort of Strangers: and there is feen a DOGE, who is changed almoſt like the fuperiours of Religious Communities, and hath little more authority.

Laſtly TURIN, the refidence of a Court, where the Virtues have long taken up their abode, will charm you with the regularity of its buildings, the beauty of its fquares, the parallellifm of its ftreets, the wit of its inhabitants; and there you will agreeably end your journey.

I have thus, as you fee, made the tour of Italy in a very expeditious manner, and at a ſmall expence, to engage you really to come thither. Moreover it is enough for a man like you, to give him only a fketch of a picture.

D I fay

I say nothing of our manners: they are not more corrupted than those of other nations, whatever malice may assert to the contrary. They only vary in the shades according to the difference of Government: for the Roman resembles not the Genoese, nor does the Venetian resemble the Neapolitan: and one may say of Italy, as well as of the whole world, that, allowing some trifling difference, it is here as elsewhere: " a little good, and a " deal of bad."

I say nothing to you before hand of the agreeable chearfulness of the Italians, any more than I do of their love for the arts and sciences; it is what you will soon know, when you become acquainted with them, and especially, as your own conversation is so charming, that it will be always a pleasure to say to you : I am your very humble and obedient servant.

I have taken the opportunity of a moment's leisure to give you an idea of my country. It is only a coarse piece of painting, whereas from another hand it would have been a charming piece in Miniature. The subject were worth attempting, but my pencil is not fine enough to execute it.

Rome, Nov. 12, 1756.

LETTER III.

To one of his Sisters.

THE loss we have suffered by the death of so many Relations and friends, tells us, my dear sister, that this life is, in reality, only a borrowed life, and that God alone essentially possesses immortality. But what ought to be our comfort is, that we shall meet together again in him, if we constantly fix our hearts on him.

The pains you tell me you suffer, ought to be more precious to you than pleasures, if you have faith. Mount CALVARY is, here below, the place of a Christian: if ever he goes up to the top THABOR, it is only to stop there for an instant.

My health continues equally vigorous, because I neither flatter nor pamper it. My stomach would sometimes be indisposed, but I tell it, that I am not at leisure to attend to it, and it then lets me alone. Study absorbs all those surd indispositions, of which man so frequently complains. It often happens that idleness is the only cause of our indisposition: and many women are ill, without knowing where their illness is, merely because they have nothing to do. People grow tired of being too well; and too great a share of health is burthenfome to people of the world.

I am glad to hear fuch good news of little MICHAEL. He is a plant, which, well cultivated, will one day produce excellent fruit: all depends on a proper culture—a man becomes every thing, or nothing, according to his education.

You lament that we fee not one another; but it is neither our figure nor our words, which form our friendfhip. Provided our affections and our thoughts bring us together, it is of no confequence at what diftance our perfons are. When we love one another in God, we always fee one another, becaufe God is every where.—He ought to be the centre of all our feelings, as he is that of all fpirits.

I embrace you moft cordially, and am fenfible of the value of the letters you write to me. They recall to my remembrance a Father, whom I knew too fhort a time; and a Mother, whofe life was a continual leffon of virtue. I never fail remembring them at the altar, any more than I do you, my dear fifter, whofe moft humble and affectionate brother and fervant I am beyond all expreffion, &c.

LETTER IV.

To Monſignor Bouget, *private Chamberlain to his Holineſs.*

Monsignor,

I Will not fail to accept of your gracious invitation, as from a man, who unites in his perſon, wit, ſcience, and chearfulneſs. If ever melancholy ſhould offer to lay hold on me, I would ſeek your agreeable converſation, the value of which Benedict XIV perfectly knows, and which would have made the ſame impreſſion on Saul as did David's harp. You have the talent of relating things in a moſt rapid and moſt intereſting manner. Mere nothings, by the turn you give them, become matter of a ſolid converſation.

It is ſome time ſince we met at the Trinity of the Mount. Our French Minims deſerve to be frequently viſited: no man can help being fond of them, who loves the ſciences and ſociety: and this fondneſs for them is encreaſed, when you are there.

When you come to ſee me, I will ſhew you my reflections on a cauſe, which will engage your attention. There are of all ſorts in the Holy Office. Some make a man laugh; ſome make him ſigh: but be not afraid of my read-

ing

ing to you any thing of the moft gloomy kind.—The great art of fociety is to know how to ferve people according to their tafte.

Chearfulnefs is the true Phyfician of the ftudious: after being confined by obftinate labour, both the mind and the heart require to be fet at liberty. It is as neceffary for the foul to expand itfelf, if we defire to recover our verdure and bloom, as it is for a tree to enjoy the open air. There are however fome people, who refemble the rofe out of flower, which fhews us nothing but bark and thorns. When I meet with them, I fay not a word; but pafs by in a hurry for fear of being pricked.

Chearfulnefs keeps off old age. With it a man always looks frefh, inftead of being wan, and wrinkled; the effect of uneafinefs and cares.

The reafon why BENEDICT XIV. enjoys fo good a ftate of health, is that he is always extremely chearful. He lays down his pen, to vent fome *bons mots*; then he takes it up again, and is never tired.

You have done very well to ingraft the Italian chearfulnefs on the French: it is the way to live an hundred years. This is what I wifh you, being, beyond what I can exprefs, MONSIGNOR, your very humble, &c.

LETTER V.

To the Most Reverend Abbot *of* Monte Cassino.

Most Reverend,

YOU do me too much honour in consulting me with respect to the date of your two manuscripts. By comparing them with the writing of the ninth Century, I take them to be of that age. Moreover one of our Authors, who lived in that age, and is little known (though we have some fragments of his on the Sacrifice of the Mass) is cited in those Manuscripts.

It is very generous in you to deign to take the opinion of a poor Franciscan, when you are the Head of an Order, perfectly acquainted with Antiquity; and which hath given the most shining and most honourable proofs thereof in every part of the world. "We should have been the greatest fools, said In- nocent XI *(Odescalchi)* had it not been for the Benedictine Monks." Besides being the glory of the Holy See, and of different Churches, for whole ages together, they were moreover the Fathers and preservers of history. It was with them the Monarchs found their

most

moſt auguſt and moſt intereſting title-deeds; and with them learning and religion were preſerved without interruption, as the moſt precious of depoſites, whilſt the thickeſt cloud ſeemed to cover the Univerſe. Notwithſtanding their riches and power, they were never known to form cabals in kingdoms, or enter into intrigues againſt the State: on the contrary, they have been of great aſſiſtance to it. We may therefore ſay, that notwithſtanding all the riches and honours they enjoy, the public gratitude hath not yet repaid them.

If I can comply with your deſire, I will, with pleaſure, go to that famous ſolitude, out of which have come a whole world of ſaints and learned men. We imagine that, by treading on the ſoil inhabited by great men, we partake of their merit.

Nothing can be added to the profound reſpect with which I am, &c.

Rome, March 5, 1748.

LETTER VI.

To Mr. STUART, *a Scotch Gentleman.*

I Have followed you in spirit, my very dear sir, both by sea, and on the Thames. While my soul alone travels in England, I shall not be insulted: whereas, were I to appear there in person, and in my Friar's garb, God knows how the Mob would use me—You must own that the Popes are a good-natured sort of men: for were they disposed to use reprisals, they would insist, that any Priest, Monk, or Friar should be allowed to enter LONDON in his habit, or that they would suffer no Englishman to come to ROME. And who would be caught there? You first of all, my dear sir, who are fond of visiting ITALY from time to time. But, I protest, I should be more so than you; and you may believe me: for I am sincerely attached to the ENGLISH nation, which has all along cherished the sciences in a distinguished manner, and with which an acquaintance may much improve us. We should be too great losers, were we deprived of seeing it, at least in some of its natives. I have a determined passion for your great Poets and your

your eminent Philosophers. With them a man becomes sublime, and perceives the world beneath his feet. I sometimes pay a visit to NEWTON by night. While all nature seems to sleep, I sit up to read, and admire him. Never did man unite, like him, science with simplicity—It is characteristic of true genius, to be a stranger to puffing and ostentation.

I depend on your bringing for me, at your return, the small manuscript of BERKLEY, that illustrious mad-man, who fancied there was nothing material in the world, and that all bodies existed only in our ideas. What a spectacle for reason, should all the learned, who have bewildered themselves with different systems, meet together, and this same Reason, after having kept *incognito*, come and enlighten them with its rays! How surprized, and abashed at the same time, would they be, they who had the vanity to think themselves more than inspired! The world hath at all times been abandoned to disputes and errours; and we ought to reckon ourselves happy, that, in the midst of so many clouds and contradictions, we have an unerring light to enable us to take the right road. I speak of the TORCH of REVELATION, which, in spite of every effort of Infidelity, will never be extinguished

guished. It is with Religion as with the Firmament, which sometimes appears to us darkened, though in itself it be no less radiant. The passions and sensual pleasures are vapours, which arise from the womb of our corruption, and deprive us of celestial truths: but the man who reflects, without being alarmed or surprised, waits for the return of a clear sky. Ought we not to know, that the fogs raised by the followers of *Celsus*, *Porphyry*, *Spinosa*, *Collins*, and *Bayle*, are dispersed? And those raised by our modern Philosophy will have the same fate. In every age have appeared some men of a singular turn of mind, who, it would seem, sometimes by force of arms, and sometimes by Fanaticism, must have overturned Christianity. They have, however, passed over like those storms, which only serve to make the face of heaven appear more clear and serene.

It is for want of principles to go upon, that people suffer themselves to be puzzled with sophisms. The most despicable objections are looked on as unanswerable, by a man who knows nothing. In Religion every thing is connected, every thing is combined; and if we lose our hold of one single truth, we find nothing before us but abysses and darkness. Man, instead of concluding from the sight of what he enjoys, that God can undoubtedly bestow upon him more wonderful good things after this life, judges that the DEITY, almighty as he is, can go no farther; and that this world is necessarily the term of his Wisdom and Power.

I could like to see a work, which should prove, in a demonstrative manner (nor would it be a difficult task for a person, who understood natural Philosophy and Theology) that the world, as known to us, is, in truth, a riddle. Religion alone can account either for the immensity of the Heavens (the use of which the Unbeliever cannot guess) or for the miseries we suffer, of which the Philosopher cannot find out the cause; or for the ever new-arising desires which agitate us, and whose impetuosity we cannot calm.

We have sometimes touched upon these important subjects in our chat, one while at the *Villa Borghese*, another while at the *Villa Negroni*. That time is now past, and with it a part of our life; because every thing passes away, except the sincere attachment, with which I am most cordially, my dear sir, &c.

Rome, May 13, 1748.

LETTER VII.

To Signora BAZARDI.

CONSULT me not, I beg of you, concerning the Religious state of life, which your son has a mind to embrace. If I tell you that he can do nothing better, you will consider me as an interested man, who speaks in favour of his Order. If on the contrary, I answer, that he will do well not to think of it, you will presume that it is the advice of a Friar disgusted with his state of life, or of one convinced, that the life of a Cloister is a life of misery. So that, Madam, I neither say yes, or do I say no. Every object hath two sides; the question is to know which is the better, and to adopt it.

Did I foresee that a Postulant would become a great man for learning and piety, I would use all my endeavours to determine him: but as I do not know what is to come to pass, I am very much on the reserve, and never advise any one to embrace a Religious state,

I have the honour to be, &c.

Rome, May 13, 1748.

LETTER VIII.

To the Prelate CERATI.

I Cannot pardon you for depriving the public of a multitude of Anecdotes well known to you, a collection of which would be extremely entertaining. When I come to see you again, I will take my pencil with me and write down whatever you say. What would become of the sciences, if all the learned were to follow your plan? The conversation indeed might be lively; but reading, there would be none.

MONSIGNOR CERATI ought to reflect, that when he talks, he is only useful to those about him; and that were he to write, he would render service to persons at the greatest distance. A good book becomes the patrimony of the whole world; it is equally in the hands of the RUSSIAN, and the ITALIAN. The Pope ought to oblige you, under the penalty of Excommunication, to lay open, by printing, whatever you conceal from the knowledge of the public. But perhaps, as you have seen foreign nations, you will not now be so much an *Ultramontane**, but may imagine

---

* In France the exalted opinions which the Italian Schoolmen entertain of the Pope's power, are called *Ultramontane Notions*, and the supporters of them *Ultramontane Divines*. See Let. 2, 25, 47, &c.

that the judgment of a Decree of ROME can be eluded? " He has seen a great deal (said " Cardinal PORTO-CARRERO the other day, " speaking of you) he has read a great deal, " and remembers every thing; but it will be " of no service to us, as he will carry his " knowledge with him to the other world."

Too much has been written; and it makes me sigh, when I consider all those productions, which freethinking has brought forth. But too much can never be written, if we speak of those excellent subjects you are Master of. For my part I will have it in print, that you cannot be too much admired, and that I cannot too often repeat, how much I have the honour to be, &c.

LETTER IX.

To the Marquis CLERICI, *a Milanese.*

Mr. MARQUIS,

GIVE me leave to lay before you, that *James Piovi* is in the utmost distress. I will not mention to you, that he is one of the Pope's soldiers: that would be but a poor recommendation to an Austrian Officer: but I will put you in mind, that he hath six children; that he hath kept his bed for these nine months

months paft; and laftly, that he is your God-fon.

Generofity, which is your particular characteriftic, and which only feeks opportunities of giving, has here an ample field to gratify itfelf. Were you one of thofe ordinary fouls, who oblige only with regret, I fhould never have thought of importuning you. I do not like to force kindneffes; I would have them flow from the fpring, and originate in greatnefs of foul.

I fee this letter (among thofe you daily receive from fo many of the Military) like a piece of patch-work, which will divert you. The fignature of *Brother Ganganelli* can have no merit in your eyes, but by being placed below that refpect, with which I have the honour to be, fir, &c.

Rome, Sept. 9, 1748.

LETTER X.

To Madam *****.

MADAM,

TRUE RELIGION confifts neither in a neglect of drefs, or in wearing dark-coloured cloaths. The greateft part of Devotees

votees imagine, I know not for what reason, that dark colours are more pleasing to the heavenly spirits, than bright ones. The Angels however are always painted in white or sky-blue. I do not like a piety, which makes a shew of itself. Modesty depends not on the colour of our cloaths. A decency of dress and behaviour are enough to make us what we ought to be.

Observe, moreover, that if any woman be guilty of uttering scandal in company; if she be peevish, and in a rage at mankind, she is generally speaking in dark-coloured cloaths. Singularity hath so little to do with true devotion, that the Gospel orders us to wash our faces when we fast, that we may not be taken notice of by others.

My opinion therefore, Madam, is, that you change nothing in the fashion and colour of your cloaths. Let your heart belong entirely to God: let all your actions be referred to him. That is the capital point.

Had it not been for the Devotees, the world would never have thrown so much ridicule on Devotion. Almost ever full of a bitter zeal, they are pleased with themselves alone; and they would have every one become slaves to their whims; for their piety is often no more than humour.

F   Every

Every person truly pious, is patient, meek and humble—suspects no evil—is not peevish—hides the faults of a neighbour, when they cannot be excused. Every person truly pious, *laughs with those who laugh, and weeps with those who weep,* according to the advice of St. Paul, and is *wise with sobriety*; for moderation is necessary in all things.

In a word, true Devotion is charity; and whatever is done without it, is of no use towards salvation. False Devouts do little less harm to Religion, than those who have none at all. Always ready to take fire at whatever agrees not with their opinions or humour, their zeal is restless, impetuous, persecuting; and they are commonly Fanatics, or superstitious; Hypocrites, or ignorant. Jesus Christ never spares them in his Gospel to teach us to mistrust them.

When you find, Madam, that there is neither rancour in your heart, nor haughtiness in your soul, nor singularity in your actions: that you keep the Commandments of God, and of the Church without affectation, and without troubling your head about mere trifles: you may then believe that you are really in the way of salvation.

Above all things make your servants happy, by keeping from plaguing them. Tho' others, they are still ourselves, and we ought continually

to

to lighten their yoke. Ever to have a ſerene countenance, is the way to be well ſerved. True Piety preſerves at all times the ſame calmneſs and the ſame tranquillity, while falſe Devotion is varying every inſtant.

Maintain your Nieces according to their rank, and require not of them that they ſhould do exactly whatever you do; becauſe you are particularly fond of mortification.

This ſubject alone would demand a whole letter. Young people are often difguſted with Piety, becauſe too great perfection is required of them; and we ſoon tire ourſelves with works of penance, when we know not how to be moderate. A common way of life is the moſt ſafe, though not the moſt perfect. It is an exceſs to forbid yourſelf all viſits and diverſions. Take care that your Director be not too much of a Myſtic, and that his manner of directing you end not in making you rather a ſcrupulous, than a good Chriſtian.

Where is the neceſſity of plaguing one's ſelf ſo much in order to become pious? Religion teaches what we are to believe, and what we are to do; and there never will be a better Director than the Goſpel. Mingle ſolitude with ſociety; and contract ſuch acquaintance, as may neither throw you into melancholy, nor lead you into diſſipation.

Vary your reading. There are some sorts amusing, and may succeed such as are serious. When St. *Paul* lays down the rules of decent conversation, he allows us to say things merry and pleasing: *Quæcunque amabilia.**

We should serve God like slaves, did we imagine that we sinned in every thing we do. The yoke of the Lord is the lightest and sweetest of all yokes. *Love God,* said St. Austin, *and do what you will*; for then you will do nothing, but what is agreeable to him; and you will act with regard to him, as a child does with regard to a Father whom he loves.

Above all things be charitable to the poor, especially as you have it in your power to assist them. Humanity is the pedestal of Religion; and whoever is not charitable, is not a Christian.

I do not advise you, by any means, to give to Monasteries. Besides that they will never be in want of necessaries, it is, moreover, an injustice to impoverish families in order to enrich them. People never cease crying out against the rapaciousness of the Monks and Friars; and we must not give the world room to make any new complaints on that head. Our reputation ought to be our riches; and that reputation ought to be grounded on disinterestedness, and the practice of every virtue.

* Whatever things are lovely. Eph. iv. 8.

Though a friend to my profession, I would never engage any one to bestow largesses on us, or to become a Religious. I dread giving room to reproaches and repentance, as I should dread tiring you, were I to make this letter any longer, which has no other merit in my eyes, than the opportunity it procures me of assuring you of the respect with which I have the honour to be, Madam, &c.

Rome, Jan. 2, 1749.

LETTER XI.

To the Rev. Father **** *a Franciscan Friar.*

I HAVE been for three days together, my dear Friend, scrawling whatever you seem to wish for. I have endeavoured to put in this Discourse the Pathetic, the Sublime, the Simple and the Temperate; so that there will be something to please the different tastes. You must take pains to get it well by heart, and to deliver it in a proper manner, not only so as to satisfy yourself, but also your audience, which will be both very numerous, and made up of persons of great distinction.

This little work will shew some marks of hurry; but it will have the more fire on that account. When I am in haste, my imagination kindles like a *Volcano*. I call in all my ideas, my thoughts, my perceptions, my feelings,

ings, and thefe boil up together in my head, and on the paper in a furprifing manner.

Notwithftanding the warmth you will find in this production, I have placed it in as much order as I could. I fhall be fatisfied, if you are fo; and I earneftly wifh you may.

The war rages more furioufly than ever. This I have from Flanders, where fortreffes fall like tiles every minute from the tops of the houfes in a ftorm. God grant that the French may be ever Conquerors! You know my attachment to that nation, and how much I intereft myfelf in their fuccefs. There is certainly fomething wanting to my exiftence. I ought really to have been born in France: my turn of mind and heart makes me judge fo.

Let not any one know that you have heard from me. Monks are cunning, and they may guefs from whence your difcourfe came, if you put them in mind of me.

I am always in the bofom of my own thoughts, which difperfe, or keep clofe together according to the work. Providence impofes on me, or which arifes from circumftances. The whole day is often a chaos, in which I perceive nothing diftinctly: I am obliged to pafs fucceffively from one bufinefs to another; and they are frequently more unlike than black and white, light and darknefs. I then throw myfelf into the *vortex*

of

of my brethren, chatting about, and laughing first at one thing, and then at another; for this I stand in need of, in order to recover a new being: so far have I gone beyond my strength. I often leave the old people to chat with the young, and we play like so many children. It is the best way of diverting one's self after profound study, and it was the practice of the celebrated MURATORI.

Adieu: love me, because you ought to do so, since I am, as I have been, and ever will be, your best friend,

Convent of the Apostles.

LETTER XII.

To a Prebend of OSIMO.

SIR,

RELIGION, shut up from all eternity in the bosom of God, shewed itself at the moment the universe sprang forth from nothing, and came and rested in the heart of ADAM. This was her first temple on earth, and from thence the most fervent desires continually exhaled towards heaven. EVE formed in innocence, as well as her husband, shared with him the inestimable happiness of blessing, every instant, the Author of their being. The birds with their warbling notes joined in this divine concert, and all nature added its applause.

Such was Religion, and such its worship,
when

when sin entered the world, and defiled its purity. Then Innocence fled, and Repentance endeavourd to supply its place. ADAM, banished from the terrestrial paradise, found no longer any thing but brambles and thorns, where he had before gathered the finest flowers, and the most exquisite fruits.

The righteous ABEL made to God a burnt-offering of his own heart, and sealed with his blood the love he had for justice and truth. NOAH, LOT, ABRAHAM, ISAAC, JACOB, mutually engaged to observe the law of nature, the only Religion then pleasing to God.

MOSES appeared like a new star blazing on Mount *Sinai*, near the sun of righteousness; and the Decalogue was given him to be executed in its purity. Claps of thunder were the external sign of this new covenant, and the Hebrew people became the depositaries of a law written by Wisdom itself.

Notwithstanding the zeal of MOSES, JOSHUA and all the leaders of the people of God, the Christian Religion alone formed Adorers in spirit and truth. Whatever was holy, before its existence, appertained to it; and when, emanating from the WORD INCARNATE, it appeared in the universe, it established itself on the ruins of *Judaism*, as the daughter of predilection*, and changed the face of the whole world.

* Filia dilecta.

Evil

Evil desires, as well as evil actions, were interdicted; and the most pure and most sublime virtues germinated in the blood of a multitude of Martyrs.

The Church succeeded the Synagogue; and the Apostles, who were its pillars, had successors, to be renewed to the end of time. According to this most heavenly plan, and most divine oeconomy, the reality succeeds the shadow; for the whole ancient law was no more than a figure of JESUS CHRIST: and evidence, after death, will be the reward of faith. We shall see God as he is in himself, and rest eternally in him.

It is thus, Sir, you are to begin your work on Religion: you must go up to its source, shew its excellency, raise yourself with it to heaven, from whence it came down, and whither it is to return.

RELIGION will only then be perfectly established, when there shall be no other reign, but that of charity: for it is neither learning nor exterior magnificence that constitutes its merit, but the love of God. That is the basis of our worship; and we are mere phantoms of virtue, if we are not convinced of this truth.

I consider Religion as a chain, of which God himself is the first link, and whose length is that of eternity. Without this band every thing falls to pieces, every thing is overturned:

ed: Men are animals only worthy of contempt; nor hath the Universe any thing interesting in it. It is neither the sun nor the earth which constitute its merit, but the glory of being shut up in the immensity of the Supreme Being, and of subsisting only through JESUS CHRIST, according to the words of the Apostle: *All things were created by him and in him....and all things subsist in him.**

Take care there be nothing in your work, but what is worthy of your subject; and when, in your way, you meet with any famous Unbeliever, or celebrated Heresiarch, overthrow him with that courage which truth inspires, but without ostentation or bitterness.

RELIGION is so beautiful a cause to maintain (as uniting in its favour every testimony on earth and in heaven) that it ought not to be defended but with moderation. Efforts of wit and genius have nothing in common with truth. "It is enough to shew Religion as it is in itself," said St. Charles Borromæo, "to prove its necessity." Those men who were for having no worship at all, were either reduced to eat acorns, or abandoned themselves to the greatest enormities.

I have now made a study of Religion for upwards of forty-five years, and I am every

---

* *Omnia per ipsum & in ipso creata sunt....et omnia in ipso constant.* Col. i. 16, 17.

day

day more struck with it. It is of too elevated a nature to be the work of man, whatever Irreligion may pretend. Fill yourself with the spirit of God, before you write any thing, that you may not give us empty words. If the heart agree not with the pen, while it expresses sacred truths, the Readers are seldom affected. Penetrate their souls with the same fire, which God himself brought down on earth, and your book will produce wonderful effects.

What hath rendered the little book *de Imitatione Christi*, or *the Following of Christ*, so valuable and so moving, is that its Author (GERSEN, Abbot of *Vercelli*, in Italy) has transfused into it all that charity, with which he was himself so divinely inflamed.

GERSON is often confounded with GERSEN: it is however easy to demonstrate, that neither GERSON, nor THOMAS A' KEMPIS, was the Author of that inimitable book. It affords me, I own, an infinite pleasure, that so excellent a work should come from an *Italian*. In the fifth chapter of the fourth book there is an evident proof, that it was not written by a *Frenchman*. The Priest is there said, when he has on his sacerdotal Vestments, to bear *before him* the cross of Christ. Now every body knows that the Chasuble or upper Vestment in *France* differ from those of *Italy* in this, that the Cross in the former is on the back.

back. I have no defign however to write a differtation, but fhall content myfelf with affuring you, &c.

Rome, Feb. 6, 1749.

LETTER XIII.

To Count ALGAROTTI.

THE POPE is ever great, and ever entertaining for his *bons mots*.—He was faying the other day, that he had always loved you, and that it would give him very great pleafure to fee you again. He fpeaks with admiration of the King of Pruffia; and it muft be owned, that he is a Monarch, whofe hiftory will make one of the fineft Monuments of the eighteenth Century. See here and acknowledge my generofity! For that Prince makes the greateft jeft poffible of the Court of Rome, and of us Monks and Friars.

Your laft letter is replete with Philofophy. I have fhewn it to fome of our common friends, and they found in it the fire of the Italians, and the phlegm of the Germans. This mixture does wonderfully in the eyes of men of fenfe and genius.

Cardinal QUERINI will not be fatisfied, unlefs he have you with him for fome time at *Brefcia*. He one day told me, that he would
invite

invite you to come and dedicate his Library. He is enriching it to the utmoſt of his power, to the end, no doubt, that it may be worthy of you.

You will give new life to *Bologna* at your return thither. The Muſes are not aſleep, though leſs animated than formerly. It muſt be a wit like yours, that can electrify the Academicians.

ROME does not make me forget that city, where I formerly ſpent ſome time. The remembrance of the learned I knew there, renders it always preſent to my mind. If the will of the Pontiff did not keep me here bound with cords, I would go with pleaſure, and end my days there, as I ſee nothing in the courſe I have to finiſh, that could be more agreeable, or more to my advantage. I ſhould then poſſeſs myſelf, and be perfectly content, though the poſſeſſion would be but very ſmall. The domain of my knowledge is of ſo little extent, that when I reduce myſelf to my own being, I am confined to the moſt ſimple mediocrity.

Phyſiology comes and tells me that I neglect her. My anſwer is, that I am the greater loſer. But what would you have me to do? Theology is become my ſovereign Miſtreſs, and I am obliged to obey her without reſerve. They who know her not, take her to be a Chimæra, or a phantom; for my part, as I

conſider

consider her under every relation, and in her whole extent, I confess her to be the true light of the soul, and the life of the Elect. Whatever emanates from God; whatever hath a relation to God, or speaks of him; cannot be a futile or indifferent object. There is no harm in preaching to a Philosopher, who seldom goes to hear a sermon, *and who will not have become a great saint by residing at Potsdam.*

You are there three men, whose talents might be of great use to Religion, if you would change their direction, viz. YOURSELF, Monsf. de VOLTAIRE, and M. de MAUPERTUIS. But that is not the *ton* of the age, and you are resolved to follow the fashion.

Waiting for that prodigy, which God can operate any moment, though there be little appearance of it at present, I have the honour to be with the highest esteem, &c.

LETTER XIV.

To M. l'Abbé LAML

I HAD a desire once more to see FRESCATI, that delightsome abode, where a thousand *jets-d'eaux* uninterruptedly darting up towards the sky, are a lively image of the elevation and depression of frail mortals: I have tired
both

both my legs and my eyes with walking, and making obfervations. The country is only agreeable, in proportion as we open the two great books of Botany and Aftronomy, one of which is above our heads, the other under our feet. It is furprifing to fee how the foul elevates itfelf to the height of a ftar, and then falls down on a grain of fand: how it expands itfelf through the immenfity of the heavens, and how it folds itfelf up again: how it analyfes light, how it anatomifes an infect, how inceffantly it is defiring, and how limited its faculties are. So that we may fay with *Dante*: "That the foul is the greateft wonder of the Univerfe."

The ftudy of nature is neceffary, in order to know the Author of it. Hence *Newton* fays, that it is abfolutely impoffible for an Aftronomer, or an Anatomift, to be an Atheift. The air is not feen, though we feel its influence on every fide; and thus it is an image of God himfelf, who, though invifible, every moment gives us notice of both his prefence and agency.

I have really recovered a new life in the country, to employ it more than ever in ftudy. Death, faid an Ancient, ought to find an Emperour on his feet; and I add, a Confultor of the Holy Office with his pen in his hand. You

will

will agree with me, that I do not place myself amiss.

This last moment draws near to us every second, and time is almost nothing. Past, present and future come so close together, that there is not time to distinguish them. Scarce doth the year begin its course, when it is at an end.

I never wrote a single word; I never made a single comma; which I did not consider as a point cut off from my life. This way of seeing things is the best means to keep off ambition; and therefore I believe she never will come and knock at my door. I despise Fortune too much for her ever to make any advances towards me. I consider it however as very fortunate for me, when I can assure you of the attachment with which I am, &c.

Rome, Oct. 12, 1749.

LETTER XV.

To a Carmelite Nun.

IT seems to me, Rev. Mother, that God, by a predilection, has made choice of mountains, to signalize his glory and mercies. I see in sacred scripture the Mounts *Sinai*, *Thabor*, *Olivet* and *Calvary*, as the most privileged places of the whole Universe, for the wonders wrought

wrought on them: and I fee alfo in Church-hiftory *Monte-Caffino* and Mount *Carmel*, as the fprings from whence have flowed two Religious Orders, that do honour to Religion by their penitential lives.

St. THERESA, your illuftrious Reformatrix, is one of thofe great fouls, whom God raifed up for the good of Chriftianity. She is a Father of the Church for her learning and writings: a model of penance for her aufterities. Not a fingle cloud obfcures, in the leaft degree, any of her actions. Ever with God to hearken to him, ever with the faithful to inftruct them, ever in the fame degree of perfection, fhe is a prodigy of knowledge and fanctity.

Her works are not fufficiently known; but the fineft, undoubtedly, is that wonderful Harmony, which reigns among fo many illuftrious young women, of whom fhe is the ftock and the model.

You have no inftructions to receive, Rev. Mother, but from that great Saint. She has faid every thing, fhe has forefeen every thing, fhe has taught every thing. Nuns cannot have a better Director; and they will apply to her, if their piety have none of thofe too fenfible attachments, which hurt true devotion.

Confult therefore St. THERESA, and not Brother GANGANELLI, the moft infignificant personage I know. I only glean after those who have made a plentiful harvest; and all the correspondence I can have with you, is to desire you to pray for me. The prayers of the Carmelite Nuns are the most agreeable perfume that can mount up to the throne of God. But not to interrupt any longer the silence prescribed by your rule, I shall content myself with mentioning nothing more, than the respect with which I shall be, while life endures, your very humble, &c.

Convent of the Apostles, June 19, 1749.

LETTER XVI.

To Cardinal VALENTI, *Secretary of State.*

MOST EMINENT,

THIS Letter is the supplication of a poor Friar, who intreats you in behalf of an object, less than nothing in the eyes of a great Lord like you; but who is worthy of all your attention, if you consider him in the light of that Christian Philosophy, which brings all men upon a level, and which directs all your actions.

The person I speak of is *Dominick Baldi,* who has been long in your service, and who has been turned away for a mere start of passion. As he came from the place where I was born, and as I know he has many good qualities (and particularly that of being moſt ſincerely attached to you) I make bold to entreat your Eminence to reſtore him to your favour.

You have a great ſoul, my Lord; and I am ſure of ſucceſs, if you will but hearken to it: your own heart will be my beſt interceſſor with you—Men are not Angels—Servants have their faults; and Maſters have equally theirs alſo.

I would have waited on you to ſollicit in perſon this favour; but probably I muſt have ſtayed ſome time in the Antichamber, on account of the people and buſineſs with which you are ſurrounded; but really I am not at leiſure to loſe my time. So many burdens of every kind are layed on me, that I ſtand in need of all my ſpirits to ſupport me under them.

If you vouchſafe to hear my prayer, my gratitude ſhall be as laſting, and as extenſive, as the profound reſpect with which I am your Eminence's moſt humble, &c.

Rome, the 21ſt Inſtant.

LETTER XVII.

To the ſame.

I AM proud that an Atom has fixed the attention of an EMINENCE; and that a poor wretch, who had nothing but my mean recommendation, has again been taken into your service. This act of goodness does you the more honour, as it shews you to be a a great man, without being prepossessed against any one; that is, a PHÆNOMENON. I have the honour, &c.

Rome, the 22d Instant.

LETTER XVIII.

To the Prelate CERATI.

CHAINED down by my state of life, tormented with business, dragged away by time, I cannot so order my daily work, so as to join you. Out of the four and twenty hours I have only six for myself: so fully am I employed. I wish to God, that all those, whose time hangs so heavy on their hands, could make me a present of the moments, which are burdensome to them! It should not be to live longer, but to give myself up to study at my ease, without fear of losing my tongue.

You are happy in being at FLORENCE, where court is paid only to Monuments, Libraries, and the Litterati.—There is no fear of meeting with a bad reception from them.

I will speedily send you the Memorial you desire. I use all possible moderation in it, both because it is agreeable to charity so to do, and because works written with passion,

though

though they have truth on their side, never do any good.

It is to no purpose to boast to me of the pleasures of gardening; I cannot apply to it: all I know are the meadows and the fields. When I stand in need of a walk; chance leads me through a thousand charming by-paths, where I take a singular pleasure in losing myself.

The Pope does no more than what he ought to do, in vindicating the memory of Cardinal Noris.* It would be a cruel thing, if a man was to be a heretic, because he is an *Augustinian* or *Thomist*: that is to say, because he follows a doctrine solemnly approved by the Church.—But when a man is hurried on by Fanaticism, he reasons no longer; he sees nothing.

The good Bishop of *Spoletto* continues to enjoy the best state of health: and writes to me in as cheerful a manner, as if he was only twenty years old. He is like the Pope (Benedict XIV), who is never in the dumps. He complains of the too great dissipation of the Hermits, who live almost under his eye. It is an evil which prevails in almost all the Communities: studies, now-a-days, are performed merely from extracts. Whoever has but the

---

* A learned Divine of the last century, who maintained the doctrine of St. Augustin regarding *Grace* and *Predestination*, and whose writings some *Schoolmen* were for having condemned at *Rome*.

epidermis

epidermis of the sciences, fancies himself a great Doctor. I know not what this may lead us to; but I fear we shall insensibly fall back again into the ignorance of the tenth Century. Knowledge, like the moon, after shining with a full orb, shews only one half, and then ends in hiding itself entirely.

Sleep, which I am not willing to lose, tells me, that we must part: my comfort however is, that my friendship for you never sleeps; and that I am by night, as well as by day, irrevocably your very humble, &c.

Rome, July 8, 1749.

LETTER XIX.

To Count ****.

SIR,

I Was too much your Father's friend, and I am still too much yours, not to endeavour to recall you to yourself, at a time when you have gone so surprisingly far from yourself. Is it possible that the dear Child, whom I knew in his Father's house so sweet-tempered, so well-behaved, so virtuous, should have really forgotten what he was, and have become passionate, haughty, and indevout? It is with all the difficulty in the world that I am made to believe it: but I have it from so many hands,

and

and from those who keep you company, that there is no longer any room left for a doubt.

Come and see me, I beseech you, and, with the effusion of a heart which tenderly loves you, I will tell you, not what resentment may inspire, or prepossession may suggest, or the bitterness of reproaches may utter, but whatever the warmest affection can dictate, in order to withdraw you from the abyss, into which bad company hath precipitated you.

You shall not find in me either an imperious Monitor, or an irritated Pedagogue, but a friend, and a brother, who will speak to you, as he would to himself, with the same mildness, and the same temper. I know that youth is a boiling age; and that there is the utmost difficulty in guarding against the world, when a man of fortune is left to himself. But honour, reason, decency, religion! Ought not all these to speak louder than the passions and sensual gratifications?

What is man, my dear friend, if he consults only his own corrupted heart? Alas! I should find in myself, as well as you find in yourself, enough to lead me astray, were I not to hearken to conscience and duty: for nothing falls to the share of any of us, but lies and corruption.

I wait for you with the greatest impatience, that I may take you into my arms and embrace you. Do not be frightened at the sight

of

of my cloister or my garb: it is precisely because I am a Religious man, that I ought to have the more charity. We will weep together for the misfortune of having lost a Father, of whom you stood so much in need. I will endeavour to give you such advice, as may enable you to make him live again in your conduct of life. Affront not his memory by any irregularities.

There is nothing yet lost, if you will but hearken to me: for I am confident that the plan of life, which I shall trace out for you, will replace things in the order in which they ought to be. Do not apprehend that I shall send you to do penance either among the *Capuchins* or the *Carthusians:* I do not like extremes. Heaven will inspire us: God never abandons those who return to him. I will stay at home all day to-morrow in order to receive you.

LETTER XX.

To the same.

IS it possible, my dear Sir, that you should not only not come to see me, as I earnestly entreated you; but that you should even deny yourself, when I came to see you. Oh! what would your Father say, to whom you made a promise, at the very moment of

his

his death, that you would place an entire confidence in my advice, and that you would make it your duty to cultivate my friendship? Once more again, what would he say? Am not I the man, who have so often carried you in my arms; who with the greatest pleasure saw you grow up; who gave you your first instructions; and for whom, on a thousand occasions, you have testified the greatest affection?

Would you have me go down on my knees to beg you would restore me your friendship? I will do it: nothing is difficult or troublesome, when a friend is to be brought back to his duty.

Had you not a noble heart, and a penetrating understanding, I should despair of any change in you, and of the efficacy of my counsels: but a fine soul, and an uncommon sagacity have fallen to your share. Can you really imagine, that I want to have the pleasure of scolding you? None but bigots find a satisfaction in flying into a passion. I have happily read enough of the Gospel, which is both my rule and yours, to know how JESUS CHRIST received sinners, and how careful people ought to be of putting out the still smoaking match, or of crushing the already broken reed. I have not forgotten that *John* the *Evangelist* mounted on horseback, notwithstanding his extreme old age, to seek a young man whom he had brought up, and who had run away from him. Moreover, have you not long known me for a man, who is neither of a surly disposition, or governed by humour; but for one who can compassionate the frailties of human nature? The more you shun me, the more guilty I shall conclude you to be. Hearken not to your companions, but let your own heart speak, and I shall immediately see you: my own presses me never to give you up. I will persecute you by loving you; and I will not suffer you to breathe, till we meet together.

It is because I am your friend, that I seek after you at a time, when almost all your relations will not suffer your name to be mentioned to them.

If you dread my remonstrances, I will not speak a word; being thoroughly convinced that you will be your own accuser, and not allow me time to speak. Try, at least, one visit; and if that turn not out agreeably, I consent that you shall never see me more. But I know your soul, and I know my own; and I am very sure, that after that interview, you will not be for quitting me any more.

I naturally ought to have a greater ascendency over your mind, I who have known you for twenty years past, than all the young people who are about you, whose sole aim is to make you spend all your substance, and are your friends, only to ruin your reputation and health.

"If my tears can affect you, I solemnly protest that they are actually trickling down while
I write

I write this, and flow from no other source, than what is the most valuable in the Universe —Religion and Friendship. Come and dry them up: it will be the only way to prove, that you still remember your Father, and that you can feel for the sufferings of a Friend.

Rome, Feb. 1, 1750.

LETTER XXI.

To the Abbé NICOLINI.

THE PICTURE you draw, Sir, of infidelity, alarms me without surprising me. Besides that this was foretold in the sacred scriptures, even to the most minute tittle, the mind is capable of going wrong in every thing, when the heart is once corrupted. From a desire that there should not be a God to punish crimes, a conclusion is drawn, that there really is none: *The fool said in his heart, there is no God.** Deism insensibly leads on to Atheism. When a man has no longer any Religion, he has no longer a compass to steer by; it is the only support to which we can rationally trust.

Notwithstanding the frightful consequences which flow from the new Philosophy, I am not for irritating those who make a profession of it. There are some unconvinced, who merit compassion; because, after all, Faith is a gift of God. JESUS CHRIST, who thundered

---

* *Dixit insipiens in corde suo: non est Deus.* Pf. xiii. *Vulgate.*

cut

out against the Pharisees, says nothing to the Saducees. Unbelievers will be more easily brought back by mildness, than by severity. We assume with them a tone of pride, which hurts them sensibly, in as much as it often happens, that the answers given them, have much less of wit, than there is to be found in their conversation and writings. The most insignificant Ecclesiastic takes upon him to attack them, without reflecting, that though his zeal be commendable, his knowledge which corresponds not to it, may do more harm than good.

Neither declamations nor invectives operate conversions. We must make use of examples, reasoning and moderation, and begin by owning, that there are truly incomprehensible mysteries in Religion, and that every thing cannot be explained. There is a chain which reaches from earth to heaven, and there is no confounding an Infidel, but by keeping hold of the links. Vain declamations are no reasons. To engage with men expert in the art of sophistry, learning, method and precision are requisite.

When I meet with people tinctured with the new Philosophy, which pretty often happens, I begin by gaining their confidence, and speak to them in the most civil manner. This they feel, if they have any education, and it lessens at least their prejudices.

All that impetuous zeal, which is for calling down fire from heaven, only excites hatred.
The

The Church is reputed to have a perfecuting spirit, merely becaufe many of her Minifters fhew too ardent a zeal. A good caufe will maintain itfelf; fo that Religion, in order to gain refpect, has only to prefent itfelf with its proofs, its tradition, its works, and its meeknefs. Chriftianity of itfelf overthrows whatever is a fect, whatever favours of a revolt, whatever breathes animofity.

I have often an occafion of feeing men, who have a real deteftation for all the Religious; and thefe are the people I am eager to receive in the moft gracious manner. If I had leifure or a capacity to encounter with the new Philofophy, I have the prefumption to think, that not one of the Philofophers would complain of me. I would lay down principles that could not be denied; and fhould I meet in my way with any of thofe too famous men, who make open profeffion of Infidelity, I would fhew them, in the moft civil manner, that they have not taken the Holy Books in their right fenfe, or that they have no good reafons for denying their authenticity.

I think, indeed, that I fhould not convert them; fince it is God alone who enlightens and changes the hearts of men; but at leaft they would not be in fuch a fury againft the Defenders of Religion—We muft endeavour to gain fomething, when we cannot gain all.

If God fuffers that there fhould be Unbelievers, we ought to bear with them, the more so, as they enter into his defigns; for it is by their means that Religion fhews greater ftrength, and the righteous are exercifed in Faith.

It is no way furprifing that ages of fuperftition fhould bring on an age of Infidelity: but they are no more than paffing ftorms, which ferve only to clear the fky, and make the face of heaven appear more ferene.

In proportion to the increafe of Infidelity, the Minifters of the Gofpel ought to be attentive to render Religion refpectable by their love for ftudy, and the purity of their manners—But here is a great deal that teaches you nothing. My pen has infenfibly hurried me away without my perceiving it. It is a fault I often reproach it with, but which it cannot correct. I beg you will excufe it in favour of my intention, and in confideration of the pleafure I enjoy in affuring you of the refpectful and fincere attachment with which I am, &c.

It is fome time fince I heard from Monfignor CERATI. I am the more uneafy on that account, as he was to have given me an anfwer with refpect to a very interefting affair.

Rome, Feb. 28, 1750.

LETTER XXII.

To Cardinal CRESCENCI.

MOST EMINENT,

YOU have folved the cafe of confcience as it ought to be folved, agreeably to
the

the opinions of the moſt excellent Doctors, and above all to that of St. Thomas, whoſe ſuffrage is of the greateſt weight.

The men, of whom your Eminence ſpeaks, were not condemned by the Holy Office, as having really had an intercourſe with the Devil, but for having made uſe of the moſt ſacred words of the Maſs and of the Pſalms, to play their mad pranks. It is well known that our modern Sorcerers are not ſupernatural Agents, and that *Dæmonomania* (though, according to ſcripture, the Devil be a real Being) is almoſt ever an effect of ſuperſtition, or the work of a diſtempered brain.

I kiſs your hands with the moſt profound reſpect, waiting for the time, when we are to kiſs your feet, if the prophecy, attributed to St. Philip-Neri, take place, as every one ſays it will.

Br. L. Ganganelli.
Rome, March 3, 1750.

LETTER XXIII.

To a Gentleman of Ravenna.

I Never could have expected, Sir, that you would have addreſſed yourſelf to ſuch an obſcure Religious as I am, to pronounce on a family affair. There are here many learned Lawyers, who will decide it excellently.

Abſtracting from my incapacity in this regard, I do not like to give my opinion on
ſecular

secular affairs. I call to mind that *St. Paul* forbids every Minister of the Lord to intermeddle in any temporal business. A man, who is dead to the world, ought not to concern himself about the world. Every Religious Society, that follows not that maxim, will perish sooner or later; as every intriguing Monk or Friar, who thrusts himself into families, for the purpose of prying into their secrets, regulating marriages or wills, is as despicable, as he is dangerous.

We have too many duties to fulfil, to find time for meddling with other people's business; and we should at this day be held in detestation, if we had dared to do so. We formerly made noise enough only to know whether we had the use alone, or the property of our own Commons, without now meddling with the property of people in the world. St. FRANCIS would curse us (he who preached up nothing but disinterestedness and poverty) were he to see us employed in settling secular affairs.

All that I ought or can do, is to exhort you to concord and peace, and not to shew a criminal avidity for the goods of this transitory life, which will leave us nothing behind it, but our works. Let us take care they be good, that we may not appear empty-handed before God. I am, &c.

Rome, *March* 1, 1750.

LETTER XXIV.

To Cardinal Querini.

Most Eminent,

I Like to see a Library in your Eminence's possession, because one may be sure that it will not be covered with dust, or suffered to lie still. From the manner in which you speak of it, and the discernment of which I know you to be master, it will be worthy of the admiration of the Curious. I shall forever remember having spent one day with your Eminence, Cardinal Passionei, and several other men of learning: and that day will be the finest, and most valuable Ephoca of my life.

I saw what was most learned in *Europe*, and I drank at the fountain-head of the two finest rivers in the intellectual world. The most important questions were there discussed without ostentation, obstinacy, or pride. None but the half-learned, and half-wits make a parade of obstinacy and vanity. But what struck me still more was, that genius, which is not always found joined with erudition, issued from the bosom of knowledge, like a flash of lightening from the firmament.

I could have wished to have seen our modern Philosophers near these two great men; and the rather so, as they would have been charmed with their moderation. Some time ago I put Cardinal Passionei in mind of this anecdote; and his memory, which is ever immense,

immense, and ever at his command, repeated, in a summary way, all that had been then said.

I could very gladly, my Lord, wish to accompany you to *Monte-Cassino*. You must there appear with rays of light, like MOSES on Mount *Sinai*. It is your centre, and the cradle, where you acquired the greatest lights, to perpetuate the chain of so many illustrious men, who have been formed there.

I should think, my Lord, (if I may presume to own so much) that your last letter to the *Protestant* Ministers, is a little too dry. Your Eminence knows better than I do, how necessary unction is, when the minds of men are to be gained over. Nothing can be added to the profound respect, with which I am, &c.

LETTER XXV.

To the Rev. F. ORSI, *some time after made a Cardinal.*

REV. FATHER,

I Twice called at your Convent without having the good luck to find you at home, though you are a most sedentary Religious. My design was to thank you for the volume you sent me. I felicitate ITALY for the happy production, with which you have enriched it. Monsieur *Fleury* stood in need of a Writer to fill up the voids of his history: for it must be confessed (notwithstanding the respect I have for his memory) that he has slightly passed

over

over several important facts. Perhaps he had not the necessary notes on some articles—But a person ought to think twice before he condemns so great a man.

I cannot however pardon him for telling us scarce any thing concerning the Church of RAVENNA, so famous in the annals of history for a multitude of events relative to its EXARCHS. There is sometimes a danger in aiming at being too concise: sketches are given instead of pictures.

We reproach Monf. *Fleury* with being too zealous for the *Gallican Privileges*:* and the French will accuse you, Rev. Father, of maintaining, with too much ardour, the *Ultramontane* opinions.

Such is the difficulty of writing, so as to please all governments. Judicious people, however, allow both the French and the Romans their different claims, as there is nothing in this dispute which regards Faith. Every country has its opinions, as every individual has his fancy.

I wish your labours may meet with the great reward they deserve, not for your glory,

---

* The *Gallican Privileges*, or the *Liberties of the Gallican Church*, are grounded on these two maxims, viz. 1st, That the power given by Christ to his Church is purely spiritual; and extends neither directly nor indirectly to temporal concerns. 2d, That the plenitude of power, which the Pope has, as Head of the Church, is to be executed according to the canons received by the whole Church: and that he himself is subject to the judgment of a General Council, in the cases mentioned by the Council of Constance. *Fleury Instit. au Droit Eccles.* P. 2. c. 35.

but for that of the Church; as you stand not in need of the purple, to render you illustrious. For my part, I look on myself as the most honoured of mankind, when you vouchsafe to receive with cordiality the sincere and respectful sentiments, with which I am irrevocably, &c.

Rome, June 11, 1750.

LETTER XXVI.

To a PRELATE.

MY LORD,

SINCE I first began to write, my hand ought to have been worn out by this time; but it is more vigorous than ever, when I am to trace out the sentiments with which you inspire me. Though fully employed, I have nevertheless done whatever you ordered.

I have seen the person, and have overcome the opposition made at first to what you desired: the poor orphan will be taken care of. The misfortunes of others render me singularly eloquent: it is then that my soul, my heart, and mind speak all at once.

Monks and Friars are reproached with doing no good to any but themselves: were this really the case I would never be either: but it is after all a mere calumny, which I will not undertake to refute. There are human miseries in Cloisters solely because men are there; and we find men every where. This hinders not however many virtues being seen in Cloisters. I am ashamed of myself (I solemnly protest) when I consider some venerable personages with whom I live. They are taken up with good works from morning to night. The world forms a judgment of Religious Communities only from a few scandals, which sometimes unhappily break out, without being willing to weigh the talents and virtues, which are perpetuated in them.

When men can be brought to honour the Religious state, it will become very honourable; and in it will be found men *powerful in works and words*, when ever it shall be thought proper to seek after them. Emulation is absolutely necessary in a Cloister to keep up a love for study: ambition and scandal are the ruin of it. An ambitious or hypocritical Religious, who makes a profession of humility, while he is puffed up with pride; a man meanly clad, and who only seeks after riches; a pretender to devotion, who gives himself out as a servant of God, while he is no more than a slave to his passions, is a monster both in Church and state.

When I reflect that there are Religious men, who damn themselves for a miserable superiority, liable to a thousand vexations and troubles, I am at a loss to define man; and I only say, that it is damning one's self for a very trifle.

Oh my Cell! my books! my work! what should I suffer, were I forced to quit you, to be whirled round in the vortex of business
and

and honours? the very title of MAJESTY is no indemnification to a man for the loss of his liberty, when he becomes a Monarch.

I was taught from my tender infancy, that the honour of having an immortal soul, is the greatest glory that can be enjoyed, and I have happily ever remembered it.

I would not say so much to all the world, for there are few capable of comprehending it; but you, who relish the inestimable pleasure of existing and thinking, perfectly understand me. I embrace you with my whole heart, and am without reserve your servant and friend.

Rome, Nov. 6, 1750.

LETTER XXVII.

To Monseigneur HENRIQUEZ.

MY LORD,

YOU condescend to consult me, whereas it is I who stand in need of consulting you. Your learning and piety are well known, and every body acknowledges you to be an excellent guide, and a most learned Doctor.

To obey you however, I will tell you that the matter in trust must be given to PETER, (notwithstanding he has had the misfortune to change his belief) though designed for him by JOHN, solely in consideration of his attachment to the Catholic Religion. It is only necessary to acquaint him with the intention of his Benefactor, when he was so
kind

kind as to leave him that fum. But I do not think that the Truftee can deprive him of it, on account of his change of Religion.

Your Lordfhip tells me, that there are fome people who pretend that it may be given to a Monaftery; but I prefume to fay (though a Friar myfelf) that it would be a wrong application of it: Firft becaufe it ought to be given the perfon, to whom it belongs: fecondly, becaufe, in every divifion of effects, the preference ought to be given to the families: thirdly and laftly, becaufe the poor, who have no means of fubfifting, are principally to be affifted.

Providence is the refource of Religious Communities, and that, rather than human means, ought to be their fupport. No Religious Order is any farther deferving of efteem, than as it imitates JESUS CHRIST.— But recourfe is often had to temporal views in order to preferve a Monaftery from decay, without reflecting, that a true Chriftian has no abiding city; and that nothing happens without the will of God.

I fubmit however my opinion to yours, as I am never obftinately attached to my own fentiments. I expofe them according to the dictates of my confcience, and I take all poffible care that it may be enlightened; for there is nothing fo bad, but what may be done (even under a perfuafion of doing good) where there is no other guide to direct, but an ignorant Devotion. I have the honour to be, &c.

LET-

LETTER XXVIII.

To the Abbess of a Monastery.

Rev. Mother,

FROM the account you have sent me, it appears that you do not know how to shew resolution and firmness on proper occasions. What will become of the Rule, if your Nuns are carried away with dissipation, and you suffer them to lead you as they please? Dissipation, and above all the *Parlour**, are the ruin of Nunneries. There is nothing but retirement, and a due employment of time, that can keep up any order in the different Religious Communities. The Cloister becomes an insupportable yoke, when the world is seen, and we keep its company: the more we see of it, the more are we disgusted with our state of life.

It is my advice, that you should often call together the whole Community in your own apartment; and that, like a good Mother, who loves her children, you should speak to them, with effusion of heart, on the necessity of complying with their duties. I would then have you use your endeavours in order to persuade them, in a proper manner, that your conscience reproaches you with being too easy and condescending; and that if you are obliged to shew some appearance of severity, it is because you have a soul to save.

* A room in a Nunnery, where the Nuns are allowed to speak to Externs through an iron grate.

Let. xxviii.   P. CLEMENT XIV.

When the Nuns perceive that you are not governed by humour, but by a fear of failing in your duty to God, they will hearken to you with refpect; otherwife they will be of the number of the foolifh Virgins, without either oil or light in their lamps, when they are to go and meet the Bridegroom. This would be the moft afflicting misfortune that could happen: and it would be then, after having exhaufted every refource of prudence and charity, that recourfe muft be had to the lawful authority of fuperiors to introduce a Reformation.

But I prefume, Rev. Mother, that you will not come to that extremity. There will be grumbling againft you for fome little time; but the anger of Nuns is a cloud which paffes over like a fhower, unlefs there be cabals and parties formed: for in that cafe it is God alone who can difperfe them.

It is difficult to oppofe a Superior in a Nunnery, who intreats, conjures, and humbles herfelf; who makes ufe of tears, rather than reproaches, in order to move and perfuade. Ah! would to God, that were the ordinary language of all Abbeffes! For Alas! there are but too many, who inebriated with a chimerical Nobility, without any other merit than a multitude of whims, and a deal of pride, live feparately from the Nuns, and spend one part of their days at the toilet and in the parlour. They are *foolifh Virgins* (and perhaps moreover may they not deferve that name) who are the ruin and scandal of Communities, in which they live like drones in a bee-hive, only to eat the honey, and to put every thing in disorder.

You have reduced me, Madam, to a cruel trial by consulting me: for I have no talent for the direction of souls, more particularly of Nuns. My sentiments are the same as those of our Father St. Francis (you will excuse my being so ingenuous): He used to say, " God has deprived us of wives by inspiring us with a desire of entering into Religion: but I fear the Devil has given us sisters to be our plagues." He knew how difficult a thing it was in general to direct Nuns, though there are some very tractable, and very sensible. Not even a single Community can be found, wherein there is not some one worthy of the highest elogiums.

After what I have said, Madam, I take the liberty to beg that you would apply no more to me, especially, as I shall not have time to answer you; and because I cannot say more than what your Rule tells you. Talk little to your Directors, but say a great deal to God: and peace will flourish again in your Abbey. I wish it for your sake, and for the honour of Religion, as I am with all possible respect, &c.

Rome, Nov. 10, 1750.

LETTER XXIX.

To the Abbè LAMI, *Author of a Periodical Paper at* FLORENCE.

I Always see your sheets with pleasure, my dear Abbè: but I could wish you would specify the grounds of the censures you pass. Instead of saying, for instance: " The style of such a work is incorrect; and that there are trifles in it, which spoil the beauty of the book:" you ought to shew them, and point them out. A Rule always stands in need of an example

How would you have an Author amend, or the public adopt your way of thinking, if you pass your censure in a vague manner, without shewing the passage, where the Writer hath been guilty of neglect?

There is not a book, of which it may not be said, that it contains some oversights or affected phrases. When a person speaks thus only in general terms, he gives room for suspicion that he has but just cast an eye, in a hurry, over the work, of which he gives an account; and that he wanted to get rid of his task.

It is also another omission, not to shew the finest passages in a book. The good taste of a Journalist requires, that he should pay an attention to this article. If a work be not worth reading, it would be better to let it pass unnoticed, than to use invectives against the

Writer. It is an act of cowardice to criticize a work with bitterness, for no other purpose, than to set the public a laughing at the expence of the Author.

It were to be wished that ROME would follow the method of PARIS, and that we might here see several periodical works appear succeffively. We have only a pitiful *Diario* (Journal) which contains mere fiddle-faddle, and teaches nothing. The function of an enlightened Journalist is as necessary, as it is honourable, in a country where literature is cultivated. No one knows better than I do, what a country owes to a Writer, who reduces himself to a state of captivity every week or every month, in order to give an analysis of the books that are printed, and to make known the genius of his nation. It is the least expensive, and most expeditious way to diffuse learning, and to teach people to form a right judgment of what they read.

I should have no idea of French Literature, but for the French Journals which some friends have the complaisance to send me. When a man is severe, but never biting; when exact, but never punctilious; when just, but never partial, he fulfils his task to the satisfaction of the public. Mine is done, whenever I can renew to you the sentiments of esteem and affection, with which I am, &c.

Rome, March 2, 1750.

LETTER XXX.

To Count ***

IT is incredible, my most intimate friend, how much your three visits have comforted my soul. The tears you shed in my presence; the confession you made to me, clapping your cheek to mine, pressing my hands, protesting that you never would forget the eagerness with which I sought after you, promising me, in the strongest manner, to repair your past life, and to labour seriously to enter again into the favour of God—all this will never be effaced from my memory and heart. I all along used to say to myself: he has had too Christian an education not to return again to his duty; I shall see him; his going astray is only a storm, which will soon blow over. The calm is returned, God be praised; for it is him alone, my dear friend, and not me, you are to thank.

Since you desire a plan of life drawn up by me for your direction, I will trace out for you, in a plain manner, what my weak lights, and strong friendship can inspire me with: and it shall be short. The commandments of God, those first and sublime laws, from whence all others emanate, are reduced to a few words. When precepts are clear and grounded on reason, as well as productive of our own happiness, they stand in no need of commentaries or dissertations.

You

You will read every morning the parable of the prodigal fon, and recite the *Miferere*, or the 50th pfalm* with a contrite and humble heart: and that fhall be all your prayers. You will read fome pious book during the courfe of the day; not like a flave performing his tafk, but like a child of God, who is returned to his Father, and who looks for every thing from his mercy. Read not for a long time together, for fear of taking a diflike to reading. Contract the happy cuftom of hearing Mafs as often as you can: and never omit to do fo on Sundays and Holidays. Keep yourfelf in the pofture of a fupplicant, who begs pardon, and hopes to obtain it.

Make it a point of duty every day to beftow fome alms on the poor, to repair the injury you have done them, by giving to criminal pleafures and fuperfluities, what belonged to them. Renounce all that company, which has withdrawn you from God, yourfelf, and your true friends: and form new connections; fuch as honour, decency, and religion may own. It is an eafy matter to get rid of our companions in debauchery, without being rude to them. A perfon tells them civilly of the plan of life he is determined to purfue: he is for engaging them to conform to it: he talks to them of the regret he feels for what is paft; and the good refolutions he has formed refpecting the time to come: after this

---

* 51ft in the Englifh tranflation.

he sees them no more: or should they appear again in his company, it is a proof they have changed their conduct: and then, instead of shunning them, he receives them with greater pleasure than ever.

Often walk out, lest too great retirement plunge you into melancholy. Contrive also to have always with you either a man of mature age, or a virtuous young man. Go out alone, as seldom as you can help it; especially at first, before your resolutions are well strengthened. It may happen, that indulging wandering thoughts, and soon growing tired of yourself, you may seek out such occasions, as will plunge you again into the precipice.

Take some amusing, but instructive book, to keep up a modest cheerfulness. Grief is a rock to young people, when on their conversion. They draw a parallel between their former dissipation, and the serious life now prescribed them: and the conclusion is, that they return to their former irregular courses.

Keep an exact account of your debts and your income; and, by your frugality, you will be able to pay your Creditors—A man is always rich, who can deny himself; as he is always poor, who refuses himself nothing.

Settle something for life on the woman you seduced, (provided always that she keeps at a distance from you) that want may not oblige her to continue in an irregular course. Make known your intentions to her by writing; at the same time, ask her pardon for having de-
bauched

bauched her; conjure her to forget creatures, and to attach herself henceforward only to the Creator.

When an occasion offers, refuse not to engage at a small game for company's sake; it will be an innocent amusement; and by thus complying, you will not expose yourself to the raillery of worldlings, who seek every pretext of ridiculing piety.

Dress like other people, according to your rank, without being either a fop or a sloven. True Devotion dreads extremes: it is always counterfeit, when it affects dirty cloaths, hanging down the head, an austere look, and a whining language.

Send away the servants who have been accomplices in your intrigues, and sharers in your iniquities; though it would be proper to edify them, after having scandalized them. But it is to be feared, that knowing your weakness, they may lay snares to bring you back to the ways of perdition—You are yet too young not to surround your heart with a double fence and a double ditch.

Live with your new servants (whose good conduct and fidelity ought to be well attested) as a master who understands the duties of humanity; as a Christian, who knows that, in the sight of God, we are all equal, notwithstanding the inequality of conditions. Set them a good example; watch over their behaviour, without being either a plague to them, or a spy; and you will gain their affection

tion by your mildnefs and benevolence—Nothing can give greater pleafure, than to make thofe who are about us, happy.

I exhort you to vifit the Chapel, which Cardinal Cibo (whofe memory I infinitely refpect) built for himfelf in the inclofure of the *Carthufians.* Rather than blend his afhes with thofe of his illuftrious Anceftors, which are inclofed in the moft fuperb tombs, he chofe to be buried among his Domeftics, whofe Epitaphs he himfelf compofed, referving for his own only thefe words full of humility: HERE LIES CIBO, AN UNCLEAN WORM.*

This fepulchre is totally concealed from the fight of men: but God, who fees every thing, will know how to fhew it at the laft day: and that circumftance will be an overwhelming reproach to thofe proud ones, who are vain, even in their graves.

You muft think of fome employment. A man always does ill, when he is doing nothing. Sound your capacity; confult your tafte; interrogate your own foul; but, above all, addrefs yourfelf to God, that you may know what is fitteft for you, either in the Military or Civil line. You are no longer qualified for the Ecclefiaftical ftate. No one ought to carry into the fanctuary, the remainder of a heart polluted with the commerce of the world; unlefs the Lord fhould manifeft his will in an extraordinary manner: a thing indeed very rare,

---

* HIC JACET CIBO, VERMIS IMMUNDUS.

rare; and the inftances of it are much more to be admired, than imitated.

Your friends will think hereafter of marrying you; and my advice is, not to defer it too long. Marriage, when entered on with purity of heart, preferves young people from a multitude of rocks and fhelves: but do not rely on me to look you out a wife. I made a promife to God, at the very time I embraced the Religious ftate, never to meddle with marriages, or laft wills and teftaments. A Monk or Friar is a man buried, and ought to give no figns of life, but in fpiritual concerns: for the foul never dies.

Your kinfman, a man fo difcreet, of fuch integrity, and fo obliging (with whom I have happily reconciled you) has it in his power to find out a proper match for you. When a perfon fettles for life, Religion and Reafon ought to be more confulted than inclination. Marriages, grounded folely on love, are feldom attended with lafting happinefs. That paffion is admirable in Paftorals and Romances; but of no ufe in practice.

I fay nothing of your expences or table. With the principles I lay down for you, they cannot but be moderate. Often invite to dinner fome virtuous friend. I do not like to fee you alone; and you muft be fo, as little as poffible; except in the times of prayer and reading. *Woe be to him, that is alone,** fays the fcripture.

* *Væ foli.* Eccl. 4. 10.

Go only now and then to your country feat. If you live there conftantly, and efpecially at this time, you will bury your good refolutions, as well as your education. Rural fociety only leads to diffipation; and however little we keep there, it ends at laft in becoming ruftic, ignorant, and clownifh. Hunting, love, and the bottle too often employ the whole time of Gentlemen, who live continually in the country. The town polifhes the manners, adorns the mind, and hinders the foul from contracting ruft. Be not over nice with refpect to the hour of your getting up, and going to bed. Order is neceffary in every ftate of life; but reftraint and monotony too often only contract the foul.

If you fee Religion in full, as it ought to be feen, you will find there none of thofe puerilities, which a falfe devotion has introduced. Never open any of thofe Myftical and Apocryphal books, which, under pretence of nourifhing piety, only amufe the foul with trifling practices, and leave the mind as much without light, as they leave the heart without compunction. The treatife on TRUE DEVOTION, by the celebrated MURATORI, will fecure you from all the dangers of falfe Credulity. I advife you to read that book over and over again, that you may profit by it.

Do not take counfel indifferently of every one: for in the maladies of the foul, as well as in thofe of the body, every one is for giving his advice. Shun Bigots as much as the giddy and diffipated: both one and the other will hinder you from arriving at the end we propofe. I rely not on your converfion, till you have tried yourfelf for a long time. It is no eafy thing to pafs from a life of licentioufnefs to the practice of virtue. For this reafon I defired you to take our honeft *Francifcan* for your Director: he was your Father's friend and mine. He is an excellent Mafter of a fpiritual life: and if he keeps you for fome time from partaking of the facred myfteries, it is only to affure himfelf, on good grounds, of your change; and to follow the conftant practice of the Church. Fear not his being fevere: he joins the tendernefs of a Father to the firmnefs of a wife director: he will not, like fome ignorant Confeffors, overburden you with exterior practices. If you have finned through pride, he will prefcribe practices of humility: if through fenfuality, he will employ thofe of mortification; judging, with reafon, that the wounds of the foul cannot be cured by a few prayers repeated in a hurry, but by labouring at a reformation of the heart. For want of this method, the greateft part of finners fpend their whole lives in offending God, and in confeffing their fins.

Above all, let there be no excefs in your piety, nor run into any extremes: that would be the way foon to relapfe again into vice.

This, my dear child, my dear friend, is what I thought myfelf under an obligation of fketching out for you. I could not do it
with

with greater tenderness, were I to write it with my blood. You would make me die of grief, if the resolutions, you lately took in my presence, were to come to nothing. What encourages me is, that you are without guile, that you love me, that you are thoroughly convinced of my sincere attachment to your welfare; and lastly, that you have experienced an irregular life to be an assemblage of vexations, remorses and torments.

Hearken to the voice of a Father, who cries out to you from the bottom of his tomb, that there is no happiness here below, but for the friends of God; and who summons you to keep the promise you formerly made him, of living, with the assistance of heaven, like a good Christian.

I am more yours than my own, &c.

Convent of the Apostles, Nov. 20, 1750.

P. S. I shall certainly reconcile you with all your family, except, perhaps, with the Marchioness R——, who, I believe, is too much of a devotee to pardon you. I expect you on Saturday to take chocolate with me, and to communicate to you a letter from poor *Sardi*, an old servant of your Mother, and who is really in want. It will not take you up much time to come from *Viterbo* to *Rome*, especially if your horses can keep from falling.

LETTER XXXI.

To Prince San-Severo, *a Neapolitan.*

Prince,

I Return you moſt humble thanks for the civilities you heaped on Mr. *Weſtler*, on account of a letter of recommendation from one ſo little as I am, of no note either among the Grandees or the learned. He is quite proud of the kind reception he met with. He never ſpeaks, without enthuſiaſm, of your contrivances for advancing the progreſs of Phyſiology, and the glory of Phyſiologiſts. There are always ſome new diſcoveries, equally uſeful and curious.

Naples is the fitteſt city to exerciſe the genius of the learned. It preſents, on every ſide, ſuch a variety of *phænomena*, that one cannot help taking notice of ſome of them. Its mountains, its ſubterraneous paſſages, its ſtones, its waters, and the fire, with which it is, in a manner, penetrated, are ſo many objects which one could wiſh thoroughly to examine.

I am not ſurpriſed, Prince, that the King himſelf ſhould be pleaſed with your labour and your ſucceſs. Every Monarch, who is ſenſible of his own glory, knows how that of the learned (when he protects them) is ſtrongly reflected back on himſelf. If geniuſes, capable of great things, found encouragement amongſt us, Italy would, once more, ſee men of the greateſt abilities iſſue from her womb. The

germ

germ of talents is still there: and it only wants cherishing in order to flourish in a glorious manner.

But the Artists begin to lose that creative genius, which heretofore wrought prodigies. The finest paintings, as well as the finest statues made now-a-days, seem to be only copies: one would say, that the pencil is forced to work against the grain. There is a coarseness in the features, instead of the delicate softness admired in our first painters; and we have not, at present, that expression, which constitutes the very life of painting.

We are richer in Authors. We have still some, who, for energy of style, and beauty of images, may rank with the ancients, such as Abbè *Buona-fede* of the Order of *Celestins*.

For this we are obliged to our own tongue. It engages us to cultivate Literature, as you engage, by your talents, every one to tell you, that there is nothing more pleasing than to assure you of the sincere respect and admiration, with which, &c.

Rome, Jan. 17, 1751.

LETTER XXXII.

To a Friar of his acquaintance, made Provincial.

I AM so little affected with dignities, that I have not courage enough to pay my compliments to those, who are invested with them. They are an additional servitude to be placed to all the other miseries of humanity,

nity, and the more to be dreaded, as they infpire pride. Man is unhappy enough in not diftinguifhing between himfelf, and fome trifling honours (which can be compared only to the bark of a tree) and in forgetting, at the fame time, an immortal foul, to feed on fome chimerical prerogatives, which laft only for a few days.

Even in Cloifters, where every thing ought to be difintereftednefs, felf-abnegation, humility, men pride themfelves on certain employments, as if they had the command of a Kingdom.

I make thefe reflections to you the more willingly, as your turn of mind places you above all honours; and as the authority you have now acquired, is folely to be exercifed to promote the happinefs of others. I am perfuaded, that you will blend meeknefs with feverity: that no cloud will be feen on your brow, nor unevennefs of temper in your conduct; that you will ever be the Brother of thofe, whofe Superior you are become; that you will endeavour to employ them, according to their inclination, and their talents; and that you will make no other ufe of fpies, than for the purpofe of difcovering thofe, whofe modefty makes them conceal their merit.

You will therefore do honour to yourfelf, in proportion as you difcharge the duties of your Office. Every one will wifh for the moment of feeing and poffeffing you, while the vifits of fome Provincials are as much
dreaded

dreaded as a storm. Above all, my dear friend, take care of the aged and young people; so that the former may meet with assistance, and the latter encouragement; for this ought to be your study. Here are two extremes, which, though they appear very distant, almost touch one another; since every young man grows older each step he takes. Observe moderation in every thing; and reflect, that it is better to carry mildness to an excess, than to give yourself over to too much severity.

Speak with dignity of religion, and never speak of it but on proper occasions. Those are always shunned, who are forever preaching. The sermons of Jesus Christ to his Disciples are not long, but they are *spirit and life.* Words have much greater force, when they come like a dart. Let there be nothing affected in your carriage. There are some who fancy that a man in office must be formal in every thing: but those who imagine so, have weak intellects.

I shall say nothing to you against duplicity, though unhappily too much practised among Superiors in Religious Orders. I flatter myself, from the good opinion I have of your merit, that you never will write any thing to the prejudice of another, without speaking to him several times, and previously telling him of your intentions. Dread finding any person culpable; but when you meet with such, humble yourself with this thought; " that man

man can do no good of himself." Be affable, and of easy access; a deal is lost, in the minds of those we govern, by coldness and reserve. In a word, be what you wished a Provincial to be, when you were an inferior: though we too often require of others, what we would not do ourselves. Make a distinction between faults, from the motives and circumstances; and know that, if there are some which require punishment, there are also others, which ought to be overlooked; because every man has his imperfections.

Trust few with your secrets; but when you do trust any, let it not be by halves: for the rest is guessed at, and there is no obligation of keeping the secret. Have no predilection for one rather than another, unless for eminence of merit. In that case we are authorized by the example of JESUS CHRIST himself, who testified a particular affection for St. *Peter*, and St. *John*.

Lastly, make the Visitation of the houses like a benign dew, so that they may regret the time, when you will be no longer in office, and may say of you: *He went through doing good.**

Love me, as I do you, and consider this letter, as an emblem of my heart.

My compliments to all our common friends, and especially to our Venerable old man, whose good advice has been of great use to me, and to whom my gratitude is immortal.

Rome, *Jan.* 31, 1751.

* *Transit benefaciendo.*

LETTER XXXIII.

To the MARCHIONESS R***.

MADAM,

YOUR refusing to change your sentiments and dispositions towards the Count, your dear kinsman, after the submissive and affecting letter he wrote to you, and the visit he paid you, is certainly enough to throw him into despair.

Is it thus God acts towards us? And what would you have the public think of your piety, when it sees you so cruelly bent on rejecting the prodigal child? I, Madam, who have not your virtue, have run after him, from the moment I heard he was gone astray; and I hope God will reward me for it.

You cease not repeating, Madam, that he has lost a deal of money; and, in a word, that he is a *bad young man.* But what is the loss of gold itself, that it should give you so much concern? You ought only to feel for the wrong use he has made of his good qualities; and to reflect that, if he really be a *bad young man*, he stands the more in need of the advice and example of the good.

Religion enjoins no such wrong practice, as to abandon a young man, because he has gone somewhat astray.

Ah! Madam, how do you know that this *bad young man* will not to-morrow be pleasing in the eyes of God, while your services will not please him? For, after all, a single grain of pride is enough to spoil the best action. The *Pharisee*, who fasted twice a week, was rejected; and the *Publican*, who humbled himself, was justified.

An universal Charity, an uninterrupted Charity, is what I will never cease repeating; and this perfectly agrees with the Morality taught in all the Christian schools, and every pulpit.

If the mercy of God depended on certain pretenders to devotion, sinners were very much to be pitied. False devotion knows only an exterminating zeal; whilst God full of patience, meekness and long-suffering, waits for the repentance of all those who have transgressed his laws.

The very blood of JESUS CHRIST claims your kindness towards your dear kinsman; and it is setting no value on it, to refuse him the entrance of your house. How do you know, Madam, that his salvation depended not on the faults of which he now repents? God often permits a man to fall into great disorders, to awake him from his lethargy. You cannot but know, that there is more joy in heaven for the conversion of one sinner, than for ninty-nine righteous, who stand not in need of repentance Besides, will you preserve resentment in your heart, while the Angels rejoice? That indeed would be frightful piety.

I tremble for all those pretenders to devotion, who affect so much severity; since God
himself

himself has declared, that he will treat us, as we have treated others. Be so good as to read St. *Paul's* Epistle to *Philemon*, in behalf of *Onesimus*, and you will then know, whether or not you ought to pardon.

It is not for us to determine, whether the heart of a man, who appears seriously concerned for his past misconduct, is changed or not. Though God alone knows it, we ought always to presume that it is so. Would you take it, Madam, to be very just in your neighbours, who are witnesses of the good works you perform, were they to pretend that you acted solely from a motive of pride? Let us leave it to the searcher of consciences to pronounce on the motive that actuates us. The brother of the prodigal son stands condemned in the eyes of Religion and Humanity, for not being properly affected by the return of his brother.

Were I your Director, (though the direction of souls has no analogy either with my employments, or my taste) I would prescribe, in order to appease your anger, that you should write to the person, who is so odious to you; that you should often see him; and even with this additional condition, that you should forget what is past.

If we regulate our piety by humour, we are only phantoms of virtue; and I most surely, Madam, presume that yours is grounded on charity; for I never judge unfavourably of my neighbour.

If

If my letter, contrary to my intention, should appear to you a little harsh, be so kind as to reflect, that I have spoken to you in that manner, less for your kinsman's sake, than for your own: for your salvation is at stake. Will you refuse to pardon him, when it is to be presumed that God himself has pardoned him!—I cannot think it.

I have the honour to be with respect, Madam, &c.

Rome, Feb. 5, 1751.

LETTER XXXIV.

To the Chevalier DE CABANE.

YOU therefore still continue, Sir, your resolution of going and burying yourself at La Trappe, and to put it out of my power to write any thing more to you for the future, except your Epitaph. As it is your final determination, I will not be so obstinate, as to continue to oppose your design; the rather so, as you have tried yourself a long time, and are past the age of life, when people take inconsiderate steps.

The worldlings will laugh at you: but at whom do they not laugh? I know not any person, any work, any proceeding, or even virtue, which have not been censured. And this ought to be a comfort to the Religious orders under the hatred borne to them, and the contempt with which they are spoken of.

At

At their first appearance they were too much extolled: a counterpoise was necessary to retain them in humility. The intentions of the Founders were certainly good, when they formed the different Institutes, we see in the Church. Even the very form of dress, they gave their Disciples, and which the world looks on as whimsical, shews their good sense and piety. They judged that it would be a means to prevent the Religious from mixing in company with seculars, and to exclude them from all profane assemblies. It was natural that men who embraced a kind of life different from the practices of the world, should have a particular dress.

Here then they are justified with regard to that point: and Ah! how easy would it be for me to apologize for them in all other respects, were I not myself a Religious man! Let any one read their Rules: let him examine their particular practices; and he cannot but own, that whatever is recommended, and practised in Cloisters, leads to God.

If they have degenerated from their first establishment; it is, because all men are frail: and that, after a certain period of time, the greatest fervour grows cool. But what was a scandal, never became a rule among the Religious Orders. In every house there are found some, who enter their protest against every deviation from the rule, and against every abuse.

Those

Those who are continually crying out against Monks and Friars; those who wish their possessions seized on, and that they were banished from every state, certainly do not know, that they were called, into the different Kingdoms, by the very Princes who endowed them, and loaded them with favours. They know not, that, if the foundations of Princes are not sacred, there is nothing in the world to be spared: that lastly, these Monks and Friars, so cruelly mauled, gained by the sweat of their brow, by their vigils, and by their toil, the bread that feeds them.

The greediness they are accused of, is a mere calumny. The BENEDICTIN Monks acquired their possessions by clearing the fields, and the Vine-yard of the Lord, in ages, when corruption and ignorance made the greatest havock. The first Disciples of St. DOMINICK, St. FRANCIS of *Assisium*, St. FRANCIS of *Paula*, never asked any thing of the Monarchs, at the time they were their greatest confidents; and when they might have obtained every thing.—Their present poverty proves this assertion.

I know that some Monasteries, by their misconduct, have merited a reformation: but the blame of that falls neither on the Monastic Rulers, nor on their Founders. A man who lives in a Cloister, as he ought to do, cannot but excite the esteem, and deservedly gain the affections of all good people. For what is a true Religious man, but a citizen of heaven; one detached

detached from the earth, who makes a sacrifice to God himself (in the person of his Superior) of his senses and his will; one who continually desires the coming of the Lord; one who instructs and edifies for the good of his neighbour; one who shews, in an ever-open countenance, the joy of a good conscience, and the charms of virtue; one who prays, labours, studies for himself and his brethren; one who places himself under the feet of all the world by his humility, and above all men by the sublimity of his hopes and desires; one who possesses nothing, but a soul in peace; one who asks for nothing, but heaven; one who, in a word, lives only to die, and dies only to live again for all Eternity?

This is what you are going to become, my dear Sir, except what regards instructing others, since you will no longer have any intercourse with mortals. That is the only thing which hurts me: for I am particularly desirous that every one should be useful to his neighbour.

Time, which is a heavy mass of lead for the greatest part of mankind, will not be burdensome to you. Each minute will seem a step towards heaven; and night will appear to you as light as day, by your then conversing with God: *Night shall be as light as day.**

You will not hear the bell, that is to call you to the Office, merely as a bell, but as the

---

* *Et nox, sicut dies, illuminabitur.* Pf. 138. *Vulg.*

Voice

Voice of God: you will not obey your Abbot simply as a man, but as a person, who holds the place of JESUS CHRIST himself, and speaks to you in his name: you will not consider penance as a restraint, to which you must submit, but as a holy kind of sensuality, which will be your delight.

You will omit none of the most minute Regulations, which retain the mind in subjection, and oppose self-will: for a Religious man keeps up his fervour, and prevents his state of life from becoming irksome by no other means, than by exactly practising whatever is recommended to him. You will moreover, Sir, preserve the liberty of the sons of God, by doing with a good heart, and a good will, whatever you will appear to do barely as an obligation.

I shall be charmed to see you, as you mention your coming; for I have no greater satisfaction than the company of true servants of God; and the more so, as they are, at this day, extremely rare. Nothing can be added, &c.

Rome, March 15, 1753.

LETTER XXXV.

To the Bishop of SPOLETTO.

MY LORD,

WHAT you wrote to me concerning the Relics of saints, does honour to your discernment and your Religion. There are two shelves to be avoided, when a man is truly a
Ca-

Let. xxxv.   P. CLEMENT XIV.   99

Catholic, *viz.* that of believing too much, and that of not believing enough. Were credit to be given to all the Relics, which are shewn in different countries, we should often be necessitated to believe, that a saint had ten heads, or ten arms.

This abuse, which has drawn on us the name of *superstitious*, has happily taken root only among the ignorant. We know in ITALY (thanks be to heaven; and the Pastors often enough inculcate it) that the Mediation of JESUS CHRIST alone is absolutely necessary; whereas that of the saints is only *good* and *profitable:* for thus it is the Council of *Trent* expresly teaches.

The Relics of the Blessed in heaven deserve all our veneration, as precious remains, which are one day to be gloriously re-animated: but while we honour them, we profess that they have no virtue of themselves; and that it is JESUS CHRIST, (of whom they are, in some sort, fragments) and the Holy Ghost (of whom they are the true temples) who communicate to them an impression entirely heavenly, capable of operating the greatest miracles.

Notwithstanding this, the worship we owe to God, is frequently distracted by that which we pay to the saints. Hence it is wisely ordained in ROME, never to place any Relics on the altar, where the BLESSED SACRAMENT is exposed, for fear of dividing the people's attention.

Our Religion (in itself so spiritual and so sublime) is unjustly taxed with encouraging abuses, of which the least footsteps will never be found in Cathedrals and ancient Monasteries.

Did we vouchsafe to hearken to the ignorant, who take no pains to be instructed, there would not be a single statue, but what has spoken; nor a saint, who has not raised the dead to life; nor a dead person, who has not appeared again: but the enemies of the Catholic Religion falsely impute to the Church of Rome all the apocryphal facts, which superstition ceases not to hand about. The common people are a set of mortals, to whom preaching is in vain: they never can be cured of their obstinacy, when once persuaded of any thing contrary to the public doctrine of the whole Church.

I lately made an English gentleman own, that the Protestants take a deal of pains to attribute continually to us absurdities which we reject, and that there was something of dishonesty in their manner of condemning us.

ITALY has all along had Pastors who were men of learning, and who were concerned for the credulity of weak minds, and at the want of faith in pretended wits. A man of sense will never judge of the Religion of a country, from what the vulgar may believe; but from the points of doctrine taught in the Catechisms and in the public Instructions.

It

It would be something very singular that ROME, the Mistress and Mother of all the other Churches; that ROME, the centre of truth and unity, should teach absurdities! It is vindicated after a noble manner in the work you have transmitted to me. I exhort you to publish it, in order to close the mouths of the enemies of the Holy See; and to let all the world know, that if there be superstitious practices in *Italy* (and perhaps more than in other places) they arise from a livelier imagination in the common people, and consequently from an imagination more apt to seize on, without reflection, whatever strikes their mind. Take care of your health, notwithstanding the zeal which eats you up; and vouchsafe to believe me with infinite respect, my Lord, &c.

Rome, March 17, 1751.

LETTER XXXVI.

To Cardinal QUERINI.

MOST EMINENT,

THE WORK I have just read over by your orders, is a production of the age, in which there are more paradoxes than arguments; more objections than solutions; more raillery than proofs; more warmth than learning; more superficies than solidity. Men of no thought will look on it, as a wonderful perfor-

performance: men of sense, as a pitiful one; but as these latter form the smaller number, the book will be in repute, and make a great noise.

Few people are competent judges of a book. If there be any thing attractive in the style, it is admired, it is spoken of with raptures, without reflecting, that the colouring is the least merit of a picture.

It must be acknowledged, my Lord, that we live in a very whimsical age. Never was there less Religion, nor was there ever so much talk about Religion: never was there more wit, nor was wit ever so much abused. People are for knowing every thing, without studying any thing: they are for deciding on every thing, without examining any thing to the bottom.

I cry not out against the age by way of recrimination. It may hate Monks and Friars as much as it pleases; and did not this hatred proceed from a hatred of Religion itself, I would never reproach it on that account. There may be some reason to complain of our too great number, as also of an engagement, sometimes too hasty, in a profession, which is to last for life—It is however proper, that people should enter therein young, to imbibe the Spirit of the Institute.

If many Religious knew how to accuse themselves, they would own that they had given occasion to complaints and murmurs by their haughty behaviour, and dissipated life. For
why

why should we dissemble or offer to hide what every one knows? But it is an act of injustice to require, that all the Religious should be bound one for another, and that the fault of an individual should be considered as the fault of all.—The sin of a brother is not that original sin, which is common to all.

You see, my Lord, that I make ample use of the permission granted me of letting my pen run on different subjects, when I have the precious advantage of writing to your Eminence. Being of the Order of St. *Benedict*, your Lordship knows that the Religious have not always time to pursue the same object. They are only the attachment and respect due to you, of which sight is never lost; and it is with both these sentiments that I am your Eminence's, &c.

Rome, *July* 3, 1751.

LETETR XXXVII.

To the Rev. Father SIGISMOND *of* FERRARA, *General of the Capuchins.*

REV. FATHER,

I AM extremely thankful, that your Apostolic excursions have not hindered you from thinking of me. I could have wished to accompany you, as I am sure I should have found, in such a journey, both instruction and edification. I should, with you, have admired how much the family of our holy Founder

was

was increased, and how abundantly virtues were perpetuated in your Order.

There is no sort of good, which the CAPUCHINS have not done; nor can they be accused of having done any thing that was bad. The alms they receive, are a salary justly due to them; since they labour, with indefatigable zeal, both in the country and in the towns, for the support of Religion, and the propagation of the Faith. There are CAPUCHINS in all the four parts of the globe; they are protected by the most barbarous princes, and have gained the love of all nations.

I executed your commission at the time appointed. I promised you to do so; and my promises are inviolable, because Religion and probity are concerned in them. Your garden, most Rev. Father, is one of my favourite walks. I prefer it to the most magnificent parks. One seems there to breathe an air uncontaminated by the depravity of the age.

I have the honour to be, most Rev. Father, with all possible veneration, &c.

Convent of the Apostles, Aug. 7, 1751.

LETTER XXXVIII.

To Madam B***, *a Venetian Lady.*

MADAM,

IT is doing me too much honour, to consult me concerning your magnificent translation of *Locke*. Is it possible that a Lady of your rank

rank should apply herself to the deepest Metaphysics in the bosom of a city, as truly immersed in pleasures, as it is in water? Here is the strongest proof that our soul disentangles itself from the senses, when it is disposed to shake off matter, and that consequently is of a spiritual nature.

I have read over and over again, with the nicest attention, the valuable Manuscript, in which you have so nobly displayed the beauties of our language, and turned, with so much elegance, the dry field of Philosophy into a beautiful flower-garden. The English Philosopher would be proud, could he see himself dressed after the Italian manner with so good a taste.

I could have wished, if possible, that your Ladyship had omitted that passage, where *Locke* seems to insinuate, that matter may think. This reflection is not that of a profound Philosopher. The faculty of thinking can only belong to a being, that is necessarily spiritual, and necessarily thinks. Matter will never enjoy the privilege of thinking, any more than darkness that of giving light: one and the other imply a contradiction—But some people are fond of venting absurdities, rather than not say something extraordinary.

I felicitate my country more than ever for having had, at all times, Ladies of learning. It would be proper to form a collection of their works, and their rare abilities. The translation of *Locke* would there hold one of the first places,

places, especially as you have found out the secret of employing, from time to time, the poetic style, in order to remove the wrinkles of Philosophy, which is apt to knit its brow, and express itself in grotesque terms.

I exhort you, Madam, to print the work, were it only to prove to foreigners, that the sciences are still in honour amongst us; and that the fair-sex in *Italy* is not so much taken up with what is frivolous, as people are pleased often to say they are.

How came you to find me out in the crowd, where my small merit has placed me? There are a great many Academicians, and especially at *Bologna*, whose judgment might be more relied on than mine. A man is not a Philosopher for having taught Philosophy, and particularly that of *Scotus*, the captious subtilty of which is nothing but a continual *Ergotism*.

There is more substance in one page of our Metaphysicians of the last age, than in all the books of *Aristotle* and *Scotus*. The same cannot be said of *Plato*, who, in an age like this, would have made an excellent Philosopher, and probably a true Christian. I find him full of matter, and noble views. He carried his sight up to the Divinity itself; nor was it obscured with any of those clouds which are met with in the writings of the ancients.

I wish, Madam, people may not find, in the last sheets of your translation, some puns which disfigure it. What of itself is majestic, stands in no need of trifling ornaments to set

it

it off. *Cicero* would be no longer what he is, should a person attempt to make him speak like *Seneca*. Excuse the liberty I take—But you love the truth; and this qualification is greater in my eyes, than whatever else renders your name illustrious.

If you can diffuse a taste for Philosophy in *Venice*, you will perform a great miracle. It is a country, where wit abounds, even among the mechanics. But pleasure is there a fifth element, which puts a stop to emulation. Both repose and time are there consecrated to it, except in the order of Senators, who, for the business they have to do, may be called the slaves of the nation. The people study nothing but mirth and jollity, even when at work. But I perceive that I shall insensibly be talking of government; and my letter will soon be guilty of high treason. I know how touchy the most Serene Republic is with regard to its usages and customs, as well as its laws.

I will therefore, Madam, confine myself to tell you what will meet with no contradiction, and what will agree with the sentiments of the whole Senate; which is, that no one can sufficiently assure you of the respect due to your understanding, birth and virtues, and of that with which I have the honour to be, &c.

Rome, Jan. 10, 1753.

LETTER XXXIX.

To the Rev. Father LEWIS *of* CREMONA, *a Religious of the Schools of piety.*

REV. FATHER,

TO take BOURDALOUE for your model in preaching, is to aim at immortality. We wanted an Orator, with your talents and spirits, to reform the style of our pulpits. We are rather Poets in our sermons than Orators, and, unfortunately, oftener pantomimes, than pathetic speakers; though the word of God demands the most noble species of eloquence, and the greatest circumspection in the manner of delivering it.

It is a miracle to me, when I consider how you have translated some volumes of BOURDALOUE. His Holiness, I make no doubt, will, with transports of joy, applaud your labour—I know how desirous he is of seeing a reformation in our manner of preaching. He is not indeed for *Frenchifying* the *Italian* eloquence (as every language has its idioms and phrases): but he wishes, that a style, which ought to be that of the Gospel, was more Christianized, and not disfigured by becoming burlesque.

The mouth of a preacher is really the mouth of God. What then must we think of a man who utters nothing but buffooneries and trifles? Whoever finds not in the sacred scripture, and the writings of the Fathers,

thers, wherewith to move his hearers, is unworthy to mount a pulpit. There are no finer images of the greatness and mercy of God, than those found in the Pfalms and Canticles: There are no histories more affecting than those of *Joseph*, *Moses*, and the *Maccabees*: There are not more striking instances of divine justice, than those of *Nadab* and *Abiud*; and that of *Belshazzar*, who saw an awful hand write in a dreadful manner, his sentence on the wall.

There are no strokes of eloquence, in all the books of the whole world, like the reflections of *Job*: they are enervated, and lose their force when a paraphrase is attempted. Let any one only collect a few of the finest passages of scripture, and adapt them properly to his subject, his discourses will be enravishing. St. PAUL, a man the most pathetic, and most sublime, uses no other language, but that of the scripture in his Epistles; and they challenge our admiration.

The greatest part of our old Collections of sermons ought to be burnt, in order to form the taste of our young preachers. It is there they seek out apocryphal and doubtful facts, citations from heathen authors, and contract a style truly ridiculous. Sentiments of compunction or terror, which arise from the exclamations, grimaces and gestures of a preacher, make only momentaneous impressions. They are no more than a clap of thunder that startles, and causes people to make the sign of of the cross; but does not hinder them from laughing the next moment.

If your method, Rev. Father, can be introduced among us, you will be the restorer of Christian eloquence; and all who are judges of it, will bless you.

I had for my Director a Religious man, full of the spirit of God, who used to sigh, whenever he heard certain preachers. When he preached to us himself, it was his heart that spoke; and, indeed, his hearers were always very much affected.

I shall see you with the greatest pleasure, whenever you are so kind as to honour me with a visit: to hearken to you, will then be my whole business.

I endeavour, in the midst of my daily occupations, always to have some moments for myself and for my friends. The soul requires that respite, to return again to work. The sciences are mountains, which cannot be climbed, without sometimes stopping to take breath.

Be careful of your health, less for your own sake, than for ours, who want to read you, hear you, and admire you. It is with this desire, so agreeable to the wishes of Religion and our country, that I have the honour to be, with all the fulness of my heart, your very humble, &c.

Conv. of the Holy Apost. March 1, 1753.

As to what regards the new modelling of the *Breviary*, which you mention to me, it
were

were much to be wished that the Holy Father would set seriously about it. But I do not agree with you in what relates to the division of the psalms. Were I consulted, I should be for having the *Beati immaculati*,* continue to be repeated every day. It is a perpetual protestation of an inviolable attachment to the law of God, and which is better in the mouth of the Ministers of the Lord, than some obscure and enigmatical psalms, often unintelligible to the generality of Priests.

I would therefore leave the little hours as they are. You will tell me, that it is to be feared, that our prayers will be said merely by rote. But are we not exposed to the same inconvenience with respect to the prayers at Mass, when they are said every day?

The notes I have received on the *Imitation of Jesus Christ*, are admirable.

* Psalm 118, Vulg.

LETTER XL.

To Count ****.

I AM, my dear Friend, a Library in your debt; but you are to pay for it. I promised to give you a list of what books might be necessary for you; and I now fulfil my promise. The list shall be only a short one, as it is not a multiplicity of books that makes learned men. To read much is of little consideration;

deration; but to read well is of essential importance.

The first book, and which I place at the head of your Library, is the GOSPEL, as the most necessary, and most sacred. It is reasonable, that the book, which is the principle and basis of Religion, should be the ground-work of your reading.

It is there you will learn to know what we owe to God, and how great are the wisdom and goodness of our Mediator, in whom we hope, and who has reconciled heaven and earth by his blood.

This book has been in your hand, almost ever since your infancy; but as you then gave little attention to it, it will now make an impression, entirely new, on your soul. The Gospel, when attentively read with the respect due to it, really appears to be the language of God. We find not there that oratorial emphasis, which characterizes the Rhetoricians, nor those syllogistical arguments, which point out the Philosopher: all is simple and plain; all adapted to the capacity of man, and, at the same time, all is divine.

I recommend particularly to you the Epistles of St. PAUL. Besides inspiring you with an aversion for false teachers, who, under the appearance of piety, destroy the spirit of it; they will penetrate you with that universal charity, which includes all, and which, better than all the masters in the world, makes us good parents, good friends, and good citizens,

We

We learn, in the school of this Apostle, the whole oeconomy of Religion, *its length, its breadth, its depth, its heigth*; in a word, the *super-eminent knowledge of Jesus Christ*,* who would be universally adored, were he better known; and by whom the intellectual and material worlds were made.

You must be perfectly acquainted with the PSALTER, as a work of the Holy Ghost; a work that inflames, while it enlightens, and, for sublimity of style, surpasses all the Poets, and Orators.

You must not overburden yourself with reading. The sacred books are not to be read, without great recollection of mind, and respect: for besides that every passage may afford a subject for ample meditation, the word of God challenges a respect quite different from that, which is shewn to the word of man.

You will take care to procure St. *Augustine's Confessions*, a work written with his tears: but a work, on which your heart, more than your understanding, must feed. You will join thereto the Collection of the finest passages of the Fathers of the Church, in order to convince yourself, that Christian eloquence alone truly elevates the soul, and that it is a thousand times more sublime, than all profane discourses, as having God for its subject, the source of whatever is great.

The IMITATION of Christ contains too much unction, and is too instructive to be left out.

It

* *Eph.* 1, 18, 19.

It is a production of *Italy*, whatever all the Differtators may fay to the contrary (for GERSEN, Abbot of VERCELLI wrote it); and in it the foul finds whatever can edify. Make frequent ufe of that little book, as of a work that abounds with confolation, adapted to every fituation of life.

Feed on the *Introduction to the Chriftian Doctrine* of F. GERDIL, the *Bernalite*; it is a book you cannot read too often. Mix the hiftory of the Church with that of the Empires and Nations, fo as not to confound your memory or ideas. The underftanding muft be kept clear, in order to form a folid and exact judgment of what we read. When you are more mafter of the French language, I advife you to read BOSSUET's *Difcourfe on Univerfal Hiftory*, and PASCHAL's *Thoughts on the truths of Religion*.

The Annals of *Italy*, by the immortal MURATORI; the Hiftory of *Naples*, by *Giannone*; the Campaigns of *Don Carlos*, by *Buonamici*; the Periodical Sheets of Abbè *Lami* (not to learn to decide, but to form your judgment) are fo many works which you muft read.

I fay nothing of the books which treat of Natural Hiftory and Antiquity; thefe are fubjects, with which an unacquaintance cannot be allowed.

You will call to mind, my dear Friend, that *Cicero*, *Virgil* and *Horace* trod the fame foil that we inhabit; that they breathed the fame air which we breathe; and therefore, as their country-

countrymen, we ought, from time to time, to read their writings, especially as they are every where strewed with sentiments and beauties. You went very well through your studies, and it will be an easy matter for you, every now and then, to enjoy the agreeable conversation of those authors.

I do not interdict you the reading of our modern Poets, with this proviso, that you use precaution in reading them, and throw not yourself, right or wrong, into every Labyrinth, Grotto or Grove you find there:. these are not places for a Christian soul. I would not have any one stay long with the Goddesses of Fable: they are indeed, in themselves, mere fictions; but too often lead to realities.

I should be better pleased to see in your hands *Pliny*'s Letters, the Thoughts of *Marcus Aurelius*, and those of *Seneca*: we there imbibe sentiments of humanity, which we cannot feel too much.

This, my dear Friend, is the Library to which I confine you, because I think books ought to be used, and not kept for mere shew. You may add however the Letters of Cardinal *Bentivoglio*.

I allow you neither Legends, nor books of Mysticism. You will find an account of the principal Saints in Church History; and the stories told of them, in *Apocryphal* books, will answer no other end, than to make you doubt of the miracles they really performed, and to diminish the respect due to them. Great men ought

ought not to be exhibited but as great men; and truth stands in need of itself alone to gain respect.

I mention not any books of Philosophy, as I do not design to send you to school again to adopt systems, and enter into disputes. I should be apprehensive of your embracing some whimsical opinion; whereas to judge impartially, we ought not espouse any one sentiment of the schools.

Philosophy has given birth to more sophisms than arguments: and, to become a true Philosopher, it is enough to have an exact knowledge of the earth and of the heavens; and a clear and precise idea of our duties, our origin, our destination. Employ your mind on these great objects in the midst of your exercises and your reading; and when you are determined on a state of life, means will then be pointed out to you, by which you may be informed of whatever is relative to it.

Good night: my pen can travel no farther: my head, fatigued with a piece of work, that hath lasted the whole day, obliges me to stop. My heart alone is still full of life and vigour, when I am to assure you, how much I am, &c.

Rome, Dec. 31, 1751.

LETTER XLI.

To Cardinal Passionei.

Most Eminent,

IF knowledge gained were to be restored like stolen goods, your Eminence would see me bring back all I know, as belonging to your Lordship: and would then be far from commending me for my pretended learning. Almost every Saturday, I go to your Eminence's magnificent Library, and fill myself as much as I can, with the excellent things I meet with there. I set out quite poor, and return home very rich: and thus it is, that private thefts constitute my whole reputation and merit: so that it is to your books, my Lord, and not to my own genius, I owe thanks.

I join, my Lord, in the pleasure which all those feel, who hearken to your Eminence in that delightful Hermitage, where science presides, virtue shines, and friendship forms the conversation. It is decreed that Brother *Ganganelli*, is to have no more than desires with respect to that object; his work is never to allow him to go and lay himself down under the shades of your Myrtles and Orange-trees. That would be something too sensual for a Friar of the Order of St. *Francis*, who ought to know nothing but mortification and poverty.

I have

I have neverthelefs, my Lord, this comfort, that I happily feel the pureſt pleaſure in performing the taſk impoſed on me; and that the reſpect, which I could ſhew you at *Freſcati*, neither could be more profound, or more extenſive, than that with which I have the honour to be here, &c.

Rome, May 8, 1753.

LETTER XLII.

To Mr AYMALDI.

THE laſt memoir you tranſmitted to me, is like thoſe uncultivated countries, in which, by chance, one meets with ſome agreeable ſpots. I am unraveling it with all the patience becoming a Religious, and the greateſt deſire of obliging you. There would be too great a voluptuouſneſs in ſtudy, did we find therein nothing but flowers. Every man who works in his cloſet, ought to conſider himſelf as a traveller, who one while meets with flowery paths, another while rugged ways.

The little publication of Father *Nocetti* the Jeſuit, on the Rainbow, is very neat and elegant. There is found in it that brilliant and poetic imagination, which embelliſhes the thoughts and ſtyle. The Jeſuits have all along cultivated the *Belles Lettres* with ſucceſs. Works of that kind are refreſhing ſtreams to me, which recal my animal ſpirits, when I am exhauſted with long and painful

painful labour: I smell at them, and am revived. You know that Erudition is the grave of the *Belles Lettres*, unless, from time to time, we allot to them a few hours, not entirely to forget them. "I am really so absorbed in profound studies (said formerly my Master in Theology) that my mind has not a smell fine enough for neat and elegant works." The taste itself is blunted, when nothing is given it to taste.

I will see the Rev. Father General of the *Dominicans (F. Bremond)* concerning your affair, and I hope I shall succeed. Besides that he is of an obliging temper to all, he has a particular kindness for me; and I will moreover put him in mind, that as St. FRANCIS and St. DOMINICK were very great Friends; and also St. BONAVENTURE and St. THOMAS of *Aquino*, it is fit that the same happy harmony should subsist between their disciples.

Adieu: take care of your health; for there are great odds to be layed, that in the Pontificate of a man of learning, your merit may lead you to something great. I desire it, much less for your own sake or mine, than for the honour of the Holy see. I have that of being, &c.

Rome, May 12, 1753.

LETTER XLIII.

To Dom GAILLARD, *Prior of the Charter-house at Rome.*

REV. FATHER,

AS you open your heart to me with regard to what passes in your Community, I will open mine to you with equal candour: and will tell you, that it were to be wished, that in an order so rigid as yours, the superiors were a little more affable and of easier access: that they would not let a week pass, without visiting the Religious in their Cells; that they would insinuate themselves in a friendly manner into their affections; and lastly, that by salutary counsels, and endearing encouragement, they would help them to bear the yoke of solitude.

The Kingdom of JESUS CHRIST is not a reign of Despotism. To make men slaves is as contrary to Religion, as it is to humanity. A vow made to obey superiors does not carry along with it an engagement to respect their humours.

It is commonly thought, that the place of a Superior is a place of authority; and that he who enjoys it, has nothing to do, but to command, and make the Religious tremble and obey: whereas the head of a Community is a man, who ought to make himself all to all, study the different characters, and sound their dispositions, in order at last to know what is hurtful to one, what does good to another,

and

and what each individual is capable of performing.

One Religious man ſtands not in need of talking, becauſe he is naturally ſilent: continued ſilence is death to another, becauſe he is a man of converſation: and it is then that a Superior muſt have different ways of acting, and excuſe one rather than another, for any ſmall breach of the Rule. No Religious Order can have any other ſpirit but that of JESUS CHRIST, who, ever meek and humble of heart, treated his Diſciples as his brethren and his friends, calling himſelf their ſervant, and performing the offices of one.

The Rule would be a real Step-mother, were it to puniſh without mercy thoſe who, through too great a livelineſs or ſlowneſs of temper, ſhould be guilty of ſome omiſſions. There are ſome Religious, whom a Superior ought more frequently to viſit, becauſe they are oftener tempted, and ſupport retirement with greater difficulty. So that, without a ſpirit of diſcretion and penetration, a Superior is no more than an Idol, whoſe government is deſpicable. There is only one manner of directing followed; and there ought to be almoſt as many different methods, as there are perſons to be directed and governed. One, if the Superior take it in head to reprimand him, goes backward in the way of ſalvation; and another makes gigantic ſtrides towards it, if no fault be overlooked in him.

The Order of the *Carthusians* merits all possible veneration, for never having stood in need either of any mitigation or reformation since its first institution; but I must own to you, that I always thought the Priors had too gloomy and too severe an air; and as they alone went to the General Chapter, they were both judges and parties.

They ought not to trouble a poor Monk for speaking a word by stealth, as they themselves often receive visits, enjoy the liberty of writing to their friends, and of going out.

A man becomes the Inquisitor of his house, when he is for punishing every thing, and overlooking nothing. There are little altercations in Communities, as well as in private families, which continue only, because a Superior has not the sense to despise them.

Visit your brethren in a quite friendly manner, and say not a word of what is past; you will then find them ashamed of their caballing. Nothing disarms anger like mildness. You will teach them that you know how to overcome yourself, when you cordially embrace them; and this will edify. There is nothing so dangerous for people in office, as to be always unwilling to own that they have been mistaken.

Accustom yourself to bury the faults of your Religious in your own house, without informing the General of them. This conduct irritates those against whom a man turns informer, and plainly evinces that he has not a talent for governing.

Such

Such is my way of thinking. Should I be mistaken, you will do me a pleasure to prove it; and if your reasons are good, I will submit: for I am neither prejudiced in my own favour, nor am I obstinate.

It is my heart that has spoken to you throughout this letter, and it is that which assures you of the sincerity of the sentiments, with which I am, &c.

Rome, June 21, 1754.

LETTER XLIV.

To the same.

THE nap taken at noon in Italy, my most dear and Rev. Father, would not have alarmed you so much, had you called to mind, that when a man is at Rome, he must live as the Romans live: *cum Romano Romanus eris.**

Is it then a scandal, is it a misfortune, that a poor Religious man should lie down for half an hour, in a country where he is overpowered with excessive heat, to return again to his exercises with greater activity? Reflect with yourself, that silence is best kept at that moment of time, you who reckon among the capital sins a single word uttered, when it is forbidden to speak. Look at Jesus Christ, when he finds his Apostles asleep: *What!* said he with the greatest kindness, *could you not watch one hour with me?*†

---

* With a Roman you must be a Roman.   † Matt. xxvi. 40.

But how do you reconcile the obedience you require of your Religious, with that you yourself refuse to the sovereign Pontiff? You cannot but know, that all the Cloisteral rules derive all their force only from the approbation of the Popes; and if he, who now reigns with so much wisdom, is pleased to dispense with your Religious in certain practices, he is absolute Master to do so. No one will dispute the Legislator's right to modify the law.

To mitigate some austerities, which depend on time, place and circumstances, is not to meddle with what is essential in the vows. *The letter kills, but the spirit gives life**; but there are some Superiors, ever of an uneasy temper, and ever afraid of the least syllable of the Constitutions being omitted. Let me beg of you to make yourself easy, both for the sake of your Religious, and for your own health. While you continue to consult me, I shall always answer you in the same manner: it is not enough to alledge conscience, we must seek to enlighten it. I embrace you with my whole heart, and am, &c.

Rome, Sept. 21, 1754.

* 2 Cor. iii. 6.

LETTER XLV.

To a RELIGIOUS *setting off for America.*

THE seas then are going to separate us; but such is the lot of human life, that some are thrown to the extremities of the world,

world, while others remain always in the same place. This however is certain, that my heart follows yours; and wherever you are, there will it be found.

If you had not laid up an ample provision of piety, I should tremble for you during a passage, where every word uttered will not be edifying, and in a country, where every example you see, will not be a model of virtue. America is the terrestrial Paradise, where the forbidden fruit is frequently eaten. The serpent is there perpetually preaching the love of riches and pleasures, and the heat of the climate makes the passions boil up.

We are sufficiently unhappy here below, in not knowing how to keep within the bounds of duty, when we see no other Superior but God; unless a lively faith be the principle of our actions: and such is the situation of the Religious in America: seeing no longer any one to direct or command them, they are lost, unless the Gospel alone bears sway in their heart.

I am persuaded that you will often beg of God the gift of fortitude, to enable you to stand out against all dangers. Whatever dispositions the Negroes have for gross vices, good may be done among them, when a man knows how to gain their confidence, and impress them with a certain degree of fear.

Reflect that God will be as near you in America, as in Europe; that his eye sees all; his justice will judge all; and that it is for him alone we ought to act. Lay down a plan of a

labo-

laborious and regular life; for if idleneſs once get the better of you, you will be inveſted with every vice, and no longer be able to defend yourſelf againſt them.

Never allow yourſelf to utter any word, that may be conſtrued contrary to Religion or good morals. Thoſe who ſeem to applaud you for it, will in reality deſpiſe you, as an unfaithful ſervant, who makes a jeſt of the maſter, whoſe bread he eats, and whoſe livery he wears.

God keep you from amaſſing. A Prieſt, who loves money, and eſpecially a Religious man, who has made a vow of poverty, is worſe than the wicked rich man, and is deſerving of more rigorous treatment.

As to the reſt, be ſociable, and gain on your Pariſhioners by a deal of civility, to the end they may ſee, that you are governed by true piety, and not by humour.

Never meddle in temporal affairs, unleſs it be to make up law-ſuits, and reſtore peace. I will pray for you to him, who commands the waves, calms the tempeſts, and never abandons thoſe that belong to him, in whatever country they are. My comfort is, that there is no diſtance for ſouls; and that by the bands of Religion and the heart, we are always neighbours.

Adieu and Adieu again; I embrace you in the moſt tender manner.

LETTER XLVI.

To the Prelate CERATI.

YOUR happiness is too great, my dear Prelate, in dividing your time between *Pisa* and *Florence*: in one of those cities your mind is at ease; and in the other your knowledge finds food and nourishment.

When I reflect that TUSCANY was the Restauratrix of the arts and sciences, I have a singular veneration for her, and my heart leaps with joy whenever I hear her name mentioned. The advantage of a most happy situation, and a most agreeable climate, rendered her worthy of that glory. One breathes there a sweet air, which seems to give new life to the soul; and at every step, we perceive the fine arts had reason to be pleased with their residence.

I knew an old man of the most embellished sense, and the most voluptuous intellect, who ordered his time so well, as to pass the spring at *Pisa*, the summer at *Sienna*, the autumn at *Leghorn*, and the winter at *Florence*. He went alternately to these four cities to imbibe the wit of the inhabitants, and diffuse his own; and to taste the sweets of the most agreeable commerce. Our manner of conversation begins to degenerate; and a person could not well now find in it that something interesting, which our Fathers introduced into theirs. It is to that amiable trifling way of the French that we owe this change.

Every

Every age has a genius which characterizes it: the same luxury which corrupts our manners, corrupts also our discourse and our writings: there is scarce any life in our conversation, in our books, or our paintings. It is a species of elegance, as slight as the intellect which produces it; and unhappily Religion itself feels something of this frivolous turn. People think that they may strip off from Christianity whatever displeases, as they strip off the trimmings of a coat.

You see these evils, you groan at the sight of them; and you have good cause to do so.

I have the honour, &c.

Rome, Sept. 2, 1754.

LETTER XLVII.

To the Abbè de CANILLAC, *Auditor of the Rota.*

I Passed by your house, my Lord, that I might have the honour of returning, with my own hands, a volume of Monsf. BUFFON. Oh! the excellent book! The excellent writer, had he not been the partisan of a system! He has an energy of style and thought, that transports and astonishes.

To ask me what I think of the *Gallican* privileges, is to shut my mouth. Besides, where is the importance of that question, if the French, as well as the Romans are Catholics, notwithstanding their different sentiments
with

with respect to this article? In former times both Popes and Kings were wrong by turns: and BENEDICT XIV. is luckily the fittest Pontiff to make what is past, forgotten. What you vouchsafe to recommend to me, shall be done, as soon as possible, and with a zeal equal to the respect, with which I am, &c.

Rome, June 6, 1754.

LETTER XLVIII.

To the Marquis SCIPIO MAFFEI.

MR. MARQUIS,

THE young Religious, whom you recommended to me, is proud of such a prerogative, nor am I less proud of your excellent letter. I will keep it as a charm to communicate to me some sparks of your learning and genius. I would gladly say a thousand things; but I am as much afraid of you, as of a spirit, and cannot speak. I call to mind the immensity of your knowledge, the merit of your publications; and the remembrance of them makes me so insignificant, that I dare not appear before you.

ITALY will for a long time boast of having given you birth; and, if VERONA is sensible of her own glory, she will erect statues to your memory. But what renders you infinitely superior to these vain honours is, that you are the humblest of men, and know your own worth less than any other.

I would never pardon time for making you grow old, without refpecting your merit, were I not convinced, as well as you, of a life in heaven that awaits us. We know that heaven is the centre and abode of all light, and that the knowledge there acquired in a moment, cannot be compared to the weak glimmerings we enjoy here below.

I fhall pay every poffible regard to the young man, you have taken under your protection. He fhall now be my fon, as he was heretofore yours, by the intereft I will take in forwarding him in the fciences and the practice of piety. He will find the fame helps in our Order, as I myfelf found to improve and form my mind; and on this occafion I may fay, without a defign of flattering my Brethren, that helps can no where be more abundant. A tafte for good books prevails; emulation is kept up; application is uninterrupted; and the incomparable SCIPIO MAFFEI is particularly efteemed. He lives in our hearts as much as he lives in his writings: this is what I can affure him, as I am more than any other, &c.

LETTER XLIX.

To Monfeigneur CARACCIOLI, *Nuncio at Venice, who died afterwards Nuncio in Spain.*

MY LORD,

I Have the honour to fend you the Decifion of the Holy Office, which, I am certain, will be agreeable to your way of thinking. I used therein my utmost zeal, to prove to you the infinite esteem I have for your virtues. Would to God, the Church had all along had Prelates as exemplary as you, my Lord, are! This is what the *Venetians* often say, and what transports me with joy, when I have the happy occasion of assuring you of all that respect with which I am, &c.

Rome, Oct. 21, 1750.

LETTER L.

To Count ***.

IF scruples once beset you, my dear Friend, you are lost: you will either return to a life of dissipation, or you will serve God like a slave. Remember that the Jewish law was a law of fear, but that the new law is a law of love. The earthen vessel to which our soul is united, allows us not to possess angelical perfection.

'Tis degrading Religion, to busy one's head about mere trifles. While there are men who pray, distractions will naturally arise in prayer; and there will be faults in their conduct, as long as they act: because every man is subject to error and vanity: *every man is a liar.**

There are none but Bigots, who take scandal at every thing, and see the Devil every where. Fulfil the law without labour of mind, or effort of imagination, and you will please

* Omnis homo mendax. *Ps.* cxv. *Vulg.*

God. Nothing retards souls so much in the progress of virtue, as injudicious scruples. Too much retirement favours illusions, and society dispels them; keep good company instead of staying alone at home. Moreover be not discouraged under temptation. Temptation is a trial, which teaches us to distrust ourselves, and affords us an opportunity of meriting the favour of God.

Come to see me, and we will together try to find out from whence the scruples, which torment you, arise. There is nothing I wish for more, than to see you a good Christian; but it would break my heart, were you to become scrupulous: every thing then would hurt you, and you would be insupportable to yourself.

I always forget to mention your good Kinswoman. It is thus my distracted thoughts, from time to time, play me a very sad trick; but the heart has no share in them. The Marchioness, more vexed, than moved with my remonstrances, is at a loss what to do. If Devotion once sets down to calculate, when a reconciliation is proposed, we must look for nothing but suspected demonstrations. However, as of a bad debt we get what we can, so you must content yourself with the very small civilities your good Kinswoman will shew you.

Persevere, my dear Friend; persevere: I am edified at your courage, and am charmed that you are pleased with the Guide I gave you. Is he not really a worthy man, and one who
will

will lead you safely to God? He has a wonderful skill in discovering the interior of persons, and a soul the best calculated for gaining their confidence.

I approve your setting something apart for charities; but I do not like that people should give drop by drop, and that they tie themselves to regular alms, so as to have nothing for those who are in extreme want. I had rather snatch a family or two from the jaws of misery, than scatter here and there a few crowns, which bring comfort to no body. It is moreover very proper to have a sum in reserve for extraordinary cases: by that means there is a remedy at hand for the most urgent occasions of distress.

Fall not into that trifling Devotion, which, without examining either birth or extraction, is for reducing every one in want, to dress and eat like the lowest class of people.

Charity never humbles any one, and knows how to proportionate itself according to circumstances and conditions. To give with pride, is worse than not giving at all. Season your charities in such a manner, that you may appear more humbled, than the person that receives them. Religion is too grand to approve of the behaviour of those mean souls, who oblige with haughtiness, and make people feel the importance of the services done them.

Content not yourself with giving; but also lend, according to the precept of the Gospel, to him in need. I know nothing more contemptible

contemptible than money, if not employed to assist our neighbour. Can the insipid pleasure of heaping up a few crown-pieces be compared to the satisfaction of making others happy here, and securing to ourselves happiness hereafter in heaven.

When you are frugal without avarice, and generous without prodigality, I shall consider you as a rich man, to whom salvation is not impossible. Prevent the wants of others without waiting till you are asked: charity puts us on guessing, that they may stand in need.

Adieu: I think it needless to repeat at the end of this letter, that I am your best friend and most humble servant. You do not certainly doubt it? If you did, you would affront me in a most sensible manner.

Rome, April 19, 1752.

LETTER LI.

To the same.

YOU ask me how it happens, that there are certain days, when given over to melancholy, without knowing any cause, we are a burden to ourselves? And I answer you:

First, it is because we depend on a body, which is not always in an equal state of health. —Secondly, because it is the design of God to make us sensible that our happiness is not to be found in this life, and that we never shall be at ease, till we leave it. It was this that
made

made the Apostle sigh after those good things that are eternal. There are mists both in the moral and physical world; and the soul has its clouds like the sky.

The best way to get rid of these troublesome thoughts, is to be fond of work. A man that is seriously employed, has no time either for sorrow or vexation. Study is the element of the soul. "You will neither be troublesome to yourself or others, says *Seneca*, if you love study." It is inconceivable how many bad quarters of an hour there are in the course of a man's life, against which labour secures him. You never will be happy here below, unless you know how to deaden the feelings of your misfortunes. He that has not any uneasiness of mind at present, either has had, or will have some, because sufferings and pains are what we inherit from our first Father; nor can we absolutely secure ourselves from them. I am with my whole heart.

Rome, April 27, 1752.

LETTER LII.

To My Lord Firniani, *Bishop of* Perugia.

My Lord,

THE Postulant * you directed to me, seems to prefer the *Augustinian* Order to that of the *Franciscans*; and so far was I from being displeased at it, that I went with him

---

* A person who desires to be admitted into any Religious Order.

myself

myself to a Religious, a friend of mine, who will take all possible care of him, and after a trial, will give him the habit of St. *Augustine*.

It values not in what Convent a person be placed, provided he has a true spirit of piety. All the Religious Orders, in my eye, are one and the same family; and luckily I have no attachment for my own Community, that can be a prejudice to any other. Moreover the *Augustinians* have at all times united learning to virtue, and one who has a real call, cannot but there receive excellent lessons.

The Father *Capuchin*, who told your Lordship so many fine things of me, scarce saw me. He judged of me, as of an optical deception, which is thought something at a distance, but is nothing near at hand. I will oblige him to recall what he has said, when he returns to *Rome*, because he will then see me nearer. It is the best way I know to correct men of the good opinion they may entertain of me. I recommend myself to your prayers, which I believe to be very efficacious with God; and I have the honour to be, &c.

Rome, *Aug.* 26, 1753.

LETTER LIII.

To the Prelate CERATI.

MONSIGNOR,

I Have just now seen your good and old Friend, Monsignor BOTTARI, and I found him, according to custom, buried in the most profound

profound reading. From that state he passed to the most picturesque conversation, which afforded me singular pleasure; for he never speaks, but he paints. Every thing is sentiment, every thing a picture; and every thing characterizes the books and persons he points at.

We conversed for a long time on the Roman Antiquities, and our different Libraries, which more or less excellent, form a wonderful collection. Two sensible Englishmen partook of our entertainment, and talked so as to be hearkened to. That nation travels to great advantage, and improves by every thing it sees. The English are said to lay hold of the substance of things, while the French content themselves with the surface. But I leave you to determine whether, with respect to the commerce of life, it is not better to be agreeably superficial, than gloomily profound.

It was a saying of Cardinal BENTIVOGLIO, that, " when a man wanted to think, he ought to see the English; and the French, when he wanted to converse." I open my Cell both to the one and the other with the greatest pleasure; though I own to you, at the same time, that there is something in the French vivacity, which particularly attracts me. There is a pleasure in meeting with one's self; for you know that I am neither dull, nor a man of few words.

You must have read the book, that Father MASSOLENI, of the *Oratory*, sent you. You will

will find it as interesting, as neatly bound. I see you over head and ears in that work, without being able to quit it. The studious man really enjoys pleasures, which surpass all those of the world. But hush! This is a secret known only to the studious, and must not be divulged.

I have the honour to be, &c.

Rome, Nov. 13, 1753.

LETTER LIV.

To a Franciscan Friar.

I Find something in myself, that puts the pen in my hand, and whispers in my ear that I must write to you, and let you know, that it is a long time since I enjoyed that sweet pleasure; and that it is my friendship for you, which now procures me that happiness.

It must be owned, as St. AUGUSTINE tells us, "That there is something sweet in friendship;" and that, "Whoever knows not the sweetness thereof, ought to exclude himself from society." The Saviour of the world canonized it by his particular attachment to St. JOHN; and we see that the greatest saints have cultivated it with a most religious attention.

Continue, therefore, ever to be my good friend. Though the world says that Monks and Friars love nobody, I have found, in the Cloister, the most sincere and obliging hearts:

hearts: but I shall not be believed, for people are resolved that we must be in the wrong. But what of that, provided we taste no less the sweetness of friendship; and I am no less your servant and friend.

Rome, Dec. 29, 1754.

LETTER LV.

To Lady PIGLIANI.

YOUR keeping your two Daughters with you is not a concern of no consequence: the quality of a Mother imposes on you the most important duties. The world will be continually thrusting itself in between you and your children, if you take not care to keep it off; not with that austerity, which excites murmurs, but with that prudence, which gains confidence.

Your Daughters will be no more than hypocrites, if you overload them with instructions, or if you make them uneasy; whereas they will love Religion, if, by your examples, and mildness, you can render it amiable to them.

Persons of twenty years of age, are not to be governed like those of ten. Different ages, as well as the different conditions of life, require different treatment, and different lessons.

Keep up, as much as you can, a taste for good books and work; but with that liberty and ease, which ties not down to a minute; and with that discretion, which knows how to make a difference between living in a Cloister, and in the world.

Marry your Daughters according to their fortune and rank; and force not their inclination, unless they should want to marry with spendthrifts or debauchees. Marriage is the natural state of mankind: to dispense therewith is an exception from the general rule.

Without being in love with the maxims and practices of the world, make not yourself ridiculous with respect to its usages. Piety becomes a subject of raillery, when shewn with any external singularities: the wise woman shuns being pointed at—When our birth demands a particular dress, we must wear it; but always with that decency in form and manner, which is agreeable to modesty.

You will take care that the young Ladies frequent company. True Devotion is neither rude nor unsociable: injudicious solitude irritates the passions, and it is often safer for young people to see choice company, than to be alone. Inspire cheerfulness, that they may not appear to drag along piety—Let your recreation consist in taking a walk, or sitting down a little to play a moderate game; and when they are to apply to study, neither mention such as are profound, nor the abstracted sciences, which serve only to make the sex vain and talkative.

Above all things gain their love: it is the greatest pleasure, to which a Mother can aspire, and the greatest prerogative she can enjoy,

joy, since she is thereby empowered to do what good she pleases.

Take care that your servants have religion and honesty: they are capable of every vice, if they have not the fear of God. We ought to act towards them neither with haughtiness nor with familiarity, but to treat them as men, and inferiors. Justice is the mother of order: every thing is in its place, when a person behaves with equity.

Never punish but with pain to yourself, and always pardon with pleasure.

Frequent your Parish-church, that the sheep may often meet with their Pastor. It is a practice agreeable both to the holy canons, and ancient usage.

Your own prudence and discretion will teach you the rest. I rely much on your sense and your good disposition, as you may be truly assured of the respectful consideration with which I have the honour to be, &c.

Rome, Nov. 15, 1754.

LETTER LVI.

To Count ALGAROTTI.

MY DEAR COUNT,

CONTRIVE matters so, in spite of your Philosophy, that I may see you in heaven; for I should be very sorry to lose sight of you for an Eternity.

You

You are one of thofe rare men, both for heart and underftanding, whom we could wifh to love even beyond the grave, when we have once had the advantage of knowing them; no one has more reafons to be convinced of the fpirituality and immortality of the foul than you have. The years glide away for the Philofophers, as well as for the ignorant; and what is to be the term of them, cannot but employ a man who thinks.

Own that I can manage fermons fo, as not to frighten away a *bel Efprit*; and that if every one delivered as fhort, and as friendly fermons, as I do, you would fometimes go to hear a preacher. But barely hearing will not do; what is heard muft pafs on to the heart; it muft germinate there; and the completely amiable ALGAROTTI muft become as good. a Chriftian, as he is a Philofopher: then fhould I doubly be his fervant and friend.

Rome, Dec. 11, 1754.

LETTER LVII.

To Monfignor ROTA, *Secretary of the Decipherer's Office.*

I Believe, *Monfignor*, that it will be proper to fix a rallying hour, that we may be able to meet with one another: I beg you would be fo kind as to let me know it, and I fhall moft certainly take care not to fail coming.

There is nothing I regret with more concern, than the time loft in Anti-chambres.

Time is the moft precious gift God has beftowed upon us; and man throws it away with a profufion as cruel, as aftonifhing.

Time, alas! is abandoned to pillage, every body comes, and fnatches away a piece from us; and in fpite of all my attention and defire to preferve it, I fee it flip through my hands; and fcarce can I fay, "it is going", but it is already gone.

I expect your orders to wait on you at your own houfe, and to affure you, that if there be any moments to fee you, there is not one, in which I am not with equal attachment and refpect, Monfignor, your very humble, &c.

Rome, Jan. 3, 1754.

LETTER LVIII.

To the GONFALONIER *of the Republic of St.* MARINO.

MY VERY DEAR FRIEND,

Although you be no more than petit fovereign of a very fmall ftate, you have a foul that puts you on a level with the greateft Princes. It is not the extent of Empires, which conftitutes the merit of Emperors: a Father of a family may have many virtues; and a GONFALONIER of St. MARINO great reputation.

I find nothing fo delightful as to be at the head of a fmall Canton, which one can fcarce find in the map, where difcord and war are unknown,

unknown, and where there are no ſtorms, but when the ſky is darkened; where there is no other ambition, than that of maintaining one's ſelf in ſilence and mediocrity; and where all things are in common from the cuſtom kept up of helping one another.

How this little corner of the earth pleaſes me! What a happineſs is it to live there, and not in the midſt of that tumult which diſturbs great cities; not in the midſt of Grandeurs, which make the little ones ſigh; nor in the midſt of luxury, which corrupts the ſoul, and dazzles the eyes! It is a place, where I would with pleaſure fix my *tabernacle*, and where my ſoul has long been through the friendſhip I bear to you. There is not a heavier burden than Sovereign power: but yours is ſo light, that it hinders you not from walking; eſpecially when I come to compare it to thoſe Monarchies, which cannot be governed, but by multiplying one's ſelf, and having one's eyes every where.

Every thing is a ſnare for a Prince at the head of a vaſt kingdom. At the time he thinks people are making court to him, they are ſeeking to deceive him. If he follows irregular courſes, he is flattered in them. If he be a man of piety, thoſe about him play the hypocrite, and make a farce of Religion. If he be cruel, he is told that he is juſt: and thus he never hears the truth.

He muſt often deſcend into his own heart to find out truth. But how much is he to be pitied,

pitied, if it be not found there! The only reason why History is filled with the reigns of so many bad Princes is, because they chose to live remote from truth. She is the only true friend that Kings have, when they are disposed to hearken to her; but here they are often deceived: for they consider her only as a troublesome monitor, that must be kept off or punished.

For my part, as I have loved her from my most early infancy, I think I shall continue to love her, were she to say the harshest things to me. She is like those bitter medicines, which, though disagreeable to the taste, restore health. She is certainly better known at St. MARINO, than any where else. In great Courts she is only seen obliquely; but you see her strait before you, and receive her with joy.

I shall not send you the book you want to see. It is quite a shapeless production, badly translated from the French, and swarms with errors against Faith and Morals. Nothing however is talked of but *Humanity*, which now-a-days is a fine word artfully substituted in the place of *Charity*; for *Humanity* is no more than a heathen virtue, whereas *Charity* is a Christian one. Modern Philosophy likes nothing that belongs to Christianity, and thus it shews to the eyes of reason, that it is pleased only with what is defective.

The ancient Philosophers, who had not the lights of faith, nor the happiness of knowing the true God, wished for a Revelation: and the modern ones reject that which no body can difown. But here they betray themfelves: for had they an upright heart and a pure foul; had they the *Humanity* they pretend to have, they would receive, with tranfports of gratitude, a Religion, which condemns even wicked defires; which exprefly enjoins the love of our neighbour; and promifes an eternal reward to thofe who have affifted their brethren, and have been faithful to their God, their King and their Country.— A virtuous man cannot hate a Religion, which preaches nothing but virtue.

Therefore, when I continually fee flowing from the pen of thofe writers, who anathematize the Chriftian Religion, the words *Legiflation, Patriotifm, Humanity*, I fay, without fear of a miftake, thefe men are making a jeft of the public; and inwardly, they have neither *Patriotifm*, nor *Humanity*.—The mouth commonly fpeaks from the abundance of the heart.

It is on this ground I would gladly have attacked the new Philofophers, had I thought myfelf ftrong enough to engage with them. They might have cried out againft my way of reafoning, becaufe I fhould have preffed them clofely; but they would not complain of my want of temper. I would have fpoken to them, as a moft tender friend; like one as zealous for their happinefs, as for my own; like a writer of truth and an impartial man, who would acknowledge their talents, and have

often

often done justice to the excellency of their understanding. I have presumption enough to think they would have liked me, though their Antagonist.

I shall not execute this plan, because I enjoy not here that happy tranquillity, which is breathed at St. MARINO: it is there a person enjoys a quietude, that has something heavenly.

This ease, however, must be baneful to the sciences and the *Belles Lettres*, since there are not seen, in the immense catalogue of famous men, any Writers Citizens of St. MARINO. I advise you to spur on your subjects, while you are in place. But make haste; for it is not of your reign that it was said: *and of his reign there shall be no end.** Your countrymen have natural parts; you have only to promote their exertion.

Here is a letter as long as your Dominions, especially if you consider the heart that dictated it, and in which you have often a good place. It is thus people write, and it is thus people love one another, when they have been at College together. Adieu.

* Luke i. 33.

LETTER LIX.

To Count ***.

I Was not willing to advise you, my dear Friend, to apply to the Mathematics, till you were well grounded in the principles of Religion. I feared that by giving yourself up to that science,

science, which admits only of what is demonstrated, you might become like so many Mathematicians, who are for subjecting our mysteries to Demonstration. The Mathematics, notwithstanding their great extent, have nothing but what is very finite, if we come to speak of God. All the lines that can be drawn on earth, all the points at which it is possible to terminate these lines, are no more than *Infinitesimals* in comparison of that immense Being, who admits of neither parallels nor ratios.

The Mathematics will give you a just way of thinking. Without them, a certain method necessary for rectifying our thoughts, classing our ideas, and settling a sure judgment, is wanting. It is easy to perceive, in reading a book (though it treats of a moral subject) whether or no the author was a Mathematician: I am seldom mistaken in this point. The most famous Metaphysician among the French, could never have composed *The Research after Truth*,* nor the learned LEIBNITZ his *Theodicea*, had they not been Mathematicians. One discovers in their publications that Geometrical order, which makes their reasoning close, strong, and above all, methodical.

Order is something so beautiful, that in all nature there is nothing but what bears its stamp; and without it there is no Harmony. So that the Mathematics may be said to be an Universal Science, which connects together all

* Father Malebranche.

the others, and expofes them in their fineft relations one to another.

The eyes of a Mathematician are generally certain and fure; they analyfe and decompofe with juftnefs. Whereas a man deprived of all knowledge of the Mathematics, fees things in a vague and almoft ever in an uncertain manner.

Strive therefore to acquire this fcience, fo worthy of our curiofity, and fo neceffary in itfelf; but fo as not to be too much taken up with it.—We muft always endeavour to be mafters of ourfelves, to whatever kind of ftudy we apply.

Had I your time and your youth, I would acquire a more extenfive knowledge of GEOMETRY. I have all along had a predilection for that fcience. My turn of mind makes me feek with avidity whatever is methodical, and I fet little value on thofe works, wherein nothing but Imagination is found.

We have three principal Sciences, which I compare to the three effential parts of our frame: Theology, which, for its fpiritual nature, is like our foul; the Mathematics, which for their combination and juftnefs, exprefs our reafon; and Natural Philofophy, which for its mechanical operations, reprefents our bodies: and thefe three Sciences, which ought to be in perfect harmony, when each keeps within its own fphere, neceffarily elevate us towards their Author, the fource and plenitude of all light.

I for-

I formerly, while at *Afcoli*, fet about a work, the defign of which was to fhew the perfect agreement which fubfifts between all the fciences. I pointed out their fource, their end, and the relation they had one to another: but the exercifes of the Cloifter, and the Leffons I was obliged to give, hindered me from finifhing it. I have fome pieces of it, which I will look out from among my papers; and, if they will amufe you, you may read them. There are fome ideas in it, and fome fight of things: but it is only a rough fketch or draught of a work, which you muft fill up, while you read, as you are capable of doing it.

Philofophy, without Geometry, is like Medicine without Chemiftry. The greateft part of our modern Philofophers are guilty of falfe reafoning, merely becaufe they are no Geometricians. They take fophifms for truth, and if they lay down any true principles, the confequences they draw from them are falfe. Study alone does not make a man learned; nor does the knowledge of the fciences make him a Philofopher. But we live in an age, when people are impofed on by founding words; and a man thinks himfelf a genius, when he ftrikes out any thing new or fingular. Truft not thofe writers, who are more taken up with ftyle than matter, and who venture any thing for the pleafure of furprifing.

I will fend you, the very firft opportunity, a treatife on Trigonometry; and, if neceffary,
I will

I will prove Geometrically, that is, to a demonftration, that I am ever your beft friend.

Rome, June 22, 1753.

LETTER LX.

To a Religious of the Conventual Friars-Minors.

YOU are in the wrong, Rev. Father, to imagine that I take no concern in our General Chapters. I am fenfibly interefted in them; not indeed like one ambitious of promotion, but like a friend of our Order, who earneftly wifhes that learning and piety may enjoy the firft places in it. A Superior, who is barely a man of learning, may do a deal of harm; and he, who has nothing but devotion, may do ftill more. "Where there is no learning, nothing can be done:" this is a judicious reflection of *St. Therefa*. Befides learning and piety, a Superior ftands in need of wifdom and difcretion; for the difference between teaching and governing is very great. It has even been obferved, that no Writers whatfoever, even thofe who give the fineft leffons to Monarchs, are fit for adminiftration. Good fenfe has often been of more ufe than great parts, or even genius, towards governing men with prudence. A man of too great parts has too many ideas, and he is ever changing.

I exert all poffible zeal, to get thofe chofen fuperiors, who are the fitteft for government, but without any view to myfelf, and without intrigue.

intrigue. I choose no other Empire than my Cell; and scarce can I there keep my imagination and thoughts in order. Man is so often tossed about by his own desires, that he does not always do what he would, though he be at liberty to act, or not to act.

I shall propose at the next meeting what you desire; and I presume it will be agreed to, as far as one can answer for a multitude of opinions, and different dispositions. Truth ought naturally to drag all men along with it; but it shews itself in so many different aspects, that every one forms his judgment from the light in which he sees it.—The view varies according to our ideas and our interest.

Be convinced that I am, as heretofore, ever ready to oblige you, ever your servant and good Friend.

LETTER LXI.

To Cardinal SPINELLI.

MOST EMINENT,

THE book will be approved of, as it deserves. Whatever certain Fanatics may alledge against it, it contains nothing, but what is very orthodox, and very practicable. If a Pharisaical spirit is suffered to go on, we shall have nothing in the Church, but trifling practices of Devotion; and Religion, which in itself is so beautiful and sublime, will become a circle of superstitions.

People

People are generally not much captivated with what tends to the reformation of the heart; they take a pleasure in growing old, without rooting up their bad habits, relying on some prayers, which they patter over in a hurry, and think sufficient to carry them to heaven.

It is not surprising that the world should seduce us: but it is inconceivable how men, who value themselves on opposing its maxims, do not guard souls against this seduction. There are *Pharisees* in every age, and will be to the end of the world. They build up *white sepulchers*, instead of erecting temples to the Eternal; and lull the Faithful asleep, by amusing them with practices, which neither influence the understanding or heart.

It were to be wished that every one had your Eminence's eye. What abuses would be reformed! What false practices suppressed! When a Pastor nourishes his mind with nothing but the sacred scripture, the Councils and Fathers, there is no fear of his Diocese falling into superstitious practices. MURATORI said that "trifling devotions were like balls for taking out spots in cloaths, which remove the spots only in appearance, to make them larger."

Though overpowered with labour, I will give your Lordship a proof, by undertaking what you have imposed on me, that I never will decline the happiness of convincing you of that sincere respect, with which I am, &c.

Rome, July 3, 1752.

LETTER LXII.

To the Abbé LAMI.

I KNOW not where I am in the midſt of the diſorder that reigns in my cell and in my head. Every thing is in confuſion: I muſt write to an Author as methodical as you are, to clear up ſuch a Chaos.

Your laſt letter on Poetry would have been a maſter-piece in my eyes, had you but characterized the Poetic genius of each nation. The *Italians* are not Poets after the manner of the *Engliſh*; nor the *Germans* after the manner of the *French*. In the firſt principles they reſemble each other; but they differ in warmth and enthuſiaſm. The *German* Poetry is a fire that gives light; the *French* a fire that crackles; the *Italian* a fire that burns; the *Engliſh* a fire that blackens.

In our poetical pieces we heap too many images one upon another; we ought to uſe them more ſparingly, if we would have them excite a livelier ſenſation. Nothing awakes a reader better than ſurpriſing him; but this cannot be done, when the things capable of producing that effect, are too much multiplied.

Happy that temperate genius, which equally in Poetry, as in Proſe, manages with delicacy the Epiſodes and ſituations! I ſoon grow tired of a garden, where I find nothing but caſcades and groves; whereas one enchants me, when I find in it only here and there verdant alcoves, and pieces of water-works. Violets gain infinitely by being only half seen through a thick foliage. A flower that conceals itself from sight, excites the greater curiosity.

Beauties are only relative. If every thing was equally grand, the eyes would soon tire with admiring. Nature, which ought to be the model of every writer, varies its landscapes in such a manner, that they never fatigue the sight. The finest meadows are found in the neighbourhood of the most simple Valley, and often a delightful river runs at the foot of a lonesome hill.

Repeat these lessons, my dear Abbè, in order, if possible, to correct our Poets of that effusion of beauties, which are no more than so much gold heaped up without order or taste. Your sheets are as much esteemed, as your genius is admired; and when a Journalist has acquired that double glory, he may talk like a master, well assured that attention will be paid to what he says.

When I was a young scholar, I lost one of my companions, to whom a sympathy of nature had intimately united me. Alas! After many a solitary walk together, many a reflection on things we did not then understand, but which we were desirous of understanding—he died: and I thought nothing could better mitigate my grief, than to address to him some verses; being convinced, even at that age, that we only changed life, when we seemed to die.

I praised, above all, his candour and his piety; for he was really an example of every virtue. But this elogium, as I was then made sensible, was faulty on account of the paintings, with which it was overcharged. I introduced into it all the beauties of the country, and did not allow my readers time to breathe.—It was a tree choaked with too much wood, and a luxuriancy of leaves, so that no fruit was seen on it.

From that moment, I never again attempted verse. I contented myself with reading the Poets, and I endeavoured to find out their faults and their beauties. What vexed me was, that my work, being full of imperfections, would never be handed down to posterity, and that my Friend, on every consideration, deserved the honour of immortality.

Never will he be blotted out of my heart; and thus it is friends have a resource in sentiment, when their mental abilities are not capable of making a return of friendship—This is my case with regard to you. Abstract from my thoughts, and think only on the attachment I have vowed to you; and you will find, that, if I am not a good speaker, I am at least a true friend, and a good servant.—Make a trial of me. *Rome, Dec.* 10, 1755.

LETTER LXIII.

To Baron KRONECH, *a German Gentleman.*

I Know not which to admire most in you, Mr. Baron, your understanding or your pleasing manner. Nothing can prove better than your

your example, how much the GERMANS are possessed of the qualities requisite for friendship. All of them, with whom I have been acquainted, had the best of souls.

If you continue to employ yourself in what is useful, you will be an honour to your nation, and to all who know you. I felicitate myself, that mere chance procured me the pleasure of your agreeable conversation. I have all along been a gainer by being communicative, having thereby met either with persons, who merited the warmest attachment; or unhappy beings, who stood in need of helps and counsel.

There is something so sweet in obliging, that a person cannot go too far to meet those in his way, when led on by this motive. I wish this letter might have no end, for the pleasure I take in talking to you; but I must recollect what I owe to my choir-duties, my ordinary labours, and the fear of tiring you. Accept therefore without ceremony the vows I make for the sight of you here again, that I may once more tell you how much I have the honour to be, &c.

LETTER LXIV.

To M. DE LA BRUYÈRE, *the Chargè des Affaires of France, at the Court of Rome.*

SIR,

I Went to your house with a design of stealing at least an hour of your time, to turn it to my own profit; but there was no getting
into

into that valuable cabinet, from whence you correspond with that of Versailles, in a manner so much to your own honour, and to the advantage of your amiable nation. I came quickly away (I who am no farther a Politician, than not to be one) and on my return home, I said to myself, I must never be seen at your house again, till I am sent for.

Did I know, however, the hour you destine to your favourite Ladies, the *Belles Lettres*, I would strive to get to the speech of you. Something would come from your excellent memory, and your lively imagination, which would embellish mine; and then my company would be worth something.

I always regret having heard only half of that certain Manuscript read, where Rome, represented such as she is, gives full satisfaction to curiosity. Flowers and fruits are there blended together, and form the prettiest basket that can be presented to persons of taste. My soul is eager to hear the rest: and I think you are too polite not to gratify it.

You could not choose a happier Epocha to paint Rome to advantage, than the reign of Benedict XIV. He seems to give new life to this city in the eyes of Foreigners, and the sciences assume a new lustre to make their court to him. So true it is, that nothing is wanting but a Monarch to give life and motion even to things inanimate.

If by chance you should have an hour with which you do not know what to do, send for
Ganga-

Ganganelli; and he will give proof that neither study, business, nor visit, can detain him, when proof is to be given of the zeal with which I have the honour to be, &c.

LETTER LXV.

To the same.

SIR,

YOU are really too generous in granting me three hours of your time, and leaving them to my choice. To-morrow, since you give me leave, I will come and enjoy the benefit of your courtesy. It is to no purpose for me to tell my intellect to dress in *gala,* and set itself off in an elegant taste; I am sure it will be able to do nothing, but admire you. Its timidity, joined to its small acquisition, will hinder it from exhibiting any brilliancy. Expect, therefore, to be at the whole expence of our entertainment—You alone will be vexed at that, for your modesty is equal to your learning.

Notwithstanding the pleasure I take in seeing you, I should still take more, had you yet with you the Duke de *Nivernois,* whose heart and understanding every one extols. He is a Nobleman who is learned only with the learned, and whose knowledge, as I may say, is interlaced with roses and jessamies.

I will let you see a production of one of our young Religious, which will convince you, that not only erudition, but even taste may
be

be found in Cloisters. When talents are exercised, as well as encouraged, we see plants, which had been looked upon as barren, produce the finest fruit.

I have the honour to be, &c.

Rome, May 3, 1753.

LETTER LXVI.

To Cardinal QUERINI, *Bishop of Brestia.*

MOST EMINENT,

YOUR Eminence does me too much honour, and has too great an opinion of my weak abilities, when you disdain not to consult me on the method of studying and teaching Theology.

There was formerly only one way of exhibiting this sublime science, which, springing from God himself, as from its source, spreads itself through the whole Church, like a most majestic and overflowing river; and this is called *Positive Divinity.*

The Professors contented themselves (out of respect, no doubt, for the sacred doctrine of Scripture, Councils and Fathers) with simply laying before the eyes of the Students the Morality and Dogmas of the Gospel. Thus were the Commandments of God formerly laid open before the eyes of the Jews, without any commentaries, and they fixed them in their memory, and in their heart, as what concerned them most, and was to constitute their happiness. The

The Church, in every age agitated by storms, (though seated on the holy mount, whose foundations are eternal) saw from time to time rise out of her bosom rebellious children, who learned the art of *Sophistry*; and it was their artificial language that obliged the defenders of the faith to make use of the *syllogystic* form.

Every body knows the Epocha, when certain Doctors bristled themselves up with *Enthymems* and *Syllogisms*, to drive, even from their very last entrenchments, the Heretics, who squabbled about the meaning of every text of scripture, and about every word in it. Thomas, the *Angel of the school*, Scotus the *subtle Doctor*, thought themselves obliged to follow the same form; and insensibly their method, supported by their brilliant reputation, prevailed in the Universities.

As all things commonly degenerate, it was impossible to bring *positive Divinity* into use again; and the manner of teaching in the schools, which got the name of the *scholastic* method, ran entirely upon distinctions and words. By endeavouring to render every thing clear, every thing became obscure; and very often no answer was given to any thing, by endeavouring to answer every thing.

Besides that this *Ergotism* appertained only to Philosophy, it had the appearance of rendering problematical the most certain truths; and this was the more vexatious, as the questions agitated were in themselves ridiculous; and they split

split hairs even about the mysteries of Religion, whose sublime depth ought to stop every man that thinks.

Since the *scholastic* method however has the advantage of helping the memory, by giving a form to the arguments; since moreover the abuses with which it is reproached, never obscure the sacred truths, whose reign is as lasting, as that of God himself, it has been thought proper to retain it.

I have therefore, my Lord, always thought, that the *scholastic* Method, modified in the manner it is taught in the *sapienza* at Rome, and in the first schools of the Christian world, might still subsist without enervating Morality, or altering the Dogmas, provided the Professors were perfectly men of learning, so as not to take mere opinions for points of Faith.

Nothing is more dangerous than to give a thing as a matter of Faith, which is merely a matter of opinion, and to confound a pious belief with what is revealed. A true Theologian never uses any distinctions, but such as are solid and real; and draws his consequences only from such principles as are clear and precise.

A truth is no way better proved, than by the common doctrine of all the Churches; a point to which our modern Theologians do not pay sufficient attention. The Dogma of the Eucharist never appeared more solidly established, than when a perfect conformity of doctrine, with regard to that point, was shewn between the Roman-Catholics and the Greek Schismatics.

Theology,

Theology, therefore, in order to be solid and luminous, that is to say, to preserve its most essential attributes, stands only in need of a clear and simple exposition of all the Articles of Faith; and then it appears supported with all its proofs and authorities.

If a person, for instance, would establish the truth of the Mystery of the INCARNATION, he must prove, that as God can only act for himself, he must have had in view, at the creation of the world, the ETERNAL WORD, by whom the Universe and ages were made; and that, "when he formed *Adam*, as *Tertullian* expresses it, he already traced the lineaments of JESUS CHRIST." This agrees with the doctrine of St. *Paul*, who teaches in the most express manner, that every thing exists in that divine Mediator, and subsists through him alone. *All things were created by him, and in him .... and things subsist by him.**

He next proves from the figures and the prophecies (which he shews to be authentic) that the INCARNATION is their object, and that there is nothing in the sacred books, but what directly or indirectly refers thereto. He then shews the time when, and the place where, this ineffable mystery was accomplished, by examining the character of the signs which accompanied it, of the witnesses who attested it, of the prodigies which followed it; and unfolds whatever Tradition has handed down on that subject.

* Omnia per ipsum & in ipso creata sunt.... & omnia in ipso constant. *Col.* i. 16, 17.

It is then he shews the authority of the Fathers of the Church, the force of their reasoning, the sublimity of their comparisons; and he makes use of the *Scholastic* method to disentangle the sophisms of the Heresiarchs, in order to fight them with their own weapons, and to conquer them.

Thus *Positive* Theology resembles a magnificent garden, and the *Scholastic* a thick-set fence surrounding it, to prevent mischievous animals from getting in to lay it waste.

If, when I filled the Divinity-chair, I taught Theology exactly after the Scholastic method, the reason was, that being a brother of *Scotus*, I could not be dispensed with from teaching *Scotism*. It would ill become a particular to endeavour to change the manner of teaching in an Order, of which he is a member: it might be attended with some dangerous consequence, though no one ought servilely to embrace whimsical opinions.

As to you, my Lord, who in quality of Bishop, have an incontestible right over Doctrine, and can give it what form you please, I entreat you to recommend it to your Theologians, that they make use of the *Scholastic* method with discretion, for fear of enervating Theology.

I shall believe that they correspond with your lights, if I see them go to drink at the fountains, instead of barely copying manuscript treatises on Theology; and if they content themselves with expounding the doctrine
of

of the Church, without giving themselves up to disputes, or imbibing a party spirit.

That spirit, my Lord, is the more dangerous, as, under its influence, people give us their own opinions, instead of those eternal truths, which every one ought to respect; and abandon themselves to altercations, which, under pretence of maintaining the cause of God, extinguish charity.

Suffer none to deny the OMNIPOTENT EFFICACY of GRACE, in order to maintain Free-will; nor under pretence of enhancing that inestimable and perfectly gratuitous gift, allow any one to destroy our Liberty; or through too great a respect for the saints, to forget what we owe to JESUS CHRIST. All the Theological truths are so connected together, that they make only one; and some of them are covered with a mysterious veil, which it is impossible to remove.

The great fault of some Theologians is, that they want to explain every thing, and know not when to stop. The Apostle, for instance, speaking of heaven says: *that the eye hath not seen, nor ear heard .... what things God hath prepared for them that love him**: and the Theologians give us a description of heaven, as if they had been there. They assign every one of the Elect his rank; and they are ready to cry out *Heresy!* should a person dare to contradict them. A true Theologian stops where he ought to stop; and when a thing is not re-

* 1. Cor. i, 9.

vealed,

vealed, and the Church has not spoken, he never presumes to decide on it. There will ever be an impenetrable cloud between God and man, to the moment of Eternity.

The figures ceased with the old Law to give place to the Reality; but Evidence is not to be found till after death: such is the œconomy of Religion. It were to be wished, my Lord, that when we speak of God, we always spoke of him with a holy awe, not as of a Being, whom we dreaded, but as of a spirit, whose immense perfections excite the greated respect and astonishment. Thus, instead of saying: " God would be unjust, or a liar; God would not be almighty, if such a thing happened:" we ought to accustom ourselves never to join such injurious words with that of God. Let us content ourselves with answering like St. *Paul: Is there injustice with God? God forbid.**

' The name of GOD is so awful and holy, that it is never to be used in pieces of wit. Is it not enough for man to exercise himself with the *phænomena* of nature, to dispute about the Elements and their effects, without making God himself the subject of their contests?

This it is that has rendered Theology ridiculous in the eyes of Freethinkers, and perhaps has taught them to introduce the name of God in all their objections and sarcasms: For how can Theology, which is nothing else but an exposition of the Providence, the Wisdom, in a word, of all the attributes of the Infinite

* Rom. ix. 14.

Being,

Being, the Almighty Being, the Being by excellence, appear a futile science, were it exhibited with dignity? Will the knowledge of a grain of sand, the sport of the wind, of an insect, which man crushes under his foot, lastly of an earth, which itself must be destroyed, be superior to the knowledge of God himself? Of that God, *in whom we are, move and live*, before whom the Ocean is only a drop of water, the Mountains a point, the Universe an atom!

A Theologian must begin his course with that immense and supreme Being. After having demonstrated his Existence absolutely necessary, and necessarily Eternal; after having sought out, even in his bosom, the creation of spirits; after having proved that every thing emanates from him as from its first Principle; that every thing breathes in him, as in its Centre, that every thing returns to him, as to its End, he displays his immense Wisdom, his infinite Goodness, from whence results REVELATION, and the Worship we pay him.

Then the Law of nature, the written law, and the law of grace appear each in their rank, according to their respective merit, and in a chronological order. Then he demonstrates how God has all along been worshipped by a small number of adorers in spirit and truth; how the Church superseded the Synagogue; how she cut off, from age to age, the rebels, who attempted to corrupt her Morality or Dogmas, and how, ever powerful in works and in words,

she

she was assisted by the greatest Doctors, and maintained in her purity, in the midst of the most frightful scandals, and the most cruel divisions.

It is necessary that those who study Theology should find real light in what is taught them, and not those false glimmerings, fitter to dazzle than enlighten; that they be led to the purest sources under the guidance of St. Augustin and St. Thomas; and that whatever savours of novelty be laid aside; that they be inspired with the evangelical spirit of toleration, even towards those, who attack the Faith; and that it be inculcated to them, that the spirit of Jesus Christ is not a spirit of bitterness and tyranny.

It is not by using invectives against Heretics, or by shewing a bitter zeal against Unbelievers, that they are to be brought to the truth; but by shewing a sincere desire for their conversion: by never speaking of them, unless to shew our sincere love for them, at the very time we refute their sophisms.

It is necessary that a Professor in Theology should contrast the Theologians of Heathenism with those of Christianity, since that would be the most effectual way to overthrow Mythology, cover with eternal ridicule the superstitions of the Ancients, and raise on their ruins the doctrine of truth.

It is still more necessary that he should avoid being systematic. When eternal truths are to be taught, we are to hold solely to the Church,

Scripture and Tradition, becaufe we are deputed by the body of Paftors, to inftruct in their name, and to exercife their authority.

Would to God this method had always been exactly followed! The Church would not have feen the moft afflicting and obftinate difputes arife in its bofom. The Paffions take the place of Charity, and the mutual hatred of Doctors produces the moft melancholy effects.

Hence it follows, my Lord, that your Eminence cannot pay too much attention to the nominating of moderate Theologians, left a bitter zeal do more harm than good. The fpirit of the Gofpel, is a fpirit of peace; and thofe who are to preach it, ought not to be men of a turbulent difpofition.

Might I prefume fo far, my Lord, I would intreat your Eminence to order a body of Theology to be drawn up, which might be for ever taught in your Diocefe, and which certainly would be adopted by feveral Bifhops. The liberty of the fchools ought to be allowed to continue only relatively to Queftions that are of themfelves indifferent; for there is only *one Baptifm* and *one Faith*.

The end of Theology was not to exercife the wit of young people, but to enlighten the mind, and elevate it to him, who is the plenitude and fource of all light.

It is proper to provide the fcholars with the beft books relating to the Treatife given them. The moft excellent manner of ftudying Religion, is to be perfectly acquainted with

with the sacred Writers, the Councils and Fathers—It is in their school we learn not to go astray; there we learn to speak of Christianity in a manner worthy of it.

I have nothing more to say, my Lord, but that a Professor in Theology ought to be a man of equal piety and learning. Eternal truths (as far as possibly it can be done) ought to pass only through lips perfectly holy. From thence results a blessing of heaven on the Master and the Scholars; and an *odour of life* for a whole Diocese. Italy has all along been happy in having Theologians, whose piety corresponds with the purity of her Theology.

Excuse, my Lord, my temerity, which would be unpardonable, had not your Eminence ordered me to give you my opinion. I submit it entirely to your Eminence's lights, having the honour to be with the most perfect obedience, and most profound respect, &c.

Rome, May 31, 1753.

LETTER LXVII.

To the Count de BIELK, *a Senator of Rome.*

EXCELLENCE,

I Will wait on your Illustrious Lordship as soon as possible, in order to examine the Manuscript your Excellency condescended to mention to me. A Religious man is no where more at his ease than at your Excellence's palace. He finds there a most delightful solitude,
choice

choice of books, and your amiable conversation. Nothing in the commerce of life is more agreeable than that Philosophic liberty, which, free from servitude, raised above grandeurs, acting without constraint, is independent of every thing, but duty.

Nevertheless you tell me that you are not happy. What then can you wish for to be so? Those haughty Romans, who inhabited the Capitol, where you reside, with all their fame and Philosophy, enjoyed not your tranquillity: they lived in the midst of storms, and you are in the centre of peace: they were always engaged in war, and Rome is now that city of which the Prophet speaks, and *whose confines are the borders of peace* *.

A man cannot be happy either in the midst of riches or noise, but only in the company of a few books, and of some friends. If we suffer ourselves to be governed by humour, we are lost.—It is the greatest enemy we have.

Your Excellence has so many resources in your own mind, that you ought not even to know what it is to be uneasy. For my part, all I know of it is only from the Dictionaries that explain the word, and truly, did it attempt to get into my cell, I would soon find a remedy: I would immediately come and improve by your knowledge, and often repeat the sentiments of respect and attachment, with which I am, &c.

Convent of the Apostles.

* Qui posuit fines tuos pacem. *Ps.* 147. Vulg.

LETTER LXVIII.

To Count ***.

WELL, my dear Friend, what are we doing? It is a long time since I have seen you: I do not deserve that privation. You know that I readily quit my pen, my work, and my books, when you pay me a visit.

Those who come to see us, neither stand in need of our studies, nor do they want to know our concerns: but that is what a great many studious people do not consider. When a person comes to see them, they are either taken up with themselves alone, or their own concerns, without reflecting, that they owe themselves entirely to their visiters.

I always made it my rule to receive kindly whoever honours me with a visit, though out of season: it is enough that he is my neighbour. Judge from hence whether or not you will meet with a kind reception.

There are now exactly ten days passed, since I saw the little Abbè. I fear; but I dare not tell you that—The art of holding one's tongue is a great virtue. Happy he who says nothing but what he ought to say! Accustom yourself to secrecy without affecting too much reserve: a mysterious man is intolerable in company: and a small share of sagacity makes it an easy matter to divine the thoughts of one, who assumes the appearance of a person who says nothing.

I am

I am not close; I however trust no one either with my correspondence or connexions. Never make use of cunning; it is a bad resource, and is moreover incompatible with probity, and is soon discovered.

I have heard the young lady spoken of, who is destined for you; and from the picture given me of her, I think she will make you happy: for I am told that she is neither a Devotee, a prude, nor a whim. I will tell you more when we meet; but let it be soon, to-morrow, to-day, just now. I am without any reserve, your servant and best friend, &c.

LETTER LXIX.

To the Rev. Father CONCINA, *a Dominican Friar.*

IT is surprising, Rev. Father, no doubt, that in so enlightened an age as ours, there should be found Casuists capable of teaching the abominations you attack. Those who think your zeal too bitter, know not what Religion requires, when its morality or Dogmas are impugned. It is then you are to say to yourself: *Cry aloud without ceasing.**

All sorts of errors would insensibly creep into the Church, were no-body to cry out against them: but no sooner does a heterodox opinion appear, or is any loose morality

* Clama, ne cesses. *If.* lviii. 1.

broached,

broached, but the sacred trumpet is clapped to the mouth, and the Pastors, who are always on the watch, stop the evil in its source.

Your work gave me sensible pleasure: I found therein that holy vehemence, which characterizes the Fathers of the Church. I could have wished to come and see you; but your occupations, as well as mine, thwart the inclination I might have to assure you by word of mouth of the respectful consideration, with which I have the honour to be, &c.

Rome, March 7, 1753.

LETTER LXX.

To Cardinal GENTILI.

MOST EMINENT,

I Will come to-morrow precisely at the hour your Eminence has appointed, like one zealous to prove, on every occasion, how much your Lordship's orders are respected by me. I cannot possibly bring with me the writing you mention, as it is not finished; but I will endeavour to supply the want of it by stretching my memory. It sometimes serves me pretty well. I am, my Lord, with the most profound respect, your Eminence's, &c.

Rome, March 7, 1752.

LETTER LXXI.

To Monseigneur Zaruski, *Grand Referendary of Poland.*

My Lord,

I Have in vain fought for the book you wanted; it is neither in our Library, nor in any other in Rome. A perfon muft be endowed with your fagacity to find it. What work is there which you have not difcovered? There is not a book in the world, but owes you homage, or one that can efcape your refearches.

You defign to perpetuate the honour the Polish nation has all along acquired, by fignalizing yourfelf by an uncommon erudition. The Copernicuses for natural Philofophy, the Hosiuses for Theology, the Faluskis for Hiftory, the Zamoiskis for the *Belles Lettres*, the Fathers of the Pious, or Charity-Schools for Erudition, the Sobieskis for the Art Military, will never be forgotten.

The Library which you have juft opened for the benefit of the public, in concert with your illuftrious Brother the Bifhop of *Cracovia*, is filled with Polish Writers, the moft diftinguifhed in every branch. It would be a pity, that fo famous a Republic fhould not keep up a love for the fciences among its fubjects, and that the natural genius of your worthy countrymen fhould remain without culture.

The wars, of which Poland has fo often been the dreadful Theatre, have made many an Author miscarry. They would have written with indelible ink the productions of their genius; but they wrote, in their own blood, the characters of their valour.

Circumstances almost constantly determine the lot of men: one stifles his aptitude for the Sciences, by becoming a soldier; another becomes eminent for his erudition, by leading a private life: and Providence orders all for the best: *It reacheth from end to end mightily, and ordereth all things sweetly**.

I could wish, my Lord, that your love for the sciences and for books, inspired you with a desire of once more seeing Rome. You formerly came thither to learn; you will now come to give us lessons, and receive the respects of every body, but particularly of him, who is your very humble, &c.

Rome, July 9, 1755.

* Pertingit à fine usque ad finem fortiter, suaviterque disponit omnia. *Wisd.* viii. 1.

LETTER LXXII.

To a Friend of his, a Religious man, nominated to a Bishoprick.

AFTER having been an humble disciple of St. *Francis*, behold you now in the rank of Apostles! It is sufficient to tell you, my dear Friend, that you are to be elevated for no other purpose, but to become in reality the
servant

servant of all, and that you are to have no splendor, but that of virtue.

In the eyes of Faith there is no dignity on earth so much to be dreaded as the office of a Bishop. He is to watch night and day over the flock of JESUS CHRIST, and to bear in mind that he is accountable before his tribunal for every sheep that goes astray. He must reproduce himself, that he may never tire; he must multiply himself, that he may be every where; he must live retired, that he may study and pray.

There are two things so essentially required of Bishops, that they cannot be worthy of their dignity, if they possess them not in an eminent degree; *Purity*, which ought to make them like the Angels themselves (for which reason they are called by that name in the sacred scripture, as appears from the first chapter of Revelation) and *Knowledge*, which in the Gospel has merited for them the honour of being called the *Light of the world*. In quality of men without *reproach*, they ought not to lie even under any suspicion with regard to their morals and conduct; and they are moreover obliged to preserve others from corruption: and for this reason are they called the *salt of the earth**. In quality of men of learning, they ought to be the eye of the blind, the foot of the lame, the light of the world. It is not enough for a Bishop that he be a man of virtue, and that he consults men

* *Matt.* v. 13.

of learning to know what he is to do; he must of himself difcern good from evil, truth from error; for he is the Judge of doctrine and manners: and if he has not the talent of judging, he will not have that of governing, but will fuffer himfelf to be impofed on.

My comfort is, that you have had a folid education, and will fee every thing with your own eyes: This is abfolutely neceffary not to become the dupe either of hypocrites or informers.

I make no doubt, but that you have already ferioufly meditated on the Epiftle of St. *Paul* to *Timothy*, and that of St. *Peter* to all the Faithful. By the firft you will have feen, that a Bifhop ought to be *irreprehenfible, fober, chafte, pacific,* not to live like thofe Chriftians, whofe hiftory is precifely that of the wicked rich man, in as much as they are dreffed in *purple* and fine *linen,* and feed every day daintily, and fuffer *Lazarus* to expire at their gate.

By the fecond you will have learned not to domineer over any Church-man intrufted to your care; for the fpirit of JESUS CHRIST is not a fpirit of domineering, but a fpirit of meeknefs and humility; fo that a Bifhop ought to confider the Parochial Clergy as his equals in the order of Chriftian charity, though they be not fo in that of the Hierarchy—His houfe ought to be their Inn.

Do not eafily excufe yourfelf from announcing the word of God, bearing in mind that St. *Paul* fays, he was not fent to baptize, but to to preach. Manage so, that there be none of the Sacraments, which you administer not from time to time, to shew your Diocesans that you are at their service in sickness, as well as in health; at their birth, as well as at their death.

Above all, be exact in visiting the domain intrusted to your care, and let not your Visitations be storms that excite fear and dread, but benign dews that diffuse joy and fecundity.

If you find by chance a fellow-labourer who has sinned, spread over him the cloak of charity, to bring him back to his duty by mildness, and to hide the scandal, as far as possible. If what he has been guilty of amount to a crime, privately engage him to quit his place; but before he does that, assure him of a support and maintenance.

I will not tell you to have a paternal tenderness for the Religious; it would be an affront. You are indebted to them for all you are, and it was at their school that you, as well as I, learned whatever we know. Visit them often in a cordial manner; it is the way to excite among them a laudable emulation, and to make them respected. To honour men, whose lives are a perpetual labour, is doing honour to one's self.—A General, who should despise his Officers, would render himself worthy of the greatest contempt.

Suffer not the piety of the faithful to be fed with false legends, or amused with trifling devotions. Watch that they be taught to have continually recourse to Jesus Christ, as to the sole and only Mediator, and to honour the Saints only with a reference to him. You are intrusted with teaching, and you ought to know what is taught.

Be nice in laying on hands, the more so, as *Italy* abounds with Supernumerary Priests, who, dragging with them ignorance and poverty, even to foreign nations, debase the dignity of the Priesthood, and disgrace their country.

Bestow no benefices but on known merit; and especially with regard to such as have the care of souls annexed to them: let them never be given to any who unite not knowledge with piety: and remember, that he who has laboured long, ought to have the preference to one who has been lately ordained.

Choose none for your associates in the government of your Diocese, but men who have grown grey in the ministry, and who command respect, as much by their age, as by their virtues. A Bishop who keeps company and advises only with young men is despised, seeing they may every instant engage him in quarrels. The Pope has no more than one Vicar-General, and consequently one will be enough for you.

Let *my Lord* be the least of your titles; and let those of *Father* and *Servant* be much dearer to you; for the figure of this world passes away, and all grandeurs with it.

Lastly,

Lastly, in the midst of riches and honours, keep no more than what is necessary to supply your real wants, and gain respect; bearing in mind that St *Paul* reduced his body to servitude, and that every Christian ought to mortify himself.

Above all things reside, and again reside. A Pastor, who withdraws from his flock without a reason, has no right to eat.

These are dreadful truths; but as we have no power to change them, we must either submit to them, or abdicate.

Let the Poor be your friends, your brethren, and even your guests at table. You cannot give too much. Alms are one of the most essential obligations of a Bishop; and these are to be bestowed in prisons, in private houses, in the public streets, and, in short, every where, in order to copy after our divine Saviour, who ceased not doing good all the days of his mortal life. But above all, give with cheerfulness: *God loves a cheerful giver**; and give so, as even to reduce yourself to want.

I have mentioned to you nothing concerning your domestic occupations, as I am convinced you will divide your time between prayer, study, and the government of your Diocese. No one tires with reading the *Scripture*, and *Fathers*, who knows their value, and lives not in dissipation; and who is sensible that the office of Bishop is a dreadful burden, and not a secular dignity.

* Hilarem datorem diligit Deus. 2 *Cor.* ix. 17.

Give

Give audience to every body; make yourself popular, after the example of our divine Master, who suffered the least children to come near him, and spoke to them with the greatest kindness. Frequently visit those of your Diocesans, who have suffered any misfortune; assist and comfort them.

It is an odious thing in a Bishop to be acquainted only with the rich and most distinguished people of his Diocese. The poor and inferior sort grumble, and not without reason; for very often, in the sight of God, they are men of the greatest worth.

If any dispute arise among the inhabitants of your Episcopal city, become immediately a Mediator. A Bishop ought not to engage in any law-suits himself; and those of others, he ought to labour to compromise.

Examine in person the Ecclesiastics, who present themselves for Orders, and take care that no childish questions, or such as are foreign to what they are obliged to know, be put to them. Watch that your Confessors observe the rules laid down by St Charles, in the tribunal of Penance.

From a pretence of business contract not a habit of seldom going to your Cathedral. The public is not satisfied with these excuses; they want to be edified; and who will pray, if a Bishop does not?

After a life so well spent, you will find yourself surrounded, at the hour of your death, with a multitude of good works. You know that

that thefe follow us to Eternity; whereas pride, grandeur, and titles, will be loft in the darknefs of the grave, and leave nothing in the foul, but a frightful void. Often read what is faid to the Bifhops pointed at in the Revelation, and tremble.

I think I have in this letter gone through all the duties of the Epifcopate; it is your's to practife them. You will have, moft affuredly, faid to yourfelf, whatever I have juft now been recalling to your mind; but you forced me to give you thefe counfels. They arife, I folemnly proteft, from the warmeft friendfhip, and the fincere defire I have to fee you labour effectually for your own fanctification, while you labour for that of others. You are doubly obliged fo to do, both as a Religious and a Bifhop.

I will wait till you are confecrated, before I write to you with more ceremony. Adieu. I embrace you with my whole heart.

Convent of the Apoftles, May 30, 1755.

LETTER LXXIII.

To the Abbè LAMI.

I AM charmed with your laft fheet. Your Criticifm is juft and rational; and it is thus that cenfures ought to be paffed without impatience, without humour, without partiality, according to the rules of juftice and good tafte. Rifing talents have often been difcouraged by too fevere a judgment being paffed

on

on them. I know not any one work, ancient or modern, in which faults have not been found, when people were difpofed to criticize every thing. Authors ftand in need of the indulgence of the Journalifts, and the Journalifts themfelves of that of the Public; becaufe there is nothing perfect in an abfolute degree.

I am obliged to you for the account you give us from time to time of the French publications. Thofe of the laft age were more nervous; thofe of the prefent more pleafing. It is much the fafhion for the beautiful to give place to the pretty: it is a diminutive derived from a fubftantive. The elogium you make of Cardinal *des* LANCES, is juftly due to him. He edifies the whole Church by the fplendor of his virtues, which in him are united to great knowledge. I fhould be well pleafed, did he live at *Rome*; I would then endeavour to gain his good graces, that I might enjoy the benefit of his great learning. He is a Pupil of the Congregation of St *Genovefa* in France, famed for fcience and piety;—He fome time wore their drefs.

There are every day fome fonnets made here, not worth a ftraw; PETRARCH muft be born again, to bring us back into the right road to Parnaffus. The Academy of the *Arcadians* is ftill kept up, but only in the air, that is to fay, on the Zephyrs, and the wings of butterflies; for they employ themfelves only in light and fportive pieces.

Often put your genius in the still; such fine things come from it, that you cannot torture it too much. Adieu: my friendship tells you the rest.

My most affectionate compliments to the Prior of the *Dominicans*. He always promises to come to *Rome;* but, like myself, he is glued to his books and his Cell.

LETTER LXXIV.

To a Gentleman of TUSCANY.

THE Education, my dear Sir, which you are for giving your children, will be no more than a Varnish, unless Religion be its basis. There are occasions to be met with in life, wherein probity alone is not of sufficient strength to resist certain temptations, and wherein the soul degrades itself, if not supported by the firm hopes of immortality.

It is necessary, in order to become happy and wise, that a man should see God, from his very infancy, as the first beginning and end of all things. Reason and Faith must inform him at the same time, that to have neither Worship nor Law, is to descend to the humiliating rank of brute beasts; and he must be convinced, that as truth is but one, so there can be only one Religion; and that, if authority did not determine our belief, every individual would have his own system and his own opinion.

You never will make your children true Christians by trifling practices of devotion.

The Christian Religion is the greatest enemy to Pharisaism and superstition. The Church enjoins duties enow, so that we need not seek to multiply them. It is but too common to neglect what is strictly commanded for the practice of what is only of counsel: because people are fonder of hearkening to whims, than to reason; and pride is perfectly gratified with singularity.

You will take care to inspire the souls of our three young Gentlemen with the most elevated sentiments, and to convince them, that the greatest Pleasure man can enjoy, is to think, and be sensible of his existence. This is a sublime voluptuousness so worthy of a mind truly heavenly, that I consider the man as miserable, or at least in a state of apathy, who is a stranger to that happiness.

The CATECHISM is sufficient to teach them the revealed truths; but in an age of Infidelity something more is wanted than the Alphabet of Religion. You will therefore fill the minds of your children with those pure and bright lights, that dissipate the clouds of modern Philosophy, and the darkness of corruption.

A few, but solid, books will make your children learned christians. They must read them with a religious attention, less with a view to consign them to their memory, than to engrave them on their hearts. Your design is not to train up young men who are to maintain a *Thesis* in the schools, but men who are

obliged

obliged, as rational Beings, to be thoroughly convinced of the eternal Truths.

When youths have studied Religion from first principles, it seldom happens that they suffer themselves to be seduced by the sophisms of Irreligion, unless the heart be totally corrupted.

Watch with the greatest care to preserve their purity unstained, not by making use of Informers and Spies, but by having your eyes and ears every where, so as to resemble the Deity, who, unseen himself, sees all.

Children must not perceive that we mistrust them, or that we watch them; for then they are discouraged and grumble; they take a dislike to those they ought to love; they begin to have an idea of the evil they never before thought of; and it is then only they endeavour to deceive. Hence the greatest part of young students, and almost all who are brought up in seminaries, act solely from fear, and are never more happy, than when at a distance from their superiors.

Be less the Master of your children, than their Friend; they will then be transparent to your eyes, and will even tell you their faults. A hundred times have young people intrusted me with what gave them uneasiness, and with what they had done amiss, because I always treated them with kindness. They will give you the key of their hearts, when they see that you sincerely wish them well, and that it hurts you extremely to reprimand them.

There are many reasons which induce me to advise a domestic education; but there are still more which hinder me from urging it. A domestic Education, generally speaking, better secures the morals; but it is so uniform, so tepid, so languid, that it discourages and prevents emulation. Besides, as it more narrowly inspects their conduct, it oftener makes hypocrites than hopeful youths.

Nevertheless, if you should find a Preceptor, who is mild, patient, sociable, and learned, and who joins condescension with steadiness, prudence with cheerfulness, temperance with amability, I would then tell you to make a trial at least, being persuaded that you would do nothing but in concert with him, and that you would not aim at being his Preceptor. There are but too many Fathers, who treat a Preceptor like a mercenary, and think themselves entitled to act the Master over him, because he receives a salary from them.

Trust not your sons, unless with a man whom you can confide in, as much as in yourself: but after that, hesitate not to leave him master of his own operations. Nothing so much disgusts a Preceptor, as to show any distrust of him, or to doubt of his abilities. Take care of the servants who are about your children; they are generally the corrupters of youth.

Let an amiable serenity ever shine on your forehead and in your eyes, and let every thing be done according to your wish without constraint

ftraint or fear—Nobody loves ftormy weather; but every body is cheered at the fight of a fine day.

Join pleafure with every kind of ftudy you propofe to your children, by infpiring them with a ftrong defire of knowledge, and a great dread of remaining in ignorance.

You muft contrive to let your children have intervals of reft from their labour, that their memory and minds may not be too much fatigued. When a perfon ftudies with a diflike, he takes an averfion to books, and only fighs after idlenefs and liberty.

Inftruct, not by punifhing, but by making them fond of your inftructions; and to this end take care to divert them with fome pieces of hiftory, and fome fallies of wit which may awake their attention. I knew at *Milan* a young man, who had been made fo fond of ftudy, that he took the days allotted for play, as a neceffary repofe indeed, but confidered them at the fame time as days of mourning. His books were his pleafure and his treafure; and it was a good Prieft, who by means of his cheerfulnefs of temper and lively imagination, had fired him with a love for all works of tafte and erudition. He would have become one of the firft among the learned in Europe, had not death ftopped him in his carreer.

Proportion their ftudies to their age, and attempt not to make Metaphyficians of them, when only twelve years old : that would not be bringing them up as young men, but as

parrots,

parrots, who are taught to repeat some words.

It is with the Sciences, as with our food. The stomach of a child requires light nourishment, and it is by degrees that it is accustomed to more substantial and solid meats.

Never fail making some book of amusement succeed the more serious reading, and to intermix Poetry with Prose. VIRGIL is no less eloquent than CICERO, and his descriptions, images and expressions give imagination and elocution to those who have none. Poetry is the perfection of languages; and if we make no use of it when young, we shall never have a taste for it. It is impossible, at a certain age of life, to read verses long together, unless a person has really a taste for Poetry.

Moderate however the study of the Poets; for besides that they often take liberties contrary to good morals, it is dangerous to be too fond of them. A young man, who talks and dreams of nothing but Poetry, is insupportable in company; his passion for it may be reckoned a madness. I except only such, whose genius is fit for that alone; and then they are indemnified for that madness, by becoming DANTES, ARIOSTOS, TASSOS, METASTASIOS, MILTONS, CORNEILLES, RACINES.

Let your children be intimately acquainted with the general history of the world, that of particular nations, especially that of their own country; and let not this be a dry study, but accompanied with short and pertinent reflections, which may teach them to form a prudent

dent judgment on events, and to acknowledge an univerfal Agent, of whom men are no more than the inftruments, and all the revolutions in nature, are effects combined and forefeen in the eternal decrees.

History is dull reading, if no more be known of it than dates and facts; but it is a book full of life, if we obferve therein the fport of the paffions, the fprings of the foul, the motions of the heart; and above all, if we there difcover a God, who, ever the mafter of events, gives rife to them, directs them, determines them according to his own will, and for the accomplifhment of his fublime defigns.

Our eyes of flefh fee nothing in the Univerfe, but a veil which hides from us the Agency of the Creator; but the eyes of faith fhew us, that whatever happens, has a caufe, and that this caufe is truly God.

Take care that fome good treatife on Rhetoric, abounding more with examples than precepts, give your fons a tafte for true eloquence. Shew them, that what is truly beautiful, depends neither on the modes nor the times, and that, though in different ages there be different ways of expreffing things, there is only one right way of conceiving them.

Infpire them with an abhorrence of that puerile eloquence, which, confifting entirely in a play upon words, is fhocking to a good tafte; and convince them, that gigantic expreffions or ideas never made part of a fine difcourfe. Although true Eloquence ought never to tire

any

any one; man neverthelefs is fo whimfical, that he is fometimes cloyed with it: and on that account, we at this day fee an affected, frivolous diction preferred to the nervous language of the Orators of the laft age.

There are certain men, and certain Epochas, which in every branch of literature have fixed the tafte; and the eyes of your children are to be perpetually directed towards thofe paintings, as towards the beft models; but not fo as to become flaves to them; for it is never allowed to be a fervile imitator of any one.

I would have the mind tower, and be itfelf; whereas it is a mere copy, when it dare not attempt invention. We have only men of wit, but we fhould have men of genius, if we did not keep too mechanically to the beaten tracks. Nothing great is done by him, who knows only one road. An inventive mind is inexhauftible, when a man knows how to dare. "Be yourfelves, think for yourfelves," would I often fay to young people under my care. It is difagreeable to fpend whole years in teaching pupils nothing elfe, but the art of repeating what others have faid.

When your children fhall have come to the age of maturity, then will be the moment to fpeak to them, like a friend, of the nothingnefs of thofe pleafures, in which the world places its happinefs; of the misfortunes they plunge their followers into; the remorfes of confcience they excite; the damages they caufe both to body and mind; laftly the pre-

cipices

cipices they sink under foot, while they seem only to strow flowers before us.

It will not be difficult for you, either by the energy of your expressions, or by some striking examples, to shew them the dangers of a life of pleasure; and to convince them, that the greatest part of the gratifications indulged beyond measure, were it not for idleness, would have nothing really attractive in them. For want of something to do, we form the most brilliant ideas of them, just as in our sleep a thousand agreeable Chimæras present themselves to our fancy.

When a son is persuaded that his Father only talks reason to him, and that his reprimands proceed from a tender affection, and not from humour, he hearkens to him; and his advice has the best effect.

Lastly, after this edifice is erected, the roof is to be raised, which I look upon as the greatest difficulty of all.—I mean the choice of a state of life. 'Tis generally the touchstone of Fathers and Mothers, and the most critical point in life for children

If you take my advice in this particular, you will allow them a whole year to deliberate with themselves on the state of life most proper for them, without ever speaking in favour of one profession rather than of another. The good education they have received, and the learning they have acquired, will successfully lead them to a happy issue; and there is the greatest room to hope, that they will then determine according to inclination and reafon.

It will afterwards be neceffary often to mention to them the advantages and dangers of each ftate, and to convince them of what importance it is, both with regard to this world and the next, to faithfully comply with the duties and obligations of the ftate of life they embrace. The Sacerdotal and Religious Profeffions will afford you ample matter to fpeak of the ineftimable happinefs relifhed in them, when a perfon has a real call from God; and the dreadful calamities experienced in thofe ftates, when a man has been fo rafh as to engage in either from human views and motives. The military life, as well as the Magiftracy, prefent of themfelves a multitude of obligations to be complied with; and in order to convince them of this, it will be enough to lay the refpective duties of each before their eyes.

After thefe precautions, and efpecially after frequently imploring the affiftance of heaven, your fons will boldly enter on the career of life they have chofen; and you will have the comfort of being able to fay before God and man, that you have confulted both their inclinations and their liberty. Nothing is of worfe confequence than for a Father to force the inclination of his Children; he expofes them to eternal regret, and himfelf to the moft bitter reproaches, and even curfes, which he has unhappily deferved.

Since

Since Providence has granted you riches, and given you birth in a diſtinguiſhed family, you will bring up your ſons according to their fortune and rank; making them however feel ſome privations, and keeping them always within the bounds of modeſty, to teach them that happineſs is not to be found in this life; and that the more elevated we are, the leſs proud we ought to be. You will take care to let them have money, both that they may learn from you not to be covetous, and be in a capacity of aſſiſting the poor. It would be proper to ſee, with your own eyes, the uſe they make of their money; and if you diſcover in them either avarice or prodigality, their allowance muſt be abridged.

In a word, my dear and reſpectable Friend, take more pains with the heart of your ſons, than with the underſtanding: if the heart be good, all will go well.

Circumſtances will teach you how you are to govern them. Appear ſometimes eaſy, ſometimes ſevere; but ever juſt and ever civil. An even temper diſconcerts young people, who will not do as they ought; for in ſpite of themſelves they feel that they have nothing to ſay in their own excuſe.

Let them have a decent liberty, that their Father's houſe may not be the moſt diſagreeable place they can be in. It is neceſſary that they ſhould like it; and that they find there, more than any where elſe, the ſweets and pleaſures which they are to expect from a Father,

ther, who is a friend of order, and kind by inclination.

My pen drags me along in spite of myself. One would say that it was sensible, and felt the sweet pleasure, that I myself feel, in speaking of your dear children, whom I love more than myself, and little less than you can love them. May God heap his blessings on them: they will be, whatever they ought to be; and the education they will receive from you, will bud forth for eternity. There are we to reap the fruit of the good advice given to youth, and there good Fathers meet their worthy children, to be eternally happy with them.

Rome, Aug. 16, 1753.

LETTER LXXV.

To the Prelate CERATI.

IF this letter conveys to you all I feel, you will not find it light; for I load it with all the esteem, affection, and admiration I am master of, to convince you more than ever, how much I respect you, and how much I love you.

I have seen the *Augustinian* Friar you directed to me, and I found him, as you said, filled with the Fathers of the Church. He has them on his lips, he has them in his heart; and he is, of all men in the world, the person who gives the greatest pleasure in turning over like a book, when his full worth is known.

St.

Let. lxxv. P. CLEMENT XIV.

St. AUGUSTINE, very juftly, is his hero, on account of his being the Univerfal Doctor, a mafter of all the fciences, and their particular favourite. Much commendation has been given to that incomparable man: but hitherto far fhort of his merit. I therefore, not long ago, advifed an Ecclefiaftic, who confulted me how he was to make his Panegyric, to fay not a word of his own, but to extract the whole from the writings of that Father; being perfuaded, that to give AUGUSTINE his due praife, a man muft be AUGUSTINE himfelf. He took my advice; and his whole Elogium was compofed of the moft fublime and moving paffages of that illuftrious Doctor. The whole was well connected, though interrupted with exclamations and flights which affected the audience.—When will our Rhetoricians and our Preachers be taught, that true eloquence does not confift either in wit or words; but that it is an expreffion of the foul, the boiling up of a heart that burns, furprifes and effects the greateft things?

There are certain moments in which great Orators feem to have no longer any ftyle or words, from an apprehenfion of debafing the fublimity of their fubject, by ftudied phrafes.

Some diftil their genius to extract eloquence; but this operation yields nothing, but forced thoughts, and bloated phrafes; whereas, had they left the energy of the heart to act alone, they would have had mouths of gold.

I find

I find nothing in most of our modern books besides mere *Elegance*; but that is far from *Eloquence*. *Elegance* pleases, and *Eloquence* drags along; and, when natural, it analgamizes itself with all the beauties of nature and wit, to shew them to the greatest advantage, and according to truth. In a word, *true Eloquence* is like that scrap of your own composition, which you shewed me some time since, wherein I discovered the very features of *Demosthenes*, notwithstanding the immense interval which ages have placed between you and him.

Nothing is more admirable than to approach the Ancients, and to keep close to them, notwithstanding the distance of time, as if we were their Cotemporaries: for it must be owned, that they have reaped and carried in all the harvest, and that we only glean after them.

Some time ago it happened, that I had composed a scientific discourse, at the desire of a friend, to be prefixed to a treatise on Geometry. I rallied every faculty of my whole soul; and in the heat of a piece of work, which lasted more than a week, I imagined I had brought forth something very interesting and quite new. But I cannot express to you how much I was afterwards suprised and confounded, to find all my thoughts scattered in a few pages of the Ancients. Nevertheless I had not plundered them; but the minds of men being circumscribed in a circle, all generations

rations are nearly alike in their manner of thinking; the tints only are quite different.

There was lately prefented to me one *Sagri* from your fchools at Pifa; and it feemed to me, that it was poffible to make a great man of him. But into what hands will he fall? The moment a young man quits the College, is the inftant to determine his fate.—It is then every thing mifcarries, or every thing fucceeds with him. I have feen fome, who had borne away every prize, and who were cited with pleafure as real geniufes of the firft rate; and notwithftanding this emphatic admiration of them, they became lefs than nothing. Criminal pleafures invefted them, or they betook themfelves to mechanical employments; or their mind, which had made an effort, felt the effects of that laborious operation, and could do nothing more. It is a forward fruit which charms by its colour as well as novelty, and withers while it is admired, and juft going to be gathered.

What pains are to be taken, before the mind is perfected! All I know is this, that mine thinks itfelf accomplifhed, when, by a communication of ideas, it partakes of yours, and affords me an opportunity of reiterating to you my fentiments of attachment and refpect.

Rome, Aug. 27, 1754.

LETTER LXXVI.

To Cardinal QUERINI.

MOST EMINENT,

THE various reflections your Eminence makes on the different ages that have rolled away since the commencement of the world, are worthy of a genius like your own. I seem to see Reason weighing all these ages; some are like lingots, others like leaves of tinsel. In reality there are some so solid and others so light, that they form the most astonishing contrast. Ours, without contradiction, bears the stamp of lightness beyond any other: but it pleases and seduces, especially by the good offices of the French, who have communicated to us an elegance which we find agreeable in spite of ourselves.

Our Forefathers would have grumbled, and with reason: however did they live in our time, they would suffer themselves to be carried away with it like ourselves; and contrary to their inclination, the lightness of our discourse and our pretty agreeable manner of writing would amuse them.

The Roman grandeur does not take up with such pleasing trifles; but the Romans of these days are no longer the majestic people they formerly were. French elegance has passed the Alpes; and we received it with pleasure, at the very time we criticized it.

Your

Your Eminence, as being very fond of the French, will have eafily pardoned their genteel engaging way, though detrimental to the dignity of the Ancients. It is not amifs that in all ages taken collectively, there fhould be fparks and flames, lilies and blue-bottles, fhowers and dews, ftars and meteors, rivers and brooks; this is a perfect reprefentation of nature : and to form a right judgment of the univerfe and the different ages, the different points of view are to be united, and made one object of fight.

All ages cannot be like one another; it is their variety that enables us to judge of things; without this diverfity, a comparifon could not be made. I know a perfon would rather choofe to live in an age, which offers nothing but what is grand; but here it may be properly faid, that we muft take the times as they are, and not continually regret what is paft, by hanging to the char of the Ancients. Let us have their good tafte, and we fhall have nothing to fear from our own futility.

One cannot, without dread, confider that gulf from whence ages iffue, and that into which they again precipitate themfelves. What a number of years, days, hours, minutes, feconds are fwallowed up in eternity, which, ever the fame, continues immutable in the midft of changes and revolutions! It is a rock in the middle of the fea, againft which all the waves dafh to no purpofe. We are like grains of fand, the sport of the wind, if we do not immoveably hold faft by that fupport. It is that which fixes your Eminence, and engages you to undertake fo many luminous works, which all Europe admires, and in which Religion glories.

I never tire with reading the account of your travels, and above all your defcription of *Paris* and of *France.* Befides that the Latin may be compared to St. *Jerome's*, there are admirable reflections on whatever your Eminence faw. What an eye have you! It penetrates the effence of things, the fubftance of writings, the fouls of Writers. You had the happinefs to fee at *Paris* feveral great men, then alive, the precious remains of the age of LEWIS XIV; they muft have convinced you that, that age was not extolled without reafon.

Nothing enlarges the foul like travelling: I read all the voyages and travels I can, that I may fend my thoughts at leaft a rambling, while my body is fedentary. This is certain, that I am often at *Brefcia*, that city, my Lord, which you enrich with your example and your precepts, and where you every hour receive homages. To thefe I join, with my whole foul, the moft profound refpect, &c.

Rome, Dec. 10, 1754.

LETTER LXXVII.

To Cardinal BANCHIERI.

MOST EMINENT,

I Have not as yet seen the *Ferrarese* your Eminence vouchsafed to recommend to me; but I have already mentioned him to the Guardian of *Ara Cæli*, who will do all in his power to prove how much he values your interesting yourself in behalf of that Convent.

I could wish my occupations would allow me to travel to *Ferrara*, that city so famed for many events, and which has the happiness of possessing your Eminence, and the ashes of *Ariosto*. My first care should be to pay them a visit. Some poetic sparks might issue from them to seize on me, and enable me to assure you in verse, as well as prose, that nothing can equal the profound respect with which I am, &c.

Rome, Jan. 7, 1755.

LETTER LXXVIII.

To a Prebendary *of* MILAN.

A PANEGYRIC on St PAUL, Sir, is no small undertaking. It requires a soul as great as that of the DOCTOR OF THE GENTILES to celebrate him in a worthy manner. His elogium is that of Religion itself: he is so much interested in it, and connected with it, that it is impossible to praise him separately.

The fame spirit, the fame zeal, the fame charity is found in that great Apoſtle, as in Religion itſelf. How rapid muſt be your pen, if you deſire to deſcribe his travels and his Apoſtolic labours? He runs as ſwift as thought, when a good work is to be undertaken; and he breathes forth nothing but JESUS CHRIST, when he announces the Goſpel. From the manner in which he multiplies himſelf, one would think that he alone formed the whole Apoſtolic College. He is at one and the ſame time both on land, and at ſea, ever on the watch for the ſalvation of the faithful, ever deſiring the palm of martyrdom, ever ſpringing forward towards eternity. Never was there ſo good a citizen, ſo good a friend. He forgets nothing; he remembers the moſt trifling ſervices done him: and his heart never once beats, but it is a wiſh after heaven that has enlightened him, a movement of love for JESUS CHRIST, who converted him, an act of gratitude towards the Chriſtians, who had aſſiſted him.

A Panegyric is a ſpecies of compoſition, which is not to reſemble a Sermon: flaſhes of lightning are requiſite, but ſuch as may ſhine on a ground-work of morality, which is to be the baſis of the diſcourſe. There are no inſtructions, where there are nothing but praiſes; and whoever confines himſelf barely to inſtruction, does not celebrate his Hero.

The ſkill of the Orator conſiſts in drawing from the elogium itſelf luminous reflections,
which

which may tend to the reformation of manners. Above all things, my dear Friend, never make the panegyric of one Saint at the expence of others: nothing is a ſtronger proof of the barrennefs of the Orator's genius. Every illuſtrious perſonage has his peculiar merit; and it is an affront to a ſervant of God (who ever confidered himſelf the leaſt of all) to enhance his glory to the prejudice of another Saint.

Let there be no digreſſions foreign to your ſubject. Never loſe ſight of its being St. *Paul* whom you are to praiſe; and remember that it would be miſſing your aim, if you dwell upon any thing but his elogium.

Let nothing be languid in a Panegyric: every thing is to be rapid; and eſpecially in that of the great Apoſtle, whoſe zeal never reſted. It is neceſſary that your hearers ſhould ſee him and hear him, and that they may ſay: 'tis he himſelf; there he is! You muſt diſplay with him the whole power of Grace; you muſt, like him, ſtrike down thoſe who abridge the abſolute power of God over the human heart: you muſt thunder like him againſt falſe Prophets, and againſt the Corruptors of the doctrine of morals. In a word, you muſt give a fuccinct idea of his different Epiſtles, while you repreſent them burning with the flames of charity, and irradiating with the lights of truth.

Force no compariſons; they muſt ariſe from the ſubject: employ no uſeleſs words; they muſt

must all be inftructive: no forced phrafes; they muft all be natural. It is your heart that muft be the Orator in this difcourfe, and not your wit or underftanding: referve that for the Academies, when you have any elogium to pronounce there: but the dignity of the Pulpit, the fanctity of the Temple, the Eminence of the fubject are infinitely above antithefes, fallies of wit, and puns.

Human Eloquence was made for praifing human actions: but a divine Eloquence is required to praife divine men. The garlands which are to crown the Elect, are not to be gathered from the Poets, but from the Prophets. I am more than I can exprefs, &c.

Rome, Oct. 13, 1755.

LETTER LXXIX.

To the Abbè LAMI.

OH! my dear Abbè, I am not at all of your way of thinking with regard to the book you criticize with fo much feverity. It certainly is not fuch an indifferent performance as you would make it appear. There are in it principles, views, details, beauties which render the work interefting. A few inftances of a negligent ftyle do not totally disfigure a book. The ftyle is no more than the outer bark; and fometimes a tree is good, though the bark be of no value. Unluckily in our age people are more taken with words, than

with

with things: too often do the phrafes or turn of expreffion make the fortune of a book. I have run through a multitude of Pamphlets printed at *Paris*, which had nothing to recommend them but a rapid, feducing ftyle. A man afked himfelf what the Writer meant to fay, but he could not tell. It is not furprifing, that in a country, where people are fo very fond of drefs, and of every thing tinfel-like, that they fhould have a paffion for a production written in an elegant ftyle.

There are fome fubjects, which ftand in need of themfelves alone to captivate the attention: whereas there are other fubjects, which would not be read at all but for a brilliant ftyle: that is their pafs-port. A fkilful Writer ought to know that difference.

I fhould be pleafed, would you analyfe two works, which have lately appeared here. *Self converfation*, and *The Elements of Metaphyfics*. The former is particularly interefting, becaufe it elevates the foul on the wrecks of the paffions and the fenfes. The fecond is no lefs fo, in as much as it renders palpable the fpirituality and immortality of the foul. They are two Metaphyfical productions prefented in different lights. *Self-converfation* is fo clear and plain, that any body may underftand it: the *Elements* fo deep and abftrufe, as to forbid the greateft part the reading of them.

I confider your fheets as a perfon appointed to awaken the Italians, and to hinder them from fleeping over the fciences and literature.

ture. In a hot climate a man often requires to be roused in order to pursue his studies. The mind grows drowsy, as well as the body, unless care be taken to spur it on; and in that state a man has not a sufficiency of spirits either to read or think.

FLORENCE has ever been a city famous for literature and taste; and I fear not its degenerating, while you continue to enlighten it. A periodical work executed with discernment, diffuses light into men's minds, keeps up emulation, and supplies the reading of a multitude of works, which a person has not time to read, or has it not in his power to procure.

When I read a Journal, that gives an account of the publications in Europe, I learn to know the genius of different nations; and I perceive that the *Englishman* neither writes like the *German*, nor thinks like the *Frenchman*. This variety, which distinguishes the different nations in their way of writing and thinking, makes me believe that the moral world is really a copy of the natural world, and that the case is the same with the minds, as with their faces, which have no resemblance one to another.

Adieu. I leave you to throw myself among the thorns of Controversy, where I am sure not to find the flowers which are seen in your writings.

Rome, Nov. 5, 1755.

LETTER LXXX.

To a Parish-priest *in the Diocese of* Rimini.

IT is a great piece of rashness in you, my dear Pastor, to presume to censure your Father and mine, and the Father of all the Faithful, the Great Lambertini, for whom all the Churches have the most profound veneration. Besides that he is celebrated for his vast and sublime knowledge, for the quickness of his understanding, and his consummate prudence, he is moreover the Head of Religion, the Sovereign Pontiff, to speak evil of whom is blasphemy. You are not ignorant that St. Paul begs pardon of the High-priest of the Synagogue, though then expiring, for having called him a *whitened wall.**

The treaty which Benedict XIV concluded with Spain, and by which the Spanish Clergy are no longer to come to Rome, has prevented, I know not how many, young Eclesiastics from becoming vagabonds, and leading a licentious life. Nothing is more proper, than to see those, who are destined to the Ministry, study under the eyes of their own Bishops, who by that means learn to know them, and never lose sight of them.

Moreover, so many reasons are requisite justly to condemn a Sovereign, that unless a person knows what passes in the Cabinets of Princes, the nature of events, the consequences an affair may draw after it; and unless a man can

* *Acts* xiii. 3.

penetrate into the fouls of thofe who act, and put others on action, his judgment cannot fail of being very criminal.

Ah! Who are we, to condemn the Vicar of Chrift, and efpecially when we are ignorant of the motives he acts on, and know not what he may have forefeen? When the cafe is doubtful, the prejudice is in favour of the Judges. How can people juftify the liberty they take of cenfuring the conduct of the Sovereign Pontiff, on no other grounds than faint appearances? It is certainly affording arms to the Proteftants, and being effentially wanting in refpect towards him, whom God has placed on a throne to fee and judge, and to whom he has commanded us to hearken, as to himfelf: I go further—It is endangering one's falvation.

There are no circumftances, nor any moment of time (however our heart or our opinion may fuffer by it) wherein it is lawful to rife up againft the fteps taken by the Sovereign Pontiff, unlefs a perfon be a member of his Council. He fees what you do not fee; and, if he does not inform us of it, it is becaufe he is often tied down by fuch confiderations, as ftop both his pen and his tongue. There is a Chriftian Policy, which, without ever hurting the truth, does not tell every truth, and wraps itfelf up in a neceffary filence, when it is of advantage not to fpeak. How will you preach in your Parifh the refpect due to the Head of the Church, if people hear you ufing invectives againft him? Let us even fuppofe that he has

done

done wrong; you ought, like a Christian, like a Priest, like a Rector, to excuse him in public, and to impose an eternal silence on those who should dare to blame him. Such are my sentiments relative to the Sovereign Pontiffs. They are the anointed of the Lord, his *Christs*, who are never to be spoken against: *Touch not mine anointed ones, and treat not my Prophets with spite.**

I flatter myself that you will get the better of your prejudices, and that you will approve of my reasons; for you have a good understanding, and an upright heart. It was a warmth of imagination, that induced you to condemn BENEDICT XIV, all whose steps are weighed in the balance of the sanctuary, and in the very sanctuary of truth itself. I embrace you, my dear Rector, &c.

Rome, May 14, 1755.

* *Nolite tangere Christos meos: & in prophetis meris nolite malignari.* Ps. civ. 15. *Vulg.*

LETTER LXXXI.

To Mr MECKNER, *a Protestant Gentleman.*

I AM sorry, my dear Sir, to hear you perpetually repeating against the Church of Rome, a multitude of thread-bare objections, long since reduced to dust by M. Bossuet, a *French* Bishop, in his *Exposition of the Catholic Faith*, and his excellent work of the *History of the Variations of the Protestant Churches*.

It is impossible to follow a Protestant step by step; because instead of waiting for an answer to the question proposed, he puts another, and never gives a person time to breathe.

If you talk to me all at once about *Purgatory*, the *Eucharist*, the *Worship of Saints*, it is impossible for me at the same instant, to give an answer concerning those three points.— Controversy must go on reasoning, if we desire to understand one another; and consequently demands, that one subject should be thoroughly discussed, before we proceed to another. Without that, we shall only beat the air; and meet with the fate of all *Ergotists*, who after a deal of argumentation, conclude with remaining obstinately attached to their own sentiments.

You agreed to the method in which I proposed to proceed, viz. to prove from the Gospel itself, and from the Epistles of St. *Paul*, which you admit as an inspired work, every truth you contest; and to shew you that they have been ever taught by an interrupted Tradition.

Had it not been so, you would know the day, and the date when we introduced any innovations; unless you have a mind to persuade us, that the whole Church, in the twinkling of an eye, notwithstanding the dispersion of its members, changed its belief, without being sensible of any change itself. But what an absurdity would it be to imagine such a thing!

The

The reproaches you continually caft, my dear Sir, on the Church of Rome, refpecting the *Celibacy*, prefcribed to the Priefts, and the *Cup* taken from the Faithful in the participation of the facred myfteries, fall of themfelves, when a perfon reflects how marriage and the Priefthood are every day found united among the Greek Catholics, and that the faithful among them receive under both kinds.

Return fincerely to the Church, and the Great Pope, who this day governs it, will not reject you from his bofom, becaufe your Minifters are married men, and becaufe you defire the ufe of the cup. His prudence will fuggeft fome temperament, or means to grant you, whatever can be granted, without altering any point of Faith or Morality, but by only changing a point of difcipline, which has all along been liable to changes.

Cardinal QUERINI, who is continually eaten up with the defire of your return, will become your Mediator with the Holy Father. By returning to the Pope, you will return to him, who was formerly your head; for you feparated from us. The abufes which then prevailed in the Church (*for it is neceffary*, as Chrift fays, *that fcandals fhould come*; and even herefies) could never authorize your Anceftors to rebel and feparate.—— They had no other way but that of remonftrances; and if they had confined themfelves to thofe, without joining thereto bitternefs, gall, or a fpirit of rebellion, they

certainly

certainly would have obtained some Reformation. To cure a tumour in the body, no one thinks of cutting off a limb, or stifling a man to death.

Many Protestants would return, if some pitiful human consideration did not stop them: for it is impossible that, reading the sacred scriptures so much as they do, they should not discover in them the prerogatives of the Head of the Apostles, and the Infallibility of his Church, which can never teach any error, since *Christ* is really with it, without interruption, *to the end of the World**.

It requires only eyes to see, whether the Church of Rome, or the Protestant Church be in the right. The one appears like the holy Mountain mentioned in scripture†; and the other like a vapour, that obscures the sight, and has no solidity.

I would give, my dear Sir, the last drop of my blood to see you reunited to us: be assured that you have broken the chain, by which you held to the centre of Unity, and that you are no longer any thing but unconnected Beings, without compass, without guide, without a Head.

This God makes you feel in a dreadful manner, by abandoning you to I know not how many different errors, which form almost as many sects, as communions. And this is a proof, that when there is no longer any

* Matt. xxviii. 20. Dan. ii. 35.

authority

authority to unite the faithful, each holds to his own opinion and consequently to his own prejudices.

Do not imagine, I beg, my dear Sir, that I mean here to infult your unhappy condition. Alas! Every thing tells me that you act *bonâ fide:* but that will not juftify you in the fight of God, who requires of you a ferious examination of fo effential a point; efpecially as you can inform yourfelf, and judge for yourfelf better than any other.

The fentence a man pronounces againft himfelf, when in the wrong, is worthy of your great foul and good heart. Your candour affures me that you will feek information according to truth, and that you will not reject it, whenever you fee it. It is on the lips of good Catholics; and by hearkening to them, you will hearken to it. 'Tis what I defire with all the fulnefs of my heart from the ardent wifh I have to be eternally with you in that abode of peace, where will be found only thofe who are marked with the fign of Faith. Judge from hence of the extent of that attachment, with which I have the honour to be, &c.

Rome, May 14, 1755.

LETTER LXXXII.

To the Prince SAN-SEVERO.

EXCELLENCE,

THE Petrifications I sent you are far beneath the thanks you return me for them. I know the full value, as well as the advantage, of entering into a correspondence with a Philosopher, who delights in the study of nature, and who admires its *phenomena* and sports, only because he understands them.

The birds from the new world which you have procured for the Emperor, cannot but be very great curiosities; I doubt, however, if with the utmost care and precaution, they can be brought alive to our climates. A thousand attempts have been made by different people to bring over the Humming-bird and *Colibri*, but have always been attended with the mortification of seeing them die at some distance from our ports.

Providence in giving us the Peacock has sufficiently enriched us, so that we need not go elsewhere in search of winged beauties. *America*, in reality, has nothing grander than our finest birds; but the preference is commonly given to what is foreign, merely because it comes from a far off.

You must, my Prince, be enraptured with the undertaking of Monsieur de BUFFON, the *French* Academician, and with his first volumes, which have already appeared. I know
nothing

nothing of them as yet, but from a curfory reading of them once over; yet what I have feen, appears to me admirable. I am only concerned that the Author of a natural hiftory fhould declare for a fyftem. It is the way to make people doubt of feveral things he advances, and to have fkirmifhes to maintain againft fuch as differ in opinion from him. Moreover, whatever departs from the account given of the Creation in the book of *Genefis*, has nothing to fupport it but paradoxes, or at moft, mere hypothefes.

Moses alone, as being an infpired Author, could perfectly acquaint us with the formation of the world, and the developement of its parts. He is not an *Epicurus*, who has recourfe to atoms; nor a *Lucretius*, who believes matter eternal; nor a *Spinofa*, who admits of a material God; nor a *Defcartes*, who prattles about the laws of motion; but a Legiflator, who publifhes to all men, without any hefitation, without fear of a miftake, how the world was created. Nothing is more fimple, nothing more fublime than his firft fetting out. *In the beginning God created heaven and earth.* He could not have fpoken more pofitively, had he been a fpectator of the Creation; and by thefe few words Mythology, fyftems and abfurdities of all kinds crumble to pieces, and appear to the eyes of reafon to be nothing more than mere Chimæras.

Whoever does not fee the truth in what Moses relates, was never born to know it.

Men every day grow fond of hypotheses, void even of probability; and refuse to believe what gives us the most sublime idea of the power and wisdom of God.

An *Eternal* world offers a thousand more difficulties than an *Eternal* Intelligence; and a *Co-eternal* world is an absurdity which cannot exist, since nothing can be so ancient as God.

Besides that he is *necessarily* existent, and the Universe is not so; by what right can matter, a thing totally contingent, and absolutely inert, pretend to the same prerogatives with an Almighty Spirit, with a Spirit entirely immaterial? These are whims, which could arise only in the paroxysm of a distempered imagination, and are a proof of the astonishing weakness of man, when he is resolved to hearken to himself alone.

The history of nature would be a book sealed and closed to all generations, did they not see a God, Creator and Preserver of all things; for nothing is more strongly felt than his Agency. The Sun with all its magnificence and majestic appearance; the Sun, though adored by different nations, has neither understanding nor discernment; and if its course be so regular, as never to be interrupted for a single instant, it is owing to the impulse it receives from a Supreme Agent, whose Orders it executes with the greatest punctuality.

It is to no purpose to range with our eyes through the immense expanse of the Universe; we see the whole shut up in the immensity menfity of a Being, before whom the Univerſe is as if it were not. It would be something very ſingular, that the Univerſe ſhould enjoy the privilege of being indebted to itſelf alone for its Exiſtence and Beauty, when the moſt trifling work cannot exiſt without an Artificer. Reaſon digs for itſelf dreadful precipices, when it hearkens only to the paſſions and ſenſes: and reaſon without Faith excites compaſſion. All the Academies of the whole Univerſe may frame what ſyſtems they pleaſe concerning the Creation of the World; but after all their reſearches, all their conjectures, all their combinations, after multitudes of Volumes, they will tell me much leſs than MOSES has told me in a ſingle page; and even what they tell me, will be void of every degree of probability.—Such is the difference between the man that ſpeaks only from himſelf, and the man that is inſpired.

The Supreme Being ſmiles, from the height of the heavens, at all theſe ſenſeleſs ſyſtems, which arrange the world according to their fancy; and which ſometimes make chance the Father of it, at other times ſuppoſe it eternal.

Some people take a ſatisfaction in believing that Matter governs itſelf, and that there is no other Divinity; becauſe it is well known that Matter is abſolutely inert and ſtupid, and that nothing is to be dreaded from any thing it can do: whereas the Juſtice of a

God, who sees all things, and weighs all things, is an overwhelming idea to the Sinner.

Nothing is more beautiful than the hiſtory of Nature, when connected with that of Religion. Nature is nothing without God; but ſhe produces every thing, and gives life to every thing by the agency of God. Though ſhe be no part of what compoſes the Univerſe, he puts the whole in motion; he is the ſap, and the life of the whole. Take away his Agency, there is no longer any activity in the elements, vegetation in the plants, ſpring in the ſecond cauſes, nor revolution in the planets. Eternal darkneſs takes the place of light, and the Univerſe becomes its own grave.

Should God withdraw his hand, the ſame which happens to our bodies, when he ſtops the motion thereof, would happen to the whole world. They fall into duſt; they exhale in ſmoke: and it is not even known that they ever exiſted.

Were I ſufficiently qualified to write on natural hiſtory, I would begin my work by laying open the immenſe perfections of its Author; I would then treat of man, the maſterpiece of his works; and ſucceſſively from ſubſtance to ſubſtance, from ſpecies to ſpecies, I would go down to the Ant, and ſhew that the ſame wiſdom ſhines forth, and the ſame Almighty power acts in the ſmalleſt Inſect, as well as in the moſt perfect Angel.

Such a picture as this would have been intereſting to the lovers of truth; and the

plan,

plan, being traced by Religion itself, would render it of infinite value.

Let us never speak of Creatures, but to draw nearer to the Creator. They are the reflection of his indefectible light; and these ideas elevate us, and humble us: for man is never less nor greater, than when he views himself in relation to God. He then discovers an infinite Being, whose image he is, and in whose presence he is no more than an Atom: two apparent contrarieties, which must be reconciled in order to form a just idea of ourselves, and to avoid the two extremes of the proud Angels, and of Unbelievers, the latter of whom reduce themselves to the condition of brute beasts.

Your letter, my dear Prince, has led me to these reflections; though I acknowledge at the same time, that I find no greater satisfaction, than when an opportunity offers of speaking of God. He is the proper element of our heart, and it is only in the love of him, that the soul expands itself.

I happily was sensible, from my earliest age, of this great truth; and in consequence of that, I chose the Cloister, where, separated from creatures, I might more easily converse with the Creator. The commerce of the world is so full of noise and tumult, that we are there almost strangers to that recollection, which unites us to God.

I thought only of writing a letter; but it has turned out a sermon: except that, instead of concluding with *Amen*, I shall conclude

clude with expressing the respect due to you, and with which I have the honour to be, &c.

Rome, Dec. 13, 1754.

LETTER LXXXIII.

To Count ALGAROTTI.

IT is a long time, my dear Count, since we had any chat together, or rather since I have been at your school. An insignificant Philosoper and disciple of *Scotus*, can do nothing better than improve by the lessons of a man of learning, who has published the NEWTONIANISM OF THE LADIES.

A Philosophy of *Attraction* ought in a particular manner to be yours, by reason of your engaging and amiable character, which attracts all minds to it: but as to my part, I could wish, besides so many advantages, for that of being less a Newtonian, and more a Christian.

We were not created either to become the disciples of *Aristotle* or *Newton*. Our soul has a more noble destiny; and the more sublime yours is, the more ought you to go up towards its source.

You may tell me as often as you please, that it is the business of a Friar to preach; and I will constantly answer you, that it is the business of a Philosopher frequently to reflect from whence he came, and whither he is going— We have all of us a first beginning and a last end;

end; and nothing but God can either be the one or the other.

   Your Philosophy, in spite of all its reasoning, rests only on Chimæras, if you separate it from Religion. Christianity is the substance of the truths man ought to search after: but he loves to feed on errors, just as reptiles love to glut themselves with the mud of marshy grounds. People go a great way in search of what they might find in themselves, if they would but enter into themselves; for this reason, the great AUGUSTINE, after he had run through every Being, to see if none of them were his God, returns at last to his own heart, and declares that it is there he exists more than any where else: *I came back to myself.* *

   I hope that you will preach to me some of these days, so that each may have his turn. Ah! God grant it! But whether you moralize, or whether you joke, I shall always attend to you with that pleasure, which is felt in hearing one a person is sincerely fond of, and whose humble servant he is as much by inclination as duty, &c.

Rome, Sept. 7, 1754.

LETTER LXXXIV.

To the Abbè PAPI.

THE learned Cardinal QUERINI then, my dear Abbè, is gone to unite his science to that of God, and to fill himself from that torrent

* *Et redit ad me.*

torrent of light, which we perceive here below, as it were only through a cloud. He died as he had lived—his pen in his hand—finishing a line—and just ready to go to the Church, where his heart always was.

Mine erects to him a monument within itself as durable as my life. He had a great kindness for me; ah! for whom had he not the same? His Cathedral, his Diocese, all Italy, even BERLIN experienced the effects of his liberality. The King of PRUSSIA honoured him with a particular esteem, and all the learned of Europe admired his zeal and talents.

He was of a conciliating disposition.— The Protestants were fond of him, though he often told them round truths. It is to be regretted that he has not left us some considerable work, instead of having written only a few detached pieces. He would have swelled the *Benedictine* Library, already so voluminous, as being one of the most distinguished members of the Order of St. *Benedict*; and he would have enriched the Church with his productions.

Mr VOLTAIRE will regret the loss of him, if Poets can be susceptible of friendship. They wrote to one another in a friendly manner: one genius seeks out another. As to me, who have no other genius but that of admiring great men, I shed tears on the tomb of our illustrious Cardinal. Ah! when shall we find his equal? I have the honour to be, &c.

Convent of the Apostles, Jan. 1, 1755.

LETTER LXXXV.

To a Painter.

WHILE, my dear Sir, there is expreſſion in your pieces, you may be well pleaſed with your performance. Expreſſion is an eſſential point, and makes up for ſeveral faults, which would not be excuſed in an ordinary painter.

I have mentioned your talents to his Eminence Cardinal Porto-Carrero, and he will give you recommendations to *Spain*, as you deſire it; but nothing will make you better known than your own genius; and a genius is as neceſſary to form a Painter as it is to form a Poet. Carrachio, notwithſtanding the boldneſs of his pencil, would never have ſucceeded, without that poetic rage, which gives enthuſiaſm and fire.

There is diſcovered in his paintings a ſoul that ſpeaks, warms and inſpires enthuſiaſtic ideas. By admiring him, and filling one's ſelf with the truth and juſtneſs of his images, a man imagines he may become a Carrachio.

Let that great man, whom you have choſen for your model, breathe in you, and you will bring him to life again on the canvas. Were you only his ſhadow, you would deſerve to be eſteemed—There is ſomething real in the ſhadow of a great man.

Nature is ever to be the object, which the man, who aims at being a painter, ought to have in view; and to expreſs it well, all violent efforts are to be avoided. Painters as well as Poets become gigantic, by offering violence to their genius in compofition. When the head is properly organized for the execution of a work, a man finds himfelf hurried away by an irrefiftible impulfe to take up the pen or the pencil, and he follows his own natural bent of mind, without which there is neither expreffion nor tafte.

Rome is the true fchool where a man is to form himfelf; but whatever pains are taken, no one will go beyond mediocrity, who is not poffeffed of a genius for painting.

It is time for me to hold my tongue, as a *Confultor* of the Holy Office is not a painter, and a man runs a great rifque, when he talks of what he is only imperfectly acquainted with.

I am, Sir, &c.

LETTER LXXXVI.

To Monfignor Aymaldi.

YOU have reafon, *Monfignor*, to be aftonifhed at the happy alliance, which is to unite, for the future, the Houfes of Bourbon and Austria. There are prodigies in politics, as well as in nature: and Benedict XIV, when he heard that furprifing news, had very great reafon to cry out: *O wonderful alliance.**

* *O admirabile commercium.*—The firft words of an anthem ufed in the fervice of Candlemas-day, fignifying the inexpreffible and incomprehenfible union of the divine and human nature in the perfon of Christ.—Thefe allufions are frequent among the *Italians*, and even the great Benedict appears to have been rather too fond of them.

Monfieur

Monsieur de Bernis has immortalized himself by that political *phenomenon* as having seen things in a truer light, than Cardinal de Richelieu.

By means of this alliance, we shall have no more any wars in *Europe*, till men grow tired of peace, and the King of Prussia, ever greedy of glory, shall cease to seek after conquests. But I see Poland lie very convenient for him; and since a Hero, equally valiant and successful, ever likes to aggrandize himself, he will one day or other seize on part of it; be it only the town of *Dantzick*. Poland itself may perhaps contribute to this Revolution, in not watching sufficiently over its own territories, and abandoning itself to a thousand different factions. The spirit of patriotism among the *Poles* is not strong enough to make them defend their country at the hazard of their lives; they are too often from home not to lose their national spirit. The *English* have principles to go on; and therefore with them alone will the love of their country never be extinguished.

Europe has had all along some warlike Monarch, ambitious of extending his dominions and gathering laurels; sometimes a Gustavus, sometimes a Sobieski, sometimes a Lewis the Great, sometimes a Frederic. Empires have been enlarged more by arms, than by talents; for it hath been found that nothing has so much efficacy as the law of the stronger: it is *a King's final answer, or strongest reason.**

* *Ratio ultima regum.*

We are here happily strangers to those calamities. All is peace, and each one relishes most deliciously the fruits thereof, as I myself, in a most eminent manner, relish the pleasure of assuring you of my esteem and attachment.

LETTER LXXXVII.

To the Abbé NICOLINI.

SIR,

I AM extremely concerned that I was not at the Convent of the Apostles, when you did me the favour to call on me before your departure. I was, alas! on the banks of the *Tiber*, which the ancient *Romans* have magnified as much as they did their triumphs—In reality it is only an ordinary river either for length or breadth.

It is however a walk I am particularly fond of, on account of the ideas it raises in my mind relative to the grandeur and decay of the *Romans*. I call to my remembrance the time, when those haughty Despots kept the Universe in chains, and ROME had as many Gods, as it had vices and passions.

I return after that to my lowly Cell, where I am taken up with CHRISTIAN ROME, and where I, though the least in the house of God, labour for its advantage: but it is a task-work, and therefore almost always disagreeable: for in point of study, a man generally only loves that which he does freely.

I dare

I dare not mention the death of our common friend; it would be opening again a wound which smarts too much. I came too late to receive his last words. The loss of him is regretted like that of one of those rare men, who was too good for the age he lived in, and had all the candour of the first ages. He is said to have left behind him some pieces of poetry, worthy of the greatest Masters. He never mentioned them, which is the more extraordinary, as Poets are not more silent with regard to their writings, than with regard to their merit.

We have lately had here a swarm of young *Frenchmen*; and you must believe that I saw them with great pleasure. My chamber was not big enough to hold them; for they all did me the favour to come and see me, because they had been told, that there was a Friar in the Convent of the Apostles, who was remarkably fond of *France*, and of every thing that came from thence. They talked all together, so that the noise they made was exactly like an earthquake, though it diverted me much.

They are not very fond of ITALY, because it is not as yet perfectly Frenchified; but I afforded them some consolation, when I assured them that they would one day accomplish that *Metamorphosis*, and that I myself was become more than half a *Frenchman*.

I have the honour to be, &c.

Rome, July 24, 1756.

LETTER LXXXVIII.

To Mr STUART, *a Scotch Gentleman.*

SIR,

IF you were not in some manner affected by the mobility of the waves which surround you, I should sharply reproach you with your inconstancy; for you cannot be allowed to forget a friend, who has so sincere an affection for you. Your behaviour recals to my mind, what I have often thought, that the principal nations of Europe may be compared to the elements.

According to this comparison, the *Italian* resembles the fire, which is always in motion, flames out and crackles; the *German* is like the earth, which, notwithstanding its density, produces good pulse and excellent fruit; the *Frenchman* is like the air, the subtilty of which leaves no trace behind it; and the *Englishman* the inconstant wave, which is changing its place every instant.

An experienced Minister, with address, either chains down occasionally these elements, or sets them on jarring with one another, according to the interest of his Master. This we have seen more than once, when Europe was on a flame, and all in motion for reciprocal injuries.

Human policy sets people at variance, or reconciles them, according to its own interest, as it has nothing more at heart, than do-
minion

minion and its own aggrandizement. On the other hand, Chriſtian Policy is a ſtranger to the criminal art of ſowing diviſions, could it reap therefrom the greateſt advantage. I cannot ſet any value on a Policy without equity, for it is downright *Machiaveliſm* reduced to practice: but I have a great opinion of a Policy, which ſometimes quiet, and ſometimes in action, ſuffers itſelf to be governed by prudence; meditates, calculates, foreſees: and after having called to mind what is paſt, conſiders the preſent, perceives what is to come, and thus brings together all times, either to remain quiet, or enter on action.

It is abſolutely neceſſary that a good Politician ſhould be thoroughly acquainted with hiſtory, and the age he lives in; that he know the ſcale of the ſtrength, and mental abilities of thoſe who appear on the ſcene of the world; ſo that he may intimidate if there be weakneſs, reſiſt if there be courage, take an advantage if there be raſhneſs.

The knowledge of men, much more than of books, is the ſcience of a good Politician. It is of great importance in any buſineſs to have an exact knowledge of thoſe who are to be employed and put on action. Some are only good at ſpeaking, others have courage to act; and all conſiſts in not miſtaking their characters. Many a Politician miſcarries by miſplacing his confidence. When a ſecret has once ſlipped away, there is no recovering it again; and it would be better to commit a fault by too great

great refervednefs, than by an act of imprudence: *what is not fpoken, cannot be written.*

The dread of being betrayed renders pufillanimous the man, who has too indifcreetly laid open his heart to others. There are occafions, when a perfon ought to feem to fay every thing, though he fays nothing; and to have addrefs enough to miflead without ever betraying the truth: for that is never to be violated.

It is not weaknefs, but wifdom to yield, when we cannot do otherwife. All depends on knowing well the moments of acting, and the difpofitions of the people we have to do with; and on forefeeing, with certainty, the effect a refiftance will produce on fuch a particular occafion.

Self-love is often prejudicial to Policy. When, hurried on by refentment, we are for triumphing over an enemy, we entangle ourfelves in fome troublefome affair, without forefeeing the confequences of it.

We muft fhake off our paffions, when we would lead men, and oppofe only a cool head to people of the warmeft tempers; and therefore it is a common faying amongft us, *that the earth belongs to the Phlegmatic.*—Great moderation difconcerts the moft impetuous adverfary.

We fhould have fewer quarrels and wars in the world, if people would but calculate how much it cofts merely to fall out and fight. It is not fufficient to have men and money

money at our difpofal, we muft likewife know how to employ them, and reflect that the chances are not always on the ftronger fide.

We have had for a long while at Rome, only a temporizing Policy, becaufe we are weak, and becaufe the courfe of events is the happieft refource for thofe who cannot refift, to difentangle themfelves from difficulties. But as at prefent this is a fecret, of which nobody is ignorant, and as our flownefs in determining is well known, it is not amifs, but even very proper, that a Pope fhould from time to time know how to be refolute; not indeed for contefted claims, but in things that are juft. Without this, the fovereign Pontiffs would be fure to be oppreffed, as often as they were threatened.

Some nations unhappily ftand in need of war to become opulent; and there are others, to whom war brings certain ruin. And I conclude from all this, that a Minifter who has the addrefs to take an advantage of thefe circumftances, is a real treafure; and when a fovereign is fo happy as to find fuch a one, he ought to keep him in fpite of all cabals.

I have been prating on a fubject, which you underftand much better than I do; but one fentence draws on another, and infenfibly a man becomes bold enough to talk of what he knows nothing about.

Such is the nature of letters: we begin them without knowing what we are going to fay. When the foul comes to fold itfelf up again, it is juſtly aſtoniſhed at its own fecundity. It is a lively image of the production of a world from nothing; for, in ſhort, our thought, which exiſted not before, ſtarts forth on a ſudden, and makes us ſenſible that Creation is not a thing impoſſible, as ſome modern Philoſophers pretend. I leave you to yourſelf; you are much better there than with me. Adieu.

Rome, Aug. 22, 1756.

LETTER LXXXIX.

*To the Rev. Father ****, nominated Confeſſor to the Duke of ****.*

WHAT a charge! What a burden!—My deareſt Friend, is it for your damnation or for your ſalvation that Providence has provided for you ſo formidable an employment? This thought ought to make you tremble.

You aſk me what you are to do to comply with the duties of your place?—You muſt become an Angel.

Every thing is a rock, every thing a ſnare for the Confeſſor of a Sovereign Prince, if he has not patience to wait the moments of God, and mildneſs to compaſſionate the imperfections of others, and reſolution to keep the paſſions within bounds. He ought more than any other to be filled with the gifts of the Holy Ghoſt, that he pour forth ſometimes fear, ſometimes hope, and always light. He muſt

must have a zeal proof against every trial, and a spirit of justice to make him weigh the interests of the people, and of the sovereign whom he directs.

He must, in the first place, endeavour to find out, if the Prince, whose Director he is, knows the duties of Religion, and his obligations towards his subjects: for alas! It is but too common a thing for a Prince to come from the hands of those who formed him, with no other science, than a very superficial knowledge of things. In this case, he is to oblige his penitent to seek instructions, and to draw from the true sources, what Religion and Policy require of a man, who is to govern others; and this, not by loading his memory with a multiplicity of reading, but by studying first principles.

You must not be a stranger to several excellent works on this subject. I know one which was made for Victor Amadæus, which has no other fault, but that of being too diffuse, and requiring too much.

When the Duke has been solidly instructed, (for he is not to be lulled asleep with trifling practices) you will recommend it continually to him to seek after the truth, and love it without reserve. Truth ought to be the Compass of Sovereign Princes. It is the way to bring down all Informers, and such as maintain their place at Court, only by knavery and flattery; and who (a thousand times more dangerous than all other scourges) ruin the Prince both for this world, and the next.

You must never cease insisting on the indispensable necessity there is of shewing that respect to RELIGION which is due to it, not by inspiring a spirit of persecution, but by recommending an Evangelical courage, which spares the persons, while it puts a stop to the scandals. You must often repeat to him, that the life of a Sovereign, as well as his Crown, has nothing to depend on, if he allows jests to be thrown out against the Worship paid to God, and if he stops not the progress of Irreligion.

You must take care, by your steady behaviour, by your representations, by your prayers, and even by your tears, that the Prince, under your direction, distinguish himself by his good works, and make them flourish in his dominions, as the means of establishing the tranquillity of the Citizens, and promoting the happiness of families, which are the true causes of population.

You must often represent to him, that his subjects are his children; that he owes himself to them by night as well as by day; in a word, every moment, in order to comfort and assist them: that he cannot impose taxes, but in proportion to their riches and labour, and so as not to reduce them to indigence and despair: and that he owes them speedy justice.

Unless

Unless you engage him to see every thing himself, you will only fulfil half your ministry. The people cannot be made happy, but by entering into every particular regarding them, and these particulars cannot be known, without descending down to the people.

Let this people, (so much despised by the great ones, who do not reflect that in a state all is the people, except the sovereign) be always present to your mind, as a sacred portion, which ought ever to employ the Prince's thoughts; a portion, which is the support of his throne, and ought to be treated with the same tenderness as the pupil of the eye.

Make the illustrious personage, under your direction, sensible, that the life of a sovereign is a life of labour; that diversions are allowed him only in the same manner as they are allowed other men, that is to say, by way of relaxation; and teach him, that he is to interrupt his lectures of piety, and even his prayers, when the state is to be assisted.

Speak to him of the terrible account he is to give to God of his administration, and not of the sentence which history will pronounce against wicked Princes after their death. It is not a motive sufficiently Christian to fix on this object the eyes of a religious Prince; for history is no more than the voice of men, and will perish with them; whereas an ever-living God, an ever-avenger of crimes, is what ought to regulate the conduct of a sovereign. It is of little consequence to the

gene-

generality of mankind, whether people speak well or ill of them after their death; but the fight of an inflexible, eternal Judge makes a dreadful impreffion on the mind.

Never impofe any of thofe vague penitential works, which confift in mere prayers; but apply proper remedies to the wounds that fhall be fhewn you; and above all things endeavour to difcover what is the predominant and ruling fin. Without that, a man may hear Confeffions for an age together, and never know his penitent.—We muft always go up to the fource of the evil, if we defire to ftop its courfe.

Take particular care to confine yourfelf within the bounds of your Miniftry, and never meddle (I do not fay in any intrigue) but in any bufinefs of the Court. It is a fhame to fee a Religious man, who ought not to be feen, but to reprefent JESUS CHRIST, difhonour that auguft function by fordid intereft, or horrible ambition.

Your whole defire, and all your views ought to have no other object, than the falvation of the Prince, who gives you his confidence. Aftonifh him by a virtue, which is proof againft every thing, and ever equally fupported. If a Confeffor renders not himfelf refpectable, and efpecially in a Court, where nothing but pretexts for not being a Chriftian are fought after, he authorizes vice, and expofes himfelf to contempt.

Inculcate earnestly into the mind of the Prince, that he has to answer to God for all the places he disposes of, and for all the ill, which is done in them, if he make not a good choice of such as are to fill them. Above all things represent to him the danger of nominating ignorant or vicious persons to Ecclesiastical dignities, and of feeding their love of ease and their avidity by a plurality of benefices. Persuade him to seek out merit, and reward such as write for the public good, and in defence of Religion. Teach him to support his dignity, not by haughtiness and pride, but by a magnificence proportionate to his territories, his strength and his revenue; at the same time to descend from his rank in order to become a man with his people, and to study their happiness.

Place often before his eyes his duties and obligations, not in a severe tone, and with importunity, but with that charity, which, as an effusion of the Holy Ghost, never speaks but with prudence, seizes the proper moments, and turns them to advantage. When a Prince is convinced of the learning and piety of a Confessor, he hearkens to him with docility, unless his heart be depraved.

If he accuse not himself of the essential faults which are committed in the administration, you must speak of them in general terms, and you will insensibly gain the point so far, as to make him acknowledge what it is of importance for you to know. You will often

often infift on the neceffity of hearing every body, and fpeedily doing them juftice. If you find yourfelf not difpofed to follow this plan, withdraw; for thefe are precepts, which cannot be tranfgreffed without rendering one'sfelf guilty both in the eyes of God and man.

The function of an Ordinary Director attracts not the attention of the public; but every body's eyes are open on the conduct of the Confeffor of a fovereign Prince. He cannot therefore be too exact in the tribunal of pennance, in taking care that a perfon, who has, by his fcandalous life, rendered himfelf unworthy of approaching the facraments in the eyes of the public, may not be feen to approach them. There are not two Gofpels, one for the people, and another for the fovereign. The one and the other will be equally judged by that unchangeable rule; for the law of the Lord remains for ever.

Princes are not only the images of God by their power and authority, which they hold from him alone; they are fo moreover by reafon of the virtues which they fhould have, in order to reprefent him. The people ought to be able to fay of their fovereign: " He governs us like the Divinity itfelf, with " wifdom, clemency and equity:" for fovereigns are accountable for their conduct to their fubjects, not indeed to lay open to them the fecrets of their cabinet, but to do nothing that may fet them a bad example.

Be

Above all things, take care not to adulterate the truth either through fear, or from any human confideration. There is no capitulating with the law of God; it has the fame force at all times, and the fpirit of the Church is always the fame. It commends at this day the zeal of the great AMBROSE, towards the Emperor THEODOSIUS, as much as it commended it formerly; for the Church never varies either in its morality or points of faith.

I pray to God, with my whole heart, that he may fupport you, and enlighten you in fo troublefome a path, where you are not to be an ordinary man, but a heavenly Guide. Then will you live like a folitary in the midft of Grandeur; like a Religious man in a place, where ufually there is little Religion; and like a faint in a land, which would devour the men of God, had not the Lord every where his Elect. I embrace you, and am, &c.

Rome, April 26, 1755.

LETTER XC.

To the Prelate CERATI.

MONSIGNOR,

THE General Chapter of the *Dominicans* is at laft concluded; the Holy Father folemnly prefided at it; and the Rev. F. Boxadors, as diftinguifhed for his merit, as his birth, is chofen Superior-General. He will govern

govern with great wifdom and courtefy, like a man of fenfe, who knows mankind, and that they were not made to be directed in a haughty, imperious manner.

Benedict XIV, who opened the feffion by a moft eloquent difcourfe, and extremely flattering to the Order of St. *Dominick*, in which there have been all along great learning and eminent virtues, defired for General the Rev. F. *Richini*, a moft modeft and learned Religious: but notwithftanding both his perfonal prefence and his wifhes, he could not fucceed.

The Pope took the thing right; and as he was coming away, laughing very heartily at his difappointment, he faid that St. *Therefa* having once afked our Saviour, why a certain *Carmelite*, was not chofen, who, he had revealed to her, was to be General, he anfwered: " It was my defire, but the Monks would " not have it fo." It is not furprifing, therefore, added his Holinefs, that the will of his Vicar was ineffectual.—Every body knows, that the Holy Ghoft is too often refifted, and that man every day hinders the operation of God by his own preverfe will.

Father *B.emond* is little regretted, though a very affable and a very virtuous man. He is reproached by fome of his Order, with blindly fuffering himfelf to be led by a Brother, whom I always miftrufted, becaufe he appeared to me a flatterer. There are few of that character, who are not deceitful. A fmooth, foothing language is feldom that of
fincerity.

sincerity.—I pity poor *F. Bremond*, without daring to blame him. Where is the man in office, who has not been deceived?

Injustice towards the Great ones is a very common thing, and those, who are not Great themselves, are particularly guilty of it. People do not consider that a multiplicity of perplexing business may be some plea in excuse for them, when they do not see every thing themselves. Happy is he, who sees Dignities and Grandeurs only at a distance, like a mountain, which he would be unwilling to climb.

I have the honour to be, &c.

Rome, July 29, 1756.

LETTER XCI.

To an English Nobleman.

I Cannot conceive, my Lord, how you, who are so well acquainted with the imperfections of humanity, with the variety of opinions, with the capriciousness of taste, and with the force of custom, should be so much surprised at our form of Government. I do not pretend to justify it; and the less so as it is neither favourable to Commerce, Agriculture, nor Population, which precisely constitute the essence of public felicity: but do you think that there are no inconveniences in other countries?

We are under a government, it is true, which is a state of Apathy, and consequently excites

excites neither Emulation nor Induſtry; but I ſee you, Mr *Engliſhman*, under the yoke of a people who drag you whatever way they pleaſe, and who, by the impetuoſity of their diſpoſition, which is above reſtraint, are in reality the ſovereign. And I ſee other nations, ſuch as the *Poles*, under anarchy; the *Ruſſians* under a deſpotic government, without mentioning the *Turks*, who dare not even ſpeak for fear of a *Sultan*, who can do what he pleaſes.

It is commonly imagined, tho' I know not for what reaſon, that an Eccleſiaſtical Government is a ſceptre of iron: but whoever has read hiſtory cannot be ignorant, that it was in reality the Chriſtian Religion, that has aboliſhed ſlavery: that in thoſe countries, ſuch as *Poland* and *Hungary*, where it unhappily ſtill takes place, the Peaſants who are under the government of the Biſhops, are not in a ſtate of Villanage; and that in fine, nothing can be milder than the government of the Popes. Beſides that they are almoſt never at war, being neceſſarily Princes of peace, they trouble nobody either for taxes, or their way of thinking.

There are certain Inquiſitions, which have occaſioned the Prieſts to be branded with the name of Perſecutors. But beſides that the Monarchs, who authorized thoſe Courts, were as culpable as the Inſtigators and Promoters of them; ROME was never ſeen to indulge the barbarous pleaſure of burning her Citizens,

becauſe

because they had not faith, or because they let fall some wicked words and discourse. JESUS CHRIST, when expiring on the cross, far from exterminating those who blasphemed him, solicits their pardon in these words: *Father forgive them.**

So much is certain, that if some Ministers of God have now and then breathed carnage and blood, they have done so through an enormous abuse of Religion, which being charity itself, preaches nothing but mildness and peace.

It is to no purpose for me to run through the different countries of the world, I see that in the midst of our indigence and apathy, we lead the happiest lives of all. This indeed we derive from the temperature of our climate and the fertility of our soil, which supplies us abundantly with all the necessaries of life.

If our government had more activity, there would certainly be more strength and vigour in it, and the circulation would be greater in the Ecclesiastical state. But who has told us, that the Government would not then become despotic? The inactivity of the Popes, who are commonly too old to undertake and execute great designs, constitutes at once both our misfortune and happiness.

They leave the fields to bring forth their fruits spontaneously, without attending either to their culture or improvement; but they never crush people with a load of taxes; and

* Luke xxiii. 34.

every

every one is sure of remaining quietly at home, without experiencing the least degree of oppression.

Rich countries are taxed in proportion to their riches; and I know not truly, whether it be better to be an inhabitant of a country flourishing by its industry, and to have such exorbitant taxes to pay, as leave but the bare means of a subsistence; or to live in a place where there is no circulation, but where a man lives in a happy ease. It appears to me, that every individual, taken separately, would rather choose to gain little, and have nothing to pay, than to gain much, and to give almost the whole away. I would rather have only five and twenty *sequins* to myself, than the pleasure of possessing a hundred, out of which I was obliged to pay away ninety.

Men are commonly misled by specious advantages in what they assert respecting the different forms of Government. The world, taken in its totality, requires, no doubt, that men should labour, that they should be active, and give mutual help from one extremity of the earth to the other, in order to keep up a correspondence, and to maintain a just equilibrium, or at least a happy harmony; but that does not prevent the possibility of there being a little corner of the universe happy, without taking part in all the enterprizes and revolutions of other countries: and we are this little spot, where the serpents of Discord never hiss, and where Tyranny never exercises its cruelties.

The

The mind of man is reftlefs, becaufe it is perpetually agitated: it loves to fee countries always in motion. Thus Conquerors who ravage countries, who fack, who kill, who invade, pleafe mankind more, than thofe beings who, fixed to the fame fpot, lead a life ever uniform, ever tranquil, and never make a fhew of themfelves to mankind by their revolutions.

Neverthelefs the life celebrated by the Philofophers and Poets is not a life of tumult. To render man happy, they banifh from his heart both avarice and ambition; and in this they agree with true Chriftians, who preach up nothing but difintereftednefs and humility.

I can affure you that I have often made an eftimate of every mode of government, and that I fhould be much at a lofs to tell you which is beft. There is none which has not its inconveniences; and this is the lefs to be wondered at, when we fee the univerfe itfelf, though governed by Infinite Wifdom, fubject to the ftrangeft revolutions. People are fometimes crufhed with thunder, fometimes afflicted with calamities, and almoft ever diftrefled either by fhocks of the elements, or by fwarms of infects. In the heavenly country alone, every thing is perfect, and it is only there that we fhall experience neither evils nor dangers.

A little lefs enthufiafm, Sir, for your own country, will make you own that there are abufes in it, as well as in others. But how can we require of an *Englifhman* not to be Enthufiaft in favour of his country! You will tell me,

that

that the liberty and property of the inhabitants are particularly respected in England; and I will reply to you, that these prerogatives, which so essentially constitute the happiness of the subject, and should always remain inviolate, are so under the government of the Popes. There every one is allowed the peaceable enjoyment of his whole property, to go and come as he pleases, without the least disturbance or molestation. The arm of power is never felt in the Ecclesiastical state; and it may be said, that the Rulers there put on rather an air of intreaty than of command. Do not conclude from these reflections, that I am an apologist for a government so defective, in many respects, as ours is; I am as sensible of these defects as you can be: but consider that there is no form of administration in the whole world, of which we cannot speak both good and ill. Let the Republican love a Common-wealth, let the subject of a Monarch love Monarchy; and then every thing is in its proper place. As for me, I am in mine, when I assure you of the respect, &c.

Rome, Sept. 27, 1756.

LETTER XCII.

To a PHYSICIAN.

IT gives me the greatest concern, my dear Friend, that your domestic affairs are still in a bad way, and that your wife, by her extravagance,

travagance, does every thing in her power to make them still worse. Nothing but patience and mildness will ever be able to affect her.— Gain her confidence, and then you will obtain whatever you please.

A man ought never to make a wife uneasy, whatever faults she may have; but all proper means are to be used to open her eyes. He must reason with her; he even must seem to enter into her views, without shewing any disposition to contradict her. Then by candid and civil representations, by a mild behaviour, by sensible reasonings and effusions of the heart, she will, by degrees, be brought to relish the morality preached to her. But a pedantic air and a moralizing tone, never should be assumed.

Above all, never complain of your wife's conduct before your children; and still less, before your servants. They will contract a habit of disrespect, or even of contempt for her.

Wives deserve consideration, the more so as it is commonly the bad humour of the husband, or domestic vexations which make them peevish. Their tender frame demands a regard, as well as their situation in life, which does not allow them to dissipate their cares so easily as men, whose lives are divided between business, study, and their different employments. Whilst the husband sallies forth either for business or pleasure, the wife necessarily remains confined at home, taken up with a hundered trifling, consequently, tiresome con-

K k   cerns.

cerns. Women who love reading have a refource: but one cannot be always reading.—Befides every woman, who reads much, is commonly vain.

I would advife you to recommend it to the Creditors to often dun your Lady, when fhe is in their debt. She will foon grow tired of fuch vifits; and you will then take the opportunity of fetting before her eyes, how great a misfortune it is to be in debt, when a perfon is unable to pay.

You will affect her by fpeaking of her children, for whom you muft lay up a fortune. She loves them tenderly; and this motive will be the beft leffon that can be given her.

I was formerly acquainted with an old Officer at *Pefaro*, who had much to fuffer from the paffionate temper of his wife. When fhe grew furious, he remained unmoved, and fpake not a word; and this filent attitude foon calmed her rage.—Wrath is difarmed by mildnefs.

How pleafed am I, my dear Doctor, that I am married to my Cell! She is a good companion that never fpeaks a word to me—who never tires out my patience—and whom I always find the fame, at whatever hour I come home—ever eafy, ever ready to receive me. The troubles of the Religious are mere nothings, when compared to thofe of people in the world: but every one fhould bear his misfortunes with patience, and confider that this life is not eternal. St *Jerome* ufed to fay, that
he

he would advise only those to marry, who were afraid in the night-time, that they might have a companion to keep up their courage; but that as he was not fearful himself, he never had an inclination to marry.

I am charmed that your eldest son has an uncommon sagacity. You must rouse the genius of the younger, as it is less unfolded, that it may shew itself. The talent of a Father is to know how to multiply himself, and to appear to his children under different characters; to one as a master, to another as a friend.

The confidence which the principal people in the city repose in you, does them honour. The frequent cures you have performed, must make them sensible, that the reproaches cast on Physicians are not always well founded. It is the fashion to be merry at their expence: but I am thoroughly convinced that there is more knowledge among them, than in almost any other profession; and that their science is not so conjectural, as is generally believed. But man, ever ingenious in deluding himself, says that it is always the Physician, and never Death that kills. Moreover, where is the man of learning, who is never mistaken? The reason why we find in books so many sophisms and paradoxes is, that though a man knows a deal, he is not therefore infallible.

What I say to you, my dear Doctor, is the more generous on my part, as I enjoy the best of health, and stand not in need of a Physician. I take my chocolate every morning:

I live

I live very temperately: I take a deal of snuff: I frequently take a walk: and with this regimen a man lives a century—But a long life is not my ambition.

Continue to love me as your best friend, as well as that of your family, and as one who desires most sincerely to see you happy.

My compliments to your dear spouse, whom I could wish to see as reasonable in her expences, as you are. But that time will come. The happiness of this life consists in always hoping.

Rome, Sept. 30, 1756.

LETTER XCIII.

To the same.

YOU will see, my friend, by the Memorials of your two Colleagues, which come with this, and who are tearing one another to pieces, that study does not exempt us from the frailties incident to human nature.

The learned, nevertheless, ought to set an example of moderation, and to leave quarrels and jealousies to the vulgar, as their proper element. Every age has been productive of literary combats, truly humiliating to reason and sense. The merit of one is not the merit of another: and I see not, why envy should be so enraged, as to cry down those, who have acquired a reputation. I could wish rather never to have read in my life, than to
conceive

conceive the least hatred against a writer. If he writes well, I admire him; if he writes ill, I excuse him, imagining to myself, that he has done his best. The greater number of slender geniuses there are, who set up for Authors, the more they detest, and tear one another in pieces. Men of genius resemble Mastiffs, who despise the insults of little curs. Men who are truly great, make no reply to the cavils of Critics—The art of being silent, is the best manner of answering satires.

Literature is more exposed to skirmishes than the sciences, because it does not require the same application of mind. The Learned in the sciences are so absorbed in study, that they have not ears to hear the rumours and murmurs of jealousy: while those who apply only to literature, disperse themselves on all sides, like light troops, and are ever on the watch to know what passes.

Hence it is, that the most odious skirmishes are often found in the *French* publications; because that nation commonly abounds more with men of literature, than men of deep learning. Their sprightly and agreeable turn of mind leads them rather to literature, than to the sciences. They are afraid of forfeiting their liberty, and restraining too much their natural gaiety, were they to give themselves up to deep researches, and tedious calculations. The man of deep learning, is almost always a man, whose name will be handed down to posterity: the man of literature, is known in his own age

age alone: and as people are in a hurry to acquire a reputation, becaufe felf-love prompts them to the prefent enjoyment of it, the man of literature, prefers the *eclat* of a day, to a glory that would laft for ages to come.

I am exceeding glad, that your remonftrances have had their effect on your young fpoufe. She will perhaps at laft become a mifer: but that you muft prevent: for fhe will then ftarve you to death; and all a Phyfician ought to know of a fpare diet, is when to prefcribe it to his patients.

I have fcarce time to read the work you mention; but as you fpeak in fo high a ftrain of its Latinity, I will endeavour to run it over. Some books I run over in the twinkling of an eye; others I dive into, fo as to lofe nothing: that depends on the fubjects of which they treat, and the manner in which they treat them.

I like a work, whofe chapters, like fo many avenues, lead me agreeably to fome interefting profpect. When I fee the roads crooked, and the ground rugged, I tire at the firft fetting out, and proceed no farther, unlefs the importance of the fubject makes me forget the manner in which it is treated.

I take my leave of you to vifit an *Englifh* nobleman, who thinks and fpeaks like an *Efprit fort*. He cannot conceive how *Rome* can canonize men, who have led holy lives: as if we did not judge of perfons by their lives: and as if God had not promised the kingdom of heaven to those who faithfully fulfil his law.

I hope nevertheless that the excellent work of the Holy Father on the *Canonization of Saints* will open his eyes. He has an infinite esteem for that Pontiff, and a high idea of his writings. Adieu.

Convent of the H. Apostles, Nov. 5, 1756.

LETTER XCIV.

To the Abbè LAMI.

I Wish, my dear Abbè, for the honour of your own country, and for that of *Italy* in general, that the history of TUSCANY, which is soon to be published, may perfectly correspond to its title.

What a noble matter to treat of, if the Writer, with equal judgment and delicacy, makes the Arts spring up in that country, where they had been buried for so many ages: and if he paints, in strong and lively colours, the Family of the MEDICIS, to whom we owe this inestimable advantage!

History brings all ages and all men into one point of view, so as to form a landscape, which agreeably attracts and fixes the eye. It gives colour to the thoughts, soul to actions, life to the dead, and makes them appear again upon the Theatre of the world, as if still living; with this difference, that it is no longer to flatter them, but to judge them.

History

History was heretofore badly written: nor do our *Italian* Historians write well even at this day. They do nothing more than heap together epochas and dates, without bringing us acquainted with the particular genius of each Nation, or each Hero.

Most men consider history, as they would do a piece of *Flanders* Tapestry, just giving a glance at it. They content themselves with seeing figures shining by the brightness of the colours; without thinking of the head which sketched out the design, any more than they think of the hand that executed it— And thus they imagine they see every thing, when in reality they see nothing at all.

I defy any man to improve by history, who attends only to the Princes, Battles and Exploits passing in review before him. But I know not any book better calculated to instruct, than history, when a person considers the progress of events, and observes how they were brought about: When he analyses the talents and intentions of those, who put every thing in motion: when he transports himself to those ages and regions, where the memorable events happened.

The reading of history furnishes an inexhaustible subject for reflection. One should weigh every fact, not as a mere trifler who doubts of every thing, but as a Critic, who is unwilling to be deceived. Young people seldom improve by history, because it is mentioned to them only as a species of writing, calculated

lated merely for the memory; whereas they ought to be told, that it is the foul, and not the eyes, which are to be employed in reading hiftorical works.

Then they will fee men extolled, who were a difgrace to humanity; others perfecuted, who were the glory of their country, and of the age in which they lived. Then they become acquainted with the refources of Emulation, and the dangers of Ambition: then they difcover that intereft is the univerfal *primum mobile* in cities, courts and families.

Hiftorians but rarely make reflections, in order to give their readers an opportunity of analyfing the perfons mentioned, and of forming a judgment of them.

There are, in all the hiftories in the world, Beings almoft unfeen, but who, neverthelefs, from behind the curtain, put every thing in motion. They efcape not an attentive reader: he gives them the honour of what flattery too often attributes to men in power. Almoft all Princes, almoft all Minifters have a hidden genius, who puts them on action, and who can only be difcovered by analyfing the Princes and Minifters in order to appreciate their worth.

It may be faid with truth, that the greateft events, which aftonifh the world, are frequently brought about by men of an inferior rank, often very obfcure in their ftation of life, and their extraction. Many women, who appeared only on the public ftage of life, as the wives of fuch a Prince, or of fuch an Embaffador, and whose names are not even mentioned in history, have often been the cause of the most glorious exploits. Their counsels prevailed and were followed; and the husbands had the whole honour of an enterprize, for which they were endebted to the sagacity of their wives.

TUSCANY affords a thousand brilliant passages in its history, which an able hand might paint in a most lively and striking manner. That part, which will give an account of the revival of the arts, and their reanimation all over Europe, by the family of the *Medicis* (Princes whose territories were so confined, and whose power was so small) will not be the least interesting. When I reflect on that Epocha, I see as it were a new world issuing out of nothing: a new sun arise to enlighten Nations. Ah! why, my dear Abbè, have not you undertaken that work? You would give it all the life, of which it is susceptible. Adieu. I am besieged, but I will not be blockaded. —They are visits of civility; and we must behave with good manners.

Rome, Nov. 8, 1756.

LETTER XCV.

To Count ***.

I Cannot express, my dear Count, all the joy I feel, when I reflect that you are now marching on with a steady pace in the paths of virtue; and that you are so much master of yourself,

yourself, as to keep your senses—your passions—your heart in perfect subjection.

Yes: we will make together the little excursion we projected. Your company is my delight, since you became a new man.

I will, with pleasure, present you to the Holy Father on your arrival here; and I can assure you he will be very glad to see you, especially when he is informed that you are remarkably fond of good books.—You will find him as cheerful, as if he were only five and twenty.

Cheerfulness is the balm of life; and what makes me hope that your present pious disposition will continue, is that you are ever of a cheerful temper. We insensibly tire of virtue, when we tire of ourselves. Then every thing becomes a burden, and we conclude by giving into the most gloomy misanthropy, or excessive dissipation. I approve very much of the bodily exercises you take. They ease the mind, and render it fit for any thing. I use them myself as much, as the retired state of a Religious man, will allow.

When you come to see me, I will tell you every thing, which the irreconcileable Marchioness alledges as an excuse for not seeing you. I always thought that her affected devotion would not let her do so good an action. Vanity prompts her not to change her conduct. You can form no idea how difficult it is for certain Devotees to acknowledge they have done wrong.

As for you; flop where you are. You have written to her; you have spoken to her; and that is certainly enough; since St. *Paul* tells us, that we must be at peace with every body, *if possible*. He knew that there were people of unsociable tempers, with whom it was impossible to live in a cordial manner. I embrace you with my whole soul, &c.

LETTER XCVI.

To the Rev. Father LUCIARDI, *a Bernabite.*

REV. FATHER,

YOUR decision is agreeable to the Councils; and I should be much surprised were it otherwise; as I have for a long time been acquainted with the extent of your learning, and the precision of your answers.

Besides the excellent books, which are your constant companions, you have always the Company of Rev. Father GERDIL, whose learning and modesty equally merit the greatest commendations—Take care of your health both for the good of Religion, and our mutual interest.

The City of TURIN, where you are an inhabitant, undoubtedly knows the value of possessing you—for merit is there both esteemed and cherished.

I should scruple keeping you any longer from your studies and exercises of piety. I therefore conclude, without ceremony, by assuring

suring you, that nobody can be more cordially, &c.

Rome, Dec. 3, 1755.

LETTER XCVII.

To the Director of a Nunnery.

I DO not felicitate you on your employment; but I will strive to persuade you to acquit yourself with all possible prudence and charity. If you follow my advice, you will very seldom go to the Parlour.* It is the place of unprofitable words, small slanders, idle reports; and an infallible occasion of exciting jealousies. For if you see one oftner than another, some of them will be coming privately to hear what passes, merely from a spirit of curiosity. This will raise cabals and parties; and a thousand constructions will be put on the least word you say.

Secondly, you will never remove the vain scruples, which will be frequently repeated to you, but by despising them, and by hearkening to them—only twice at most.

Thirdly, you must accustom the Nuns never to speak to you in the Confessional of any thing, but what regards themselves: Otherwise they will make their neighbours confession, and in only hearing the confession of one, you will insensibly learn the faults of the whole Community.

* See note on letter 28. p. 72.

Fourthly,

Fourthly, you must labour inceſſantly to maintain peace in all their hearts, by conſtantly repeating to them, that JESUS CHRIST is only to be found in the boſom of peace.

You muſt often reflect with yourſelf, that if there be a *luſt of the eyes* in all men, as St. *John* informs us; there is alſo a *luſt* of the tongue and ears in many Nuns—But will you have ſkill enough to cure them? Although it be not proper to preſcribe a ſilence, which would ſtifle them; it is at leaſt neceſſary, that thoſe ill-natured diſcourſes, which amuſe at the expence of our neighbour, ſhould be interdicted.

Have regard to the weakneſs of a ſex, which requires great condeſcenſion in the government of it. An allowance muſt be made for poor recluſe women, whoſe imagination is always at work—we muſt not add any thing to a Yoke, already heavy enough with the burden of a perpetual ſolitude.

Our Holy Father knew their wants, when he allowed them to go out once a year to viſit one another—Whatever is done from a principle of charity, merits praiſe.

There will be ſome occaſions, on which you muſt arm yourſelf with reſolution: otherwiſe you will be *directed*, inſtead of being a *Director*. Many Nuns are fond of guiding him, who has the care of their conſciences.—They do it with an air of perfect piety, without ſeeming to intend it.

It

If you flight the advice I have here given, you will repent of it; and if you have a mind to do ſtill better, you will never be ſeen by them, but in the Confeſſional, the Pulpit, and at the Altar—You will be much more reſpected on that account. There are few Directors, who loſe not a great deal by being too well known. It is a great ſcience not to ſhew one's ſelf, but on proper occaſions. Aſk me nothing more; for with regard to this ſubject you have the full extent of my knowledge. Adieu.

Convent of the Apoſtles, Dec. 19, 1756.

LETTER XCVIII.

To Count GENORI.

COUNT,

MY books, my monaſtic exerciſes, my employment, all oppoſe the pleaſure I could otherwiſe take in coming to ſee you. Beſides, what can you do with a Religious man, whoſe time is perpetually divided between reading and prayer, which would interrupt our walks and converſation?

I am ſo habituated to my hours of ſolitude and work, that I ſhould think my exiſtence at an end, were I once put out of my way. All the happineſs of a Religious conſiſts in knowing how to be alone—to pray—to ſtudy. I have no other enjoyment; and I prefer it to all

the

the pleasures of the world. I set an infinite value on the conversation of a few learned men, or a few friends, provided always that they do not encroach on the distribution I have made of my time. It never was my design to make myself a slave to a minute of those hours, which are at my own disposal, for I detest every thing that is punctilious and trifling: but I love Order; and I see nothing but the love of Order, that can maintain the harmony between the soul and the senses.

Where there is no Order, there is no peace of mind. Tranquility is the daughter of Regularity; and it is by Regularity that a man keeps himself within the sphere of his duties. All inanimate Creatures preach to us an exact Regularity. The Planets perform their respective revolutions in periodical times; and the Plants assume a new life at the moment pointed out to them. The instant is known when Day is to appear, and it never fails: the moment of Night is known, and then Darkness covers the earth.

The true Philosopher never inverts the order of time, unless forced to it by his occupations, or some usages or customs require it.

To return to natural history, which you mentioned to me, it is certain that we have studied it less than we have studied Antiquity, though the one be of far greater advantage than the other. ITALY, nevertheless, offers at every step enough to exercise, and even to satisfy all the curiosity of a Naturalist. *Phe-*
nomena

nomena are obferved there, which are feen no where elfe, and which nations faid to be lefs fuperftitious than the *Italians*, would moft certainly take to be miracles.

A French Abbè, who has been here fome time, and whom I became acquainted with at Cardinal *Paffionei's*, was in the greateft aftonifhment at the wonders which nature here prefented to his fight. I fhall never forget having gone with him to the neighbourhood of the City of *Mattei*; and although it is not far, the walk took us up near five hours; for he ftopped at every ftep. He is a man of great knowledge, and has fuch a tafte for natural hiftory, that he becomes glued to an infect or a flint, and there is no getting him away. He looked fo long at every ftone, that I was apprehenfive, he would have become one himfelf: in that cafe, I own, I fhould have been a great lofer, for his converfation is as engaging, as it is cheerful and lively. He is the fame perfon, who wrote againft the fyftems of Monf. *Buffon*. How much longer would he have ftopped, had he been fo happy as to have had you for his companion?

I have the honour, dear Count, to be, with the warmeft gratitude and the moft refpectful attachment, your very humble, &c.

LETTER XCIX.

To M. C*** an Advocate.

OH! Compliments indeed! Did you know how I love them, you would never make me any.

What is reported respecting the person in question, is grounded solely on envy and malice. Where is the man in office, where is the writer, who has not enemies? Libels and satires make no impression but on weak and badly organized heads; and it is a remark you will make, that those people, who themselves have the greatest defects and vices, always most easily give credit to calumny, and shew the greatest repugnance to see those, who have been ill used.

But misrepresentation is so much in vogue, that, according to the remark of the Holy Father, a thousand recommendations are necessary to determine a man in power to favour any one; and one word is enough to make him change his mind, and put him in a passion. This is the greatest proof of the depravity of the human heart.

We should be under a necessity of seeing nobody, were we to shut our doors against every one who is spoken ill of. Rash judgment is the thing we are most to guard against. It is shameful to condemn a brother, when we have not even proofs sufficient to accuse him.

Prepossession against others will damn the greater part of the Grandees, and especially the bigots among them, who confider it as an act of piety to give credit to all the ill they hear of their neighbour. They affect not to know that God exprefly forbids us to judge, that we may not be judged; and that a man is lefs criminal in his eyes, who has committed a fault for which he is humbly forry, than a man who rafhly accufes his brethren.

The firft rule of Chriftian charity is, that a perfon ought not to believe the ill of his neighbour, which he has not feen; and that if he has feen it, he ought to hold his tongue.

Moreover, if the perfon, you are advifed not to fee, feeks the company of good people, it is a certain proof, that he is not fo much of a libertine, as he is reprefented, or that he defigns to change his conduct. Perhaps his falvation may depend on the good example you will fet him; therefore do not difcourage him.

Charity judges not like the world; for the world has fcarce ever miffed judging wrong.

I am, &c.

Convent of the Holy Apoftles.

LETTER C.

To the Abbé L***.

SINCE you confult me, Sir, refpecting the Difcourfe I lately heard, I will anfwer you with my ufual fincerity, that I found fome excellent

cellent things in it, but that I do not like that affectation which enervates. One would imagine, that it was a work made up at a Lady's toilet, and that it had been painted. For the future, let your foul speak when you mount the pulpit, and you will speak well. Wit and ingenuity ought to be only the border of a picture, and you made it the ground of your Discourse—To be a good Orator, a man ought to take a middle way between the Italians and the French, that is to say, he ought neither to be a giant nor a dwarf.

Let not the taste of the age corrupt you; if you do, you never will be able to get rid of that affected, high-flown eloquence, which puts both thoughts and words to the rack. It is of great importance to a young man of talents to receive such advice, and above all to take it; your modesty assures me you will do so. I am, Sir, with all possible desire of seeing you a perfect Orator, your very humble, &c.

Rome, the 10*th Instant.*

LETTER CI.

To Prince SAN-SEVERO.

EXCELLENCE,

I Continue to admire your new discoveries. You bring forth a second Universe from the former, by whatever you create. This makes our Antiquarians go mad, who persuade themselves,

selves, that nothing can be interesting or beautiful, but what is very old.

It is undoubtedly right to esteem Antiquity; but I do not think that we ought to become slaves to it so far, as to extol beyond bounds a thing of no value in its self, merely because it was taken out of *Adrian's* gardens.

The Ancients, like us, employed very common things for the ordinary uses of life; and if they are to be valued in proportion to their being old, the Earth, in that respect, merits our first homages, as no one assuredly will contest its antiquity.

I can neither bear with Enthusiasts, nor those who are quite unaffected with what they read. It belongs only to such, as keep the medium between these two extremes, to see things and to judge of them, as they ought. The indifference of the unaffected deprives them of taste and curiosity; both of which however are requisite to examine and to pronounce.

The IMAGINATION, when it is under no government, is still more dangerous than indifference. It causes dazzlings, which cloud the sight, and darken reason. PHILOSOPHY itself, every day, feels the effects of its too fatal impression; though that wanton jade never ought to have any empire over it. Sophisms, paradoxes, captious arguments (the retinue of all our modern Philosophers) have no other origin than the Imagination. She is wound up according to the different whims; and has no longer any regard either to experience or truth. Your

Your Excellence muſt know theſe writings, as you have frequent opportunities of reading the productions of the times. ENGLAND, which on account of its phlegm, one would believe gave leſs into Imagination than other countries, has publiſhed to the world ſome of the moſt extravagant ideas. Their Philoſophers have dreamed even more than ours; for it was neceſſary they ſhould uſe greater efforts to lay aſide their natural character, which is that of gloominefs and taciturnity. Their imagination is like a new-lighted coal-fire, the vapour of which offends the brain.

The ſaying, that " the Imagination is the mother of dreams," is well founded. It produces even more than the Night itſelf: and they are the more dangerous, as when people indulge them, they think they are not dreaming; whereas the morning undeceives us with reſpect to the illuſions of ſleep.

I ſtill fear leſt your Chemical experiments ſhould hurt your health: they ſometimes produce dreadful accidents. But when a Natural Philoſopher is making any new eſſay, he purſues it without fear of the conſequences, as an Officer, carried away by his valour, throws himſelf at random amidſt the fire of the enemy.

I have the honour to be with equal reſpect and attachment, &c.

Rome, Jan. 13, 1757.

LETTER CII.

To a Prelate.

Monsignor,

JOIN with me in vindicating the memory of Sixtus Quintus. I was yesterday forced, in some degree, to be in a passion, when it was asserted to my face, that he was a cruel Pope, and a Pontiff unworthy to reign. It is surprising how much this character, which he never deserved, continues to be given him, and how much it gains ground.

Is it then allowable to condemn so great a man, without calling to mind the times he lived in, and reflecting that Italy then swarmed with robbers: that there was less safety in Rome itself, than in a forest: and that the most virtuous women were insulted even at noon-day?—The severity of Sixtus-Quintus, which is improperly styled cruelty, would be, at least, as pleasing to God, as the piety of Pius V.

In the reign of some certain Popes we have seen thousands of men assassinated, without the Murderers ever being punished. Then might it truly be said of those Popes, that they were cruel. But it was an act of justice, and zeal equally advantageous to the public and pleasing to God, when Sixtus-Quintus put about fifty robbers to death, in order to re-establish manners in the midst of the cities, and security in the heart of the country, at a time when there was no longer any law,

good

good order or government. I sigh, I own, when I see great men become the jest of ignorant and prejudiced Writers. More than once has Posterity itself, which is called an impartial judge, been misled by the reflections of a seducing historian, who, without a commission, placed himself on the bench, and pronounced a sentence, grounded solely on his own prejudices.

It is vain to cry out, calumny! The impression is made—the book is read; and the multitude form their judgment only from what was first written. Thus has *Gregorio Leti* rendered Sixtus-Quintus odious throughout all the regions of the Universe, instead of representing him as a sovereign, who was forced to intimidate his people, and to restrain them by the greatest examples of severity.

Nothing is more to be dreaded by all ranks of people than a Government too remiss and easy. Crimes make a thousand times more victims, than well appointed punishments. The old Testament is full of instances of justice and terrour; and God himself (whom undoubtedly nobody will accuse of cruelty) ordered them.

I will certainly come and see you very soon. That you may depend upon, as well as on the affection, with which I shall be all my life, &c.

Convent of the H. Apost. April 2, 1756.

LETTER CIII.

To a Young Religious.

THE advice you afk me, my dear Friend, with refpect to the method of purfuing your ftudies, muft be analogous to your difpofition and talents. If a livelinefs of genius be your prevailing character, you muft temper it by reading works, in which the Imagination comes in for a fmall fhare: if, on the contrary, you be flow of thought, you muft enliven your mind by familiarizing yourfelf with books full of fire.

Do not overload your memory with dates and facts, before you have ranged your ideas in a certain order, and acquired a juftnefs of reafoning. You muft accuftom yourfelf to a methodical way of thinking, and to diffipate, though without any great efforts, all the chimeras that rufh on your mind.—Whoever thinks only after a vague manner, is fit for nothing—becaufe nothing can fix his attention.

The bafis of your ftudies ought to be the knowledge of God and of yourfelf. If you dive into yourfelf, you will there difcover the Agency of him, who created you: and if you reflect on the errors of the Imagination, and the wanderings of the heart, you will feel the neceffity of a Revelation, which has revived the law after a more efficacious and lively manner.

Then may you give yourfelf up, without referve, to that fcience, which by reafoning and authority, leads us into the sanctuary of Religion. There you will drink of the heavenly doctrine published in the sacred books, and interpreted by the Councils and Fathers of the Church.

By reading them, true eloquence will become quite familiar to you; and you will early begin to take them for models, so as afterwards to meet with success in your manner of writing and preaching.

Make use of the intervals of time between your different exercises, to cast an eye, now and then, on the finest fragments of the Orators and Poets, after the example of St. *Jerome*: that is to say, not like a man, who greedily feeds on them, but like one, who culls from them whatever may contribute most to the embellishment of his style, and makes use of them to promote the glory of Religion.

The Historians will afterwards take you, as it were, by the hand, and lead you from age to age, to point out to you the different events and revolutions, which have all along agitated and busied the world. This will afford you an uninterrupted means of knowing and adoring a Providence, which directs and governs all according to its designs.

You will see, almost in every page of history, how Empires and Emperors have been, in the hand of God, instruments of justice or of mercy—how he raises them—how he pulls them down—how he creates them—how he

destroys

destroys them, himself remaining unchangeably still the same.

Read over again in the morning, what you had read the preceding evening, that your reading may be properly digested, fixed in your memory, and arranged in a certain order. Never fail to make the reading of a grave and solid work, succeed that of a book which abounds with imagination, that you may not become a party-man.

This practice renders more temperate the thoughts, which the productions of a mind too much sublimated throw into a state of fermentation: it lowers and settles a genius, which too often suffers itself to be carried beyond its proper sphere.

Take every possible opportunity of enjoying the conversation of men of learning. Happily Providence has provided for this: as, in most of our houses, there are found Religious, who have pursued their studies in a proper manner.

Neglect not the company of old men. Their memory, furnished with many facts, of which they were witnesses, is a magazine which may be rummaged to advantage—They are like some old worm-eaten, dusty, ill-bound books, which, nevertheless, contain excellent matter.

Have no passion for any particular work—any particular author—or any particular sentiment—left you become a party-man: but prefer one author to another, when you judge him to be more solid and more excellent.

Prepoffeffion and prejudices are to be guarded against with the utmost precaution; but, unfortunately, the more a person studies, the more he suffers himself to be carried away with them.

We are identified, and become as it were one and the same man with an author, who has said good things; and, insensibly, the panegyrists and adorers of all his opinions, though some of them may be very singular and fantastical. —Guard against that misfortune, and ever be more the friend of Truth, than of *Plato* or *Scotus*.

Respect the sentiments of the order of which you are a member, so far as not to attack received ideas; but be not a slave to them. We are immoveably to hold only to what is of Faith, and confecrated by the universal Church. I have seen Professors, who would have died, rather than abandon some school-opinions: my behaviour towards such men, was to pity them and shun them. Apply no further to *Scholastic* Divinity, than it may be necessary for understanding the jargon of the schools, and refuting sophists: for it is so far from making an essential part of Theology, that it is no more than the outer-bark of it.

Avoid disputes: they clear up nothing: nevertheless know, on proper occasions, how to maintain the truth and attack error with the arms which JESUS CHRIST and his Apostles have put in our hands, and which consist in mildness, persuasion and charity. The minds of men are not taken by affault; but we fucceed in gaining them over, if we know the art of infinuation.

Dread fatiguing the faculties of your foul by giving yourfelf up to intemperate ftudy—each day's trouble is enough. Never therefore entrench on the morrow, by prolonging the ftudies of the night, except when neceffity requires it.

A man, who regulates his time, and commonly allots only fome hours to work, goes on fafter, than he who heaps one moment on another, and knows not when to ftop. He who follows no order in ftudying, ends in being no more than a mere title-page of books, or a library turned topfy-turvy. Therefore love order, but without being punctilious, that you may put off your work to another time, when you are not difpofed for ftudy. A ftudious perfon is not to labour like the ox conftrained to trace the furrows in a plowed field, nor like a mercenary, who is paid by the day.

To be continually ftriving againft reft and fleep is a bad cuftom. Whatever is done unwillingly, is never well done; and when a man is too earneft in writing, he hurts his health.

There are certain days and hours, when a perfon is not difpofed for work; and then it is a madnefs to offer violence to himfelf, unlefs he be in extreme hurry—The books are few which do not fmell of a painful compofition, becaufe people too often write when they ought to take their reft.

It

It is a great art, in order to fucceed in our ftudies, to know when to begin work, and when to leave off: without this, the brain is heated, the mind is either abforbed or evaporated, and our productions are either languid or extraordinary. Learn to make a good choice of the works you read, that you may know only what is worth knowing, and make a good ufe of it. Life is too fhort to lofe any part of it in ufelefs ftudies—Unlefs we make hafte to learn, we grow old without learning any thing at all.

Above all, beg of God to enlighten you: for there is no knowledge but through him; and whoever follows not his light, is in darknefs.

Dread becoming learned, for no other end than that of acquiring a reputation: for befides that *knowledge puffs up*, and *charity edifies**, a Community is hurt, when a member makes a parade of his learning.

Let events take their courfe, and your own merit fpeak for you, in order to your advancement. If employments come not to feek you out, be content with that which is the loweft— and, take my word for it, it is the beft.

I am never better pleafed than, when after holding our Chapters, I have no other dignity, but the honour of exifting. I then congratulate with myfelf for having refufed whatever was offered me, and for having nobody to govern—but myfelf,

1 Cor. viii. 1.

The advantage which accrues from the love of study, and from conversing with the dead, is a thousand times greater than the frivolous glory of commanding the living. The finest command is that of restraining the senses and passions, and of maintaining the soul in that sovereignty which is its due.

Add moreover, that the man who applies to study, knows not what it is to be tired of himself. He thinks himself young, when he is already old: the little bustles of the Cloister are ever as far off from him, as the hurry and embarassments of the world.

I exhort you therefore, my dear Friend, not only for the advantage of Religion, not only for the good of our Order, but even for your own satisfaction, to give yourself up to a studious life. With a book—a pen—and your own thoughts—you will be happy and content, wherever you are—Both the understanding and the heart of man are an asylum, when he knows how to retire to either.

I feel with pleasure, the great confidence which you repose in me, as you might, preferably, have addressed yourself to the Fathers COLOMBINI, MARZONI, MARTINELLI. They are really men, who for their learning and talents, are capable of giving excellent counsel. Adieu: and believe me your Servant and good Friend.

Rome, June 7, 1757.

LETTER CIV.

To the Rev. Father ***, a Religious of the Congregation of Somafcha.*

THE loſs the Church has juſt ſuffered in the perſon of BENEDICT XIV. affects me the more, that in him I have loſt an excellent Protector. I came back to Rome in 1740, the firſt year of his Pontificate; and from that time he never ceaſed honouring me with his kindneſſes. If you are inclined to make his funeral oration, you will have the fineſt ſubject you can deſire. Certainly you will not forget that he performed his ſtudies with your Congregation in the *Clementine-College*, and that you gave him the firſt ſketch of that ſublime and vaſt knowledge, which makes him a Doctor of the Church, and will one day aſſociate him with BERNARD and BONAVENTURE.

Take care in this funeral oration, that your mind be elevated equally with your Hero; and that the greatneſs of ſoul, which characterized him, may be expreſſed in a becoming manner.

Aim at being the Hiſtorian, as well as the Orator, but ſo, that there be neither languor nor dryneſs in your narrration. The

---

* A Congregation of Religious men, founded in the fixteenth Century, by *Jerome Æmiliani*; a noble Venetian. The deſign of this edifying inſtitute, is the care of poor Orphans of both ſexes. It was made a Religious Order by *Pius* V. *Jerome* was canonized by *Clement* XIV.

attention of the public muſt be perpetually kept awake by great ſtrokes, worthy of the majeſty of the pulpit, and the ſublimity of LAMBERTINI.

You will in vain call to your aſſiſtance all the figures of Rhetoric, if they come not to ſeek you out. Eloquence is never beautiful, but when it flows from the ſource, and ariſes from the grandeur of the ſubject—Forced elogiums are amplifications, not elogiums.

Bring forth from the cinders of BENEDICT XIV a virtue which may ſeize your hearers, and transform them into himſelf, that they may be filled with him alone. Uſe no trivial details; tell no out of the way ſtories about him, employ no bombaſt or bloated phraſes. Blend, as much as poſſible, the ſublime with the temperate, in order to form thoſe pleaſing ſhades, which give a grace to Diſcourſes. Endeavour to chooſe a happy text, which may announce at once the whole plan of your Oration, and perfectly characterize your Hero. The Diviſion is the touchſtone of a Panegyriſt: the Diſcourſe cannot be beautiful, if that be not happily choſen.

Strew morality with diſcretion, ſo that it may ſeem to come and place itſelf; and that people may ſay: " It could not be better than " where it was: that was its place."

Dread all common places; and contrive ſo, that every body may ſee LAMBERTINI, without perceiving the Orator. Praiſe with equal delicacy and ſobriety; and give a ſpring to your praises, which may make them re-afcend to God.

Unless you move the foul by happy furprifes, and noble images, your work will be no more than an ingenious compofition: and inftead of erecting a *Maufoleum*, you will only have written an *Epitaph*.

Above all, addrefs yourfelf to the hearts of your Audience; fill them with fuch alarming truths, as may detach them from this mortal life, and may make them defcend into the tomb of the Holy Father.

Pafs lightly over the Infancy of your Hero: all men are alike until the moment reafon begins to fhoot forth its rays. Let not your fentences be either too long, or too fhort: there is nothing nervous in a Difcourfe, when parcelled out into fhort fentences.

Let your *Exordium* be pompous, without being inflated; and let your firft period efpecially announce fomething grand. I compare the exordium of a funeral oration to the portico of a Church: If I find majefty there, I form an idea of the beauty of the whole Edifice.

Exhibit, in the ftrongeft manner, Death overturning Thrones, crufhing fcepters, trampling on Tiaras, withering Crowns; and place over this wreck the genius of BENEDICT, as having nothing to fear from the deftructive hand of time; as defying death to tarnifh his glory, and efface his name.

Enter

Enter into a detail of his virtues; give an analyfis of his writings; and every where exhibit a fublime foul, that would have aftonifhed *Pagan Rome*, that edified *Chriftian Rome*, and attracted the admiration of the Univerfe.

In a word, lighten—thunder—but introduce fuch fhades, as may caufe the light to iffue out with greater brightnefs, and form the moft ftriking contrafts.

My imagination is on fire, when fo great a Pope as BENEDICT, is mentioned—a Pontiff, whofe lofs is regretted by the *Proteftants* themfelves, and whom nobody, but a *Michael Angelo* could paint.

If I have enlarged upon this fubject, it was becaufe I know you can eafily lay hold of whatever I recommend to you. A funeral Oration cannot be beautiful, but in proportion to its being picturefque, and unlefs energy and truth hold the pencil. The greater part of elogiums go down to the grave with thofe whofe elogium they are, becaufe they are no more than an *Ephemeran* piece of Eloquence—the production of wit—and whofe glittering is no more than tinfel.

I fhould be mad to fee LAMBERTINI praifed by an Orator, who was barely elegant.— Every one ought to be ferved according to their tafte; and his was ever fure and good.

Get to work, my dear Friend. I will with pleafure fee what you throw on paper, as I am convinced it will be fo many flafhes of fire, which will confume every thing unworthy

thy of such an elogy. I judge from the productions you have heretofore communicated to me, and in which I observed great beauties. It is time that our ITALY should lose its *concetti*, and assume a masculine and sublime tone, analogous to true eloquence.

I am endeavouring to form, by my counsels, some young Orators, who are at the pains of taking my advice; and I do all I can, to put them out of conceit with those extravagances, which are continually introducing into our Discourses the *burlesque* in conjunction with the *sublime*. Foreigners have reason to be shocked at so monstrous an allay. The *French* especially know nothing of such a strange whim. Their discourses indeed are often superficial, and have less of substance than surface, but we commonly find among them a well supported style.—Nothing is more shocking, than to soar above the clouds, only to fall down afterwards with a thump.

My compliments to the little Father, who, but for his deplorable state of health, would do wonders. *Rome, May* 10, 1758.

LETTER CV.

To the Abbè LAMI.

YOU will undoubtedly, dear Abbè, announce in your sheets the death of the Holy Father. He was a man of learning, who has a claim to a place in all periodical works, and to whom all writers owe elogiums.

He maintained his cheerfulness to the last, so that a few days before his death, speaking of a *Theatine*, the process of whose Beatification was to be drawn up, he said: " Great servant of God, cure me; as you act towards me, so will I act towards you: for if you obtain for me the recovery of my health, I will beatify you."

The analysis of his works will require such a one as you, to give us an account of them. It would be proper also to give some extracts, which may fall into the hands of such, as have not time to read a great deal, or are not able to purchase *Folios*.

Above all his Treatise on *the Canonization of Saints**, ought to be spread abroad everywhere. Besides that he therein talks like a Physician, a Lawyer, a Canonist, a Theologian, the subject he treats is commonly little understood.

The Public imagines that nothing more is required, than to send money to *Rome* in order to procure a Canonization: whereas it is notorious, that the Pope does not make the least profit of it, and every possible means are employed to avoid being deceived in so important an object.

* Abbè *Baudeau* has published an abridgment of that learned Treatise in 1 Vol. 12°. and it is sold by *Lottin*, jun. at *Paris*.

This is so true, that BENEDICT XIV, for whose death we now mourn, being then *Promoter of the Faith*, desired two sensible *English* Gentlemen (who were passing their jokes on the Canonization of Saints) to divest themselves of all prejudice, and to read, with the utmost attention, the verbal processes relating to the cause of a servant of God, whom it was proposed to beatify. They consented to do so; and after having read, for several days together, with the most critical disposition, the proofs and evidence, which ascertained his sanctity, and all the means made use of to arrive at the truth, they said to *Monsignor* LAMBERTINI: " If the same precautions, the same examinations, and the same severity be used with regard to all who are canonized, there is no doubt, but that things are carried even to demonstration, and evidence itself." *Monsignor* LAMBERTINI answered: " Well, Gentlemen, notwithstanding whatever you may think of it, the Congregation rejects these proofs as insufficient; and the process of the Beatification will stop there."

It is impossible to express their surprise on this occasion; and they set off from *Rome*, thoroughly convinced, that people are not canonized on slight grounds, and that there are no means either easy or difficult, which are not employed to come to the knowledge of the truth. The Beatification of a Saint, is a cause, which continues pleading often above a century

century together, and the person, who is commonly called the *Devil's Advocate*, never fails collecting every testimony to the disadvantage of the servant of God, and to make use of the strongest proofs, and the most weighty objections to invalidate his sanctity, and to diminish the worth of his actions. There are many reputed Saints, who nevertheless will never be beatified, because the testimonies in favour of their sanctity are not sufficient. Not only simple virtues are requisite (as you know very well) not only shining virtues; but even such as are *heroic*, and uninterruptedly practised to the hour of death in a most eminent degree.*

The testimony of miracles is also insisted on, whatever Unbelievers may say of it, who attribute every miracle to an over-heated imagination, or to the effects of superstition: as if God could be chained down by his own laws, and was not at liberty to suspend their execution—In that case, he would have less power than the most insignificant Monarch— But what truths are not denied, when a person is blinded by a corruption both of understanding and heart?

God often manifests the sanctity of his servants by cures: and if the prodigies operated soon after their death, continue only for a time, and then cease; the reason is, that the Deity comes not forth from his secret place but at intervals,

* In gradu heroico.

tervals, and only to fhew that his power is ever the fame; and that he is able to glorify his faints, whenever he pleafes.

Our *Conclave* is as yet only in labour; and it will not be known to the laft moment, as ufual, who is to be the new Pontiff. The whole city is now taken up with conjectures, bets and pafquinades,—fo it has been from times of old, and the cuftom will not be foon laid afide.

For my part, in the midft of this hurry, I am at *Rome*, as if I were not there; only defiring, if poflible, that we may have another Lambertini: nor do I quit my cell, but for bufinefs or relaxation. It is there I enjoy my books—myfelf—and relifh the reflections of dear Abbe *Lami*, whofe very humble Servant I immutably am, &c.

Rome, May 9, 1758.

LETTER CVI.

To the fame.

WE have at laft gotten for head of the Church Cardinal Rezzonico, Bifhop of *Padua*, who has taken the name of Clement XIII, and who will edify the *Romans* by his piety. It was contrary to his inclinations, and after many a tear, that he accepted of his dignity. What a poft, when a man is defirous of complying with all the duties of it! He muft be at the call of God, of every body and

and of himſelf; he muſt be ſolely taken up with theſe important duties; and have nothing but heaven before his eyes, even in the midſt of earthly concerns. The dignity he enters upon, is the more to be dreaded, as he ſucceeds BENEDICT XIV. and to appear great after him, will be very difficult.

CLEMENT XIII continues Cardinal *Archinto* Secretary of State. He has no better means of endearing himſelf to the crowned heads, and of rendering his Pontificate illuſtrious. A ſovereign Prince muſt either make choice of an excellent Miniſter, or do every thing himſelf. BENEDICT XIII was the moſt unhappy of mankind for having placed his confidence in Cardinal *Coſcia*: and BENEDICT XIV the happieſt in having had Cardinal VALENTI for his Miniſter.

It is the eſſential intereſt of every ſovereign, and eſpecially of a Pope, to have proper people about him. The good ſenſe and knowledge of the moſt clear ſighted Prince is impoſed on, if he ſuffer himſelf to be dazzled. Then braſs becomes gold in his eyes; and he ſupports thoſe men, whom he has once taken under his protection, whatever the conſequences may be.

An ability to diſcover the different diſpoſitions of people is a qualification ſcarce any way leſs neceſſary for a Prince. No one dares attempt to impoſe on a Monarch, who is known to be a man of penetration: while he, who ſuffers himſelf to be led, becomes the tool of those about him. Some Sovereigns have done more mischief through indolence and weakness, than through downright wickedness. A man grows tired with repeating acts of crying injustice; but he does not tire with feeling and seeing nothing.

The weaker a Prince is, the more despotic he will be: for as authority is never lost; Ministers seize on it, and become tyrants.

Another qualification, which I consider as essential to good government, is to allot to every one his proper place. The government of the moral world is like a game at chess, where every piece is moved in order, and according to its rank. If one pawn be moved instead of another, there ensues nothing but confusion.

A SOVEREIGN is not only the image of God by the eminence of his rank: he ought moreover to be so by his understanding. DAVID, though only a Shepherd, had a superior light to direct him: and that he shewed, as soon as he became King.

A Prince who is barely good-natured, is no more than what every man ought to be: and a Prince, who shews nothing but severity, has not, for his subjects, the love he owes them.

But, alas! How finely we atoms talk of the duties of Royalty: and, were we invested with it, we should not know how to act. The difference between talking and reigning is great. Nothing opposes us, when we suffer our minds to take wing, and allow our pens to run on: but when a man finds himself overpowered with business, environed with rocks, surrounded with false friends; lastly overloaded with debts, and the most weighty duties; he is frightened; he dares attempt nothing: and, from an indolence, natural to all men, he trusts the concerns of government to some subaltern, and thinks only of the pleasure of enjoying and ruling.

Certain it is, that the art of governing is very difficult. If a person enjoys an hereditary Crown, he knows the Grandeur of it, without knowing the detail of a kingdom; and is easily deceived. If on the other hand, he obtains an elective Crown; he enters on a sovereignty, to which he has not served an apprenticeship; and he appears a borrowed personage, both in the midst of honour, and in the centre of business.

When a man is placed on a throne in the decline of life, he is fit for nothing but to be made a shew of. There is nothing he dares undertake: every thing frightens him: every thing inspires him with indolence; especially if he knows not who is to be his successor. —Such is the situation of Popes, if they be too old: they are then incapable of applying to the concerns of Church and state.

But there ever will be abuses in the world: if there be none here, there are some elsewhere: for imperfections are the appendage of humanity. "There is no place, but the holy "city, says the Great AUGUSTINE, where "every

"every thing will be in order, at peace, and in charity: for there God alone will reign."

I shall go and pay my respects to the new Pontiff, not like a *Religious*, who wants to shew himself, but in quality of a *Consultor* of the Holy Office. He does not know me, nor will I put myself to any expence to make myself known. I like to remain covered with the dust of the Cloister; nor do I think myself any way dishonoured by it.

Adieu. Continue to keep up, for our sakes, the good taste of the MEDICIS; and your memory will be long preserved, though that gives you little concern. I am, &c.

Rome, July 15, 1758.

LETTER CVII.

To a PRELATE.

I Humble myself, *Monsignor*, as much as others would value themselves, for the most Eminent dignity, to which the sovereign Pontiff has just raised me. I thought I was going to leave *Rome*, from the manner in which this extraordinary event was notified to me; nor am I yet recovered from my astonishment.

It is the Order of St. FRANCIS, of which I have the honour of being a member, that was designed to be recompensed in my person: but I take no share of it to myself. I barely lend my name: for the more I consider myself, the more

more I see that I had no direct nor indirect claim to the *Cardinalate*, either from birth or merit.

If any thing can afford me comfort in the midst of the flurry which agitates my mind, it is to see myself associated with the illustrious personages, who compose the sacred College; the *latchet of whose shoes I am not worthy to untie**. I fancy, that by partaking of their virtues, I may at last acquire some of my own; and that by conversing with them, I may come to imitate them—We imperceptibly copy after those, with whom we associate. I have told my dear Brethren, that I never will be a *Cardinal* with respect to them, but that they shall still ever find in me *Brother Lawrence Ganganelli*; for it is to them I owe, whatever I am; and it was the habit of St. *Francis*, that purchased me the honours of the Purple.

You know me well enough to be convinced that I am not dazzled with my new dignity. The soul takes no colour; and it is only through it that we are of any value in the eyes of God. The Lord, by making us to his own *image* and *likeness*, bestowed more on us, than all the dignities of the world can confer. To find myself great, it is in that light only I must see myself. The purple, bright as it is, was not made for my eyes, happily accustomed to see nothing, but Eternity. This point of

* Matt. iii. 11.

view

view makes all Grandeur surprisingly diminutive: neither EMINENCE nor HIGHNESS can stand in competition with an immortal life, where nothing Great is seen, but GOD alone.

I consider Dignities as only a few more syllables added to an Epitaph, from which no one can draw any vanity; because the buried man is even below the Inscriptions read on his tomb.

Will my ashes have any more feeling, though they be qualified *Eminent?* Or shall I be better off in Eternity, when some feeble voice on earth shall say: *Cardinal Ganganelli*; or a perishable pen write it?

A new dignity, and especially that of the Cardinalate, which brings along with it a multitude of obligations, is always a new burden. There are as many duties to fulfil, as there are occasions in which a person is to speak his mind without any human respects, or considerations.

I order matters so as to perceive, as little as possible, my strange *Metamorphosis*. I shall live, as heretofore, in the Convent of the Apostles, among my dear Brethren, whom I have always tenderly loved, and on whose company I set the greatest value.

If I quit my dear Cell, in which I have enjoyed more contentment than all the Kings of the earth, it is only because I must have more room to receive those, who will do me the favour to come and see me: but I will often say to it: *May my tongue cleave to the roof of my mouth, if I ever forget thee;** I will often go to

* Ps. cxxxvi. *Vulg.*

see it, and there recall to my remembrance the many days, which have vanished like a dream.

I shall therefore change nothing in my way of life; and my dear *Brother Francis* shall make up my whole household. He is strong, he is vigilant, he is zealous; he will do for every thing. My *Individuality* has received neither more extent nor bulk since I was made a Cardinal; and I do not therefore see what occasion I have for more attendants.

Oh! I was once a good walker! And my comfort is, that I shall still walk. I will only suffer myself to be drawn, when the Ceremonial requires it; and will become *Brother Ganganelli* again as often as I possibly can. No man likes to quit himself, especially when he has lived fifty-four years without ceremony, and at perfect liberty with himself.

I hope you will come and see, not the *Cardinal*, but *Brother Ganganelli*. The former will never be at home for you; the latter will always be there, to repeat to you, that whatever post I occupy, I will, without ever ceasing, be your servant and friend.

Rome, Oct. 1, 1759.

LETTER CVIII.

To a Conventual Friar.

I Have not as yet, my old brother and friend, received the packet you sent me; but I know how to be patient, though I am naturally ly of a hasty temper. Our whole life is nothing but a series of contradictions and disappointments, which we must learn to bear, unless we would disturb our peace and hurt our health.

Father GEORGI, ever the honour of the AUGUSTINIANS, ever beloved by all that know him, has not seen the person you mention: that person's passage through the town was too precipitate to admit of the satisfaction of an interview. He saw Mr. *Tissot*, Procurator-General of the Priests of the Mission, whom I infinitely esteem on account of his personal merit, on account of his being a member of a body that preaches the Gospel to the poor with the greatest success; and lastly, on account of his being a *Frenchman*.

I must tell you, that since my promotion I experience a singular sort of combat within myself: *Cardinal Ganganelli* reproaches *Brother Ganganelli* for his too great simplicity; and, withstanding all the respect which is due to the Purple, *Brother Ganganelli* gets the better of the *Cardinal*.—I choose to live as I have hitherto lived, always poor, always retired, and much more with my brethren, than with the Great ones. It is a matter of taste; for I am far from attributing my way of thinking to a virtuous disposition.

This at least is certain, that I never shall be able to assume that cold or haughty air (call it which you please) with which men in power generally receive persons of low birth, who have any thing to do with them. To make me any person's equal, it is enough that he salute me, speak to me, or pay me a visit. Is it possible that one man should put on a proud stately look when he is to speak to another man; or that a Christian should study his expressions, his gestures, his steps, his letters, for fear of appearing too modest in his behaviour towards his brethren? Is it possible for any one to refuse giving an answer to a person, because he has no titles to shew? Were the poorest wretch on earth to do me the favour to write to me, I would answer him immediately; and should look on myself as very guilty in the eyes of God and man, were I to omit that duty. No soul is contemptible in the eyes of Religion and Humanity. Nothing, in my opinion, is so little, as a Great Man governed by pride.

I enlarge on this article, to give you to understand, that the man, in whose behalf you interest yourself, may come to me any time he pleases, and I shall be entirely at his service. He will meet with no worse reception from Cardinal *Corsini*, whose civility corresponds with his noble extraction.

If too great affability be a fault, all the Cardinals may be charged with it. Pride and haughtiness are rarely found among them— Happily there is not a Foreigner but who does us justice in that point.

You will oblige me very much in letting *Signor Antonio* know, when you see him, that the Cardinal *Datary* will not forget his affair.

Take care of the small share of health you enjoy: sit up less at nights, walk out oftner, and take less Coffee. It is the usual beverage of the Studious; but it burns up the blood; and then pains in the head, in the throat, in the breast, are dreadfully felt. I am not, however, so great an enemy to Coffee, as Mr *Thierry*, the Pretender's Physician, who formerly lived here, and gave it as his opinion, that Coffee was a real poison.

Your little Nephew came to see me on Thursday. His understanding is as lively as his eyes. He tore one of my books in sport: it is to be hoped he will hereafter have more respect for them. He told me, most ingenuously, that he would be a Cardinal. I like to see the minds of children unfold themselves: it is the eye or bud of a fruit, that begins to open, and gives pleasing hopes. He was for saying his Breviary with me. Alas! His innocence would be more pleasing to God than all my prayers! I sent my *Chamberlain* home with him; but I could not get him away, till I had given him a pair of beads. He told me he would come for another pair to-morrow. That was pretty in a child only five years old. God grant he may be one day like his Father! Adieu: I embrace you with all the fulness of my heart.

Rome, Jan. 8, 1760.

LETTER CIX.

To a Protestant Minister.

I AM extremely obliged to you, my dear Sir, for the concern you take in my health. It is (thanks be to heaven) very good; and would appear to me still better, could I employ it in any thing agreeable to you.—The pleasure of obliging ought to be found in all communions.

I wish, with my whole soul, I could convince you, that I bear all men in my heart; that they are all of infinite value to me, and that I respect merit, wherever it is to be found. If your Nephew come to Rome, as you give hopes he will, he shall find in me a person the most ardent and most desirous to testify to him all the affection I bear to you.

The Church of *Rome*, my very dear Sir, so perfectly well knows the merit of the greatest part of the Ministers of the Protestant Communions, that she would felicitate herself forever to see them in her bosom. Past quarrels would be no more thought on; nor would those tempestuous times be recalled, when every one, hurried away by passion, broke through the rules of Christian moderation: but the question would be, to unite in one Faith, grounded on Scripture and Tradition, such as it is found in the Apostles, the Councils and Fathers. No one sighs more than I do at the thoughts of what you suffered in the last

Century.—A spirit of persecution is what I utterly detest.

How much would not people gain by a happy re-union? It is then, if necessary, I would tell the last drop of my blood to run out, and be concerned that I had not a thousand lives to give, so that I might die a witness of that wonderful event! That time will come, my dear Sir, because a time necessarily will come, when there will be only one and the same Faith. The Jews themselves will come into the bosom of the true Church; and it is with this firm hope, grounded on the sacred Scriptures, that they are tolerated in the heart of *Rome*, with the full exercise of their Religion.

My soul (God knows it) is entirely yours; and there is not that thing in the world, which I would not undertake to prove to you, as well as to all yours, how dear you are to me. We have the same God for our Father, we believe in the same Mediator, we acknowledge for incontestable the articles of the TRINITY, the INCARNATION, and our REDEMPTION; and we, one and the other, sincerely desire to go to heaven. But in point of Doctrine there are not two ways of getting thither. There must be a Centre of Unity on earth, as well as a Head to represent JESUS CHRIST. The Church would be really without form, unworthy of our homage and fidelity, were it no more than a body without a head.

The

The work of the Messiah is not like that of men. What he has once eſtabiſhed, muſt laſt forever. He could not ceaſe for one inſtant, to aſſiſt his Church; and you, Sir, are a man of too much learning, to conſider the *Albigenſes* as the pillars of truth, to which you are to hold. Do me the pleaſure to acquaint all your brethren, all your flocks and all your friends, that Cardinal *Ganganelli* has nothing ſo much at heart as their happineſs in this world and in the next; and that he could wiſh to be perſonally acquainted with them all to aſſure them of it. Nothing can be added, &c.

Rome, Jan. 30, 1769.

LETTER CX.

To Count ***.

I Inform you, my dear Friend, in the ſolitude where you have been for ſome weeks, that the ſame *Brother Ganganelli*, who always tenderly loved you, is become a *Cardinal*, and that he himſelf knows not how, or why.

There are certain events in the courſe of one's life, which cannot be accounted for. They are brought about by circumſtances, and ordained by Providence, which is the principle and cauſe of every thing.

Let what will happen, whether in purple or out of purple, I ſhall be no leſs entirely yours, and ſhall be always pleaſed to ſee you, and to oblige you.

I ſome-

I sometimes feel my pulse, to know whether it be really myself or not; so truly surprised am I, that the lot which raised me to one of the greatest dignities, did not preferably fall on some of my brethren—There are several whom it would have perfectly become.

Every body says, speaking of the new *Cardinal Ganganelli:* " It is incredible that he should arrive at that dignity without some intrigue or cabal;" it is however very true that there was neither.

Oh! my books! Oh! my cell! I know what I leave, but know not what I am to find! Alas! Many a troublesome Visiter will come and make me lose my time: many an interested soul will pay me feigned homage.

As to you, my dear Friend, persevere in virtue. A man is above all dignities, when he is sincerely virtuous: perseverance is promised only to a distrust of ourselves, and to flying from the occasions of sin—Whoever is presumptuous is to look for a relapse.

When I consider that the public papers will deign to take notice of me, and transmit my name beyond the *Alpes*, to inform different nations when I have the spleen, or when I have been blooded, I laugh for pity's sake. Dignities are snares made bright and glittering in order to catch people. Few know well the disgusts and troubles of grandeur: a man is no longer at his own disposal; and let him act as he will, he has enemies.

I am

I am of St. Gregory of *Nazianzum's* way of thinking: he imagined, when the people stood in a row to see him pass, that they took him for some extraordinary animal. It is a custom, I own, that I do not like; and if that be what is called *Grandeur*, I would with pleasure bid it adieu. I consider all men as my brethren; and am pleased beyond measure, when the poorest of them draw near or speak to me.

It will be said that I am vulgar in my ways; but that is a reproach I do not mind; I fear nothing but pride. Pride is so subtle a vice, that it will do what it can to get within me, and to lay hold of me: but I shall see that all within me, and all that surrounds me, is nothing—That is the best way to keep off self-love.

Do not take it into your head to make me any compliments, when you come to see me; it is a commodity I am not fond of, and especially from a friend. But here come visits, that is to say, the thing I hate most, and which, for some days past, have rendered me insupportable to myself. Grandeur has really its clouds, its flashes of lightning, and its whirlwinds like storms: I wait for a calm, and a moment of serenity. I am without reserve, and beyond all expression, as heretofore, your good and true servant, &c.

Rome, Oct. 3, 1759.

LETTER CXI.

To Cardinal CAVALCHINI.

MOST EMINENT,

YOUR recommendations are orders; nor can I sleep with ease till I have complied with your desires. Your Eminence cannot afford me too many opportunities of testifying the full extent of my esteem and attachment—By becoming your brother, I am become more than ever your servant.

It would be proper that you and I had a private conference together relative to the affairs of the Church. Your zeal for the interests of Religion is boundless; and it is the only object which ought to employ my thoughts. We are not Cardinals merely to impose on people by outward state and shew, but to be the pillars of the Holy See. Our rank, our dress, our functions, put us in mind that we ought to do every thing (according to the designs of God, and the wants of his Church, even to the shedding of our blood) to come to the assistance of Religion.

When I see Cardinal de TOURNON fly to the extremities of the globe, to preach and maintain the Gospel in its purity, his glorious example sets me all on fire, and I find myself disposed to undertake any thing.

The SACRED COLLEGE has ever had men eminent for their knowledge and zeal, and we ought to strive to continue and renew the succession. It is not human Policy which is to regulate our steps, but the Spirit of God, that Spirit without which all our actions are barren, and with which whatever we do is right.

I know your piety, I know your learning; and that, at a proper time, and in a proper place, you will know how to speak your mind without fear.

Some people are for making the Holy Father take such steps as he may repent of hereafter: for they are no longer the same men who are about him, since the death of Cardinal ARCHINTO; and this may be attended with the most disagreeable consequences. People are not so dependant on the Holy See as formerly; and prudence requires, that regard should be had to times and circumstances. When JESUS CHRIST recommends to his Apostles *to be simple as doves*, he adds: and *prudent as serpents.** One imprudent step on the part of *Rome*, in such critical times as these, might become the occasion of much trouble. BENEDICT XIV himself, though expert at conciliating minds, would have been at a loss; but he would have taken care not to violate the rights of the crowned Heads.

The subject we have to treat on is of a delicate nature. We must not offend either the Holy Father or his Council, and, at the same time, take such measures, that he may not give ear to every thing that is said to him. As his

* Matt. x. 16.

intentions are pure, he does not suspect that he can be imposed on. He ought however to balance the advantages and inconveniences of what people are for having him to do. Whoever does not take care to calculate beforehand, is always sure to miscarry.

He affects to open his heart to certain Cardinals, and to communicate nothing to others. PORTUGAL will never desist from its present way of thinking, and I see that the other kingdoms will support it, and confirm it in its opinion.

The Monarchs live not, as formerly, unconnected with one another; they are all in friendship one with another, and they really act towards one another with such brotherly affection, that whoever has the misfortune to offend one of them, offends all; and instead of having only one enemy to deal with, he has all *Europe* against him.

Will the Holy Father, through an indiscreet zeal, struggle against all the Potentates! Will he level his thunder at the ELDEST SON OF THE CHURCH, and against his MOST FAITHFUL MAJESTY! He ought to reflect that they are not Heathen Emperors whom he is for resisting, but Catholic Princes like himself.

ENGLAND ought for ever to cure Popes of an indiscreet zeal. What would CLEMENT VII say, were he to return on earth? Would he applaud himself for what he did,* when he

saw

* Cardinal *Ganganelli* does not here censure CLEMENT for not gratifying King *Henry's* unlawful desires, but for issuing

Let. cxi.   P. CLEMENT XIV.

saw that Kingdom, formerly a Nursery of Saints, at this day, the receptacle of every sect and every error?—A man ought to know how to make a sacrifice of some things, in order to preserve the whole.

The Holy See will never shine with greater lustre, nor will it ever be less exposed to an attack, never enjoy more peace, than when it has the Catholic Powers for its defenders and support. This harmony is absolutely necessary to the glory and welfare of Religion. The Faithful would be exposed to every wind of doctrine, if the Princes unhappily had not that deference for ROME, which they ought to have; and the Sovereign Pontiff himself would see his flock insensibly fall off, and choose bad pastures, instead of those he offers.

The good Shepherd ought not only to recall the strayed sheep, but to take what pains he can, that the others go not astray. Infidelity, whose fatal blast is every where communicated, wishes for nothing more, than to see *Rome* at variance with the Potentates: but Religion likes not these divisions. No opportunity must be given to the enemies of the Church, of repeating what they have too often said, that *Rome* was intractable, and aspired at a manner of ruling dangerous to the different states.

ing out an Excommunication against him, without waiting for the powers sent by *Henry* to the Bishop of *Paris*, whose Courier did not arrive on the very day, though he arrived two days after; but alas! too late to remedy what was done.

The truth is, that every Sovereign Prince is master at home, and no foreign Power has any right to control him. Men thought differently in the times of horror and confusion; but to bring back again those times, would be a dangerous attempt. Charity, Peace, Moderation!—Such are the arms of Christians, and especially those of ROME, which ought to set examples of patience and humility to all Courts.

It must be remembered, that when PETER cut off the ear of *Malchus*, who was one of the enemies of JESUS CHRIST, he received a reprimand from that divine Saviour, and was ordered to put his sword into the scabbard.

But it would be much worse to dare to use a like sword against those who have all along defended the Holy See, and who glory in being its support.

Nothing is more dangerous than an indiscreet zeal, which breaks the already crushed reed, puts out the still smoaking match, and is for calling down fire from heaven.

I know that a Pope is obliged to maintain the immunities of the Holy See; but he must not quarrel with all the Catholic powers for a few territorial rights. To afford pretexts for crying out more than ever against the Church of *Rome*, is but stirring up the fire of Infidelity.

Whoever sees things only in part, does not see well; the whole must be considered together, and the present steps weighed with respect to what is to come. *A small spark*, says St. *James*, *sets a great wood on fire*.

Weak minds imagine that people bear an ill will to a certain Religious Order, because they are not for maintaining it, in spite of the sovereign Princes. But besides that we should draw down on them still more dreadful storms, by resisting the Potentates, we must not, for the sake of that Order alone, fall out with all the Catholic Powers.

Had I the least ill will against any one, I could never sleep. I sincerely love all the Religious Orders; and I wish with my whole soul that they could all be preserved: but I consider what is most proper to be done, when there is a necessity of acting one way or other. I do not pretend that the Holy Father ought to destroy any Order; but only that he write to the crowned Heads, and inform them that he will examine their complaints against that Religious Order, and that he really do examine them.

I suppose *Rome* exposed to the resentment of all the crowned Heads. How will she support herself in the midst of those storms? We are not as yet in heaven; and if God be to preserve his Church to the end of time, it is by inspiring its Rulers with a prudence of conduct adapted to times and places, as well as with a love of peace.

It is not to be expected, that God will perform a miracle in support of an indiscreet exertion of zeal. He leaves second causes to act; and when they take the wrong side of the question, things go on no better on that account.   They

They are only such as pretend to inspiration, who will never yield to circumstances, where Faith and Morals are not concerned—In every concern of importance, a man ought to consider how it will end, in order to avoid the greatest evils.

As I know your zeal, my Lord, as well as your learning, I flatter myself, that you will find out some means, by which (I say not the Apostolic See, which cannot perish) but the Court of *Rome*, now exposed to the greatest dangers, may be saved.

Such are my reflections, and I hope you will find them just. I can confidently assure you, that I have weighed them in the presence of God, who *sounds the reins and hearts*; and who knows, that there is neither Antipathy nor Animosity, in my heart, against any one.

I have the honour to be with every sentiment due to your great learning and rare virtues, your very humble, &c.

Convent of the H. Apostles, the 16th instant.

LETTER CXII.

To Cardinal S***.

EMINENCE,

I Had not time yesterday to discourse with you at my ease on the important affairs, which at this time agitate *Europe*, and by which

which *Rome* will suffer, unless she behave with the moderation, which the Potentates require at her hands. The Popes are Pilots, almost constantly sailing on tempestuous seas, and consequently obliged sometimes to spread all their canvas, and at other times to take in a reef, on proper occasions.

Now is the time, to use the prudence of the serpent recommended by JESUS CHRIST to his Apostles. It is undoubtedly a great misfortune that Religious men destined for Colleges, seminaries and missions; men who have written much in every branch on the truths of Religion, should be abandoned at a time, when infidelity attacks, with so much fury, all the Religious Orders: but the point to be examined, in the presence of God, is whether or not it be better to affront the Sovereign Powers, or to abandon the support of a Religious Company.

For my part, I think that (as the storm is roaring on every side, and is already perceived hanging over our heads) it would be proper for a man even to execute himself, and sacrifice whatever is the most dear to him, rather than incur the indignation of the Sovereign Powers, which cannot be too much dreaded.

Let our Holy Father and his Secretary have the most sincere affection for the Jesuits; I subscribe to their attachment with my whole heart, as I never had the least antipathy or animosity against any Religious Order; but I will still say, notwithstanding the veneration I have

have for St. IGNATIUS, and the esteem in which I hold his disciples, that there is extreme danger, and even an excess of rashness, in endeavouring to support the Jesuits in the present circumstances.

It is fit indeed that ROME should solicit in their favour, and that, in quality of Mother and Protectress of all the Orders in the Church, she should endeavour to save the Society; provided always that it undergo a reformation, according to the decree of BENEDICT XIV, and according to the desires of all, who wish well to Religion: but my opinion is, that after ROME has done what she can, she ought then to leave the business entirely in the hands of God, and of the Sovereign Powers.

ROME will ever stand in need of the protection and aid of the Catholic Powers. They are Fortresses which secure her against incursions and hostilities; so that she never is more glorious, or does she ever enjoy more authority and power, than when she seems to yield to the Potentates. It is then they support her with *eclat*, and make it a duty to publish every where, and to prove by acts of deference and submission, that they really are the docile children of the common Father of the Faithful, and that they consider him as the first of men in the eyes of Faith.

The more I call to mind those unhappy times when the Popes wandering up and down— without assistance—without an asylum—had for enemies Kings and Emperors, the more necessary

necessary do I find it that they should live at peace with the Monarchs. The Church knows only two Orders, indispensably necessary, and founded by JESUS CHRIST himself, to perpetuate his doctrine, and to bring forth children, *viz.* the Orders of Bishops and Priests.

In the first, which we call the *Fine Ages* of the Church, there were neither Monks nor Friars; which evidently shews that, if Religion stand not in need of any but its ordinary Ministers to preserve it, the Regulars, its auxiliary troops, although extremely useful, are not however absolutely necessary.

If the JESUITS have really the spirit of their state, as I presume they have, they will be the first to say: "We will sacrifice ourselves, rather than excite disturbances and storms."

As a Religious body ought not to rely on perishable riches, or temporal honours, but on a solid love for JESUS CHRIST and his Spouse; they ought to withdraw with the same joy they felt in being called, if his Vicar, the Minister and Interpreter of his words on earth, want their service no longer. Religious Orders are no longer deserving of respect, nor ought they to be continued any longer, than while they have the spirit of the Church: and as this spirit is ever the same, independently of all the different Institutes of the Regulars, each Order should comfort itself, when it comes to be suppressed—But self-love often persuades us that we are necessary, at the very time when the Potentates judge otherwise.

Were there less Enthusiasm, and more principle among men, every one would assent to these truths; and instead of rashly supporting a body, of which the Potentates complain, they would engage this very body itself to withdraw, without any grumbling or noise—But people are unhappily deceived, and imagine, that there is no meddling with a particular Institute, without attacking the very essence of Religion.

If, when a Religious Order was to be abandoned, it were required also to change any dogma of Faith, or corrupt any point of Morality, then, no doubt, a person ought sooner to die, than to assent to such proceedings. But after the Jesuits are gone, the Church will continue to teach the same truths, the Church will still subsist; and Jesus Christ will sooner raise up children to *Abraham*, out of the very stones, to maintain his own work, than leave his mystical body without aid and support—The Head of the Church is like the master of a magnificent garden, who at pleasure lops off branches from those trees, which, by spreading too wide, intercept the view.

You, my Lord, who have both zeal and knowledge: speak you to the Holy Father. It will come much better from you than from me, who look upon myself, with reason, and in every respect, as the last of the Sacred College. Shew his Holiness the abyss that people sink for themselves, by obstinately opposing the will of the Sovereign Powers. The uprightness

rightness of his heart will make him give ear to you; for it may be said, that he is determined to resist the Potentates, only because he thinks it is best so to do. I expect that generous step from your love for the Church, and I am your Eminence's, &c.

Convent of the H. Apostles, Oct. 9, 1768.

LETTER CXIII.

*To a Lay-Brother.**

AH! why, dear Brother, did you hesitate to address yourself to me? Am I therefore another man, because I have the honour to be a Cardinal? Ever are my heart and arms open to receive my dear brethren. I owe them too much to forget them, since I owe them every thing.

As you acknowledge your fault, I persuade myself that you are really sorry for it. The least deviation from virtue, in a Cloister, insensibly leads to excesses. It was not through ignorance that you sinned, and therefore the greater is your guilt: and what is still worse, your fault is become public.

Humble yourself before men, and sigh and groan in the sight of God, that you may obtain pardon. I will write immediately to your Guardian to receive you kindly.

* One who takes not orders, but does the menial duties of the house, under the tie of the three vows, Chastity, Poverty, and Obedience.

You

You fancied, dear Brother, that, by quitting your retreat, you would find infinite satisfaction in the world. Alas! The world is nothing but deceit: It promises what it never bestows: it appears to be a bunch of flowers, when seen at a distance; but near at hand, it is no more than a thorn-bush.

I pray the Lord may touch you in a sensible manner; for every good motion comes from him. You must resume your exercises with the greatest fervour, and force those, who may blame your going astray, to admire you. Be persuaded that you will ever be dear to me, and that I weep most sincerely with you for the fault you have committed. Your most affectionate.

CARDINAL GANGANELLI.

Convent of the H. Apostles, Nov. 18, 1764.

LETTER CXIV.

To the Rev. Father, Guardian of ****.

IF you have any affection for me, I beg of you, Rev. Father, to receive with tenderness of heart Brother ****, who has scandalously departed from his duty. But he is come to himself—he weeps—he promises; and what ought to move you more than all this is, that JESUS CHIST, our model, teaches us how we ought to pardon. Contemplate him, I beg of you, dying on the cross, even for the salvation of those who crucified him; and then

I shall

I shall not doubt of obtaining what I requeſt. Such is the depravity of human nature, that I am much leſs ſurpriſed, than alarmed, at the exceſſes man runs into. A motion of pride, a little ſelf-complacency, is enough to make us loſe the grace of God; and from that inſtant behold us capable of every crime!

The more the Lord has preſerved us from thoſe exceſſes, which are a juſt ſubject of mourning, the more compaſſion ought we to have for thoſe who have fallen into them: for it is the pure effect of his mercy, and we can attribute nothing to ourſelves on that account.—Your Religious will bleſs their Guardian, when they ſee with what tenderneſs he receives the ſtrayed ſheep.

My deſign in writing is, not to deſire that you would remit the penance preſcribed by the Conſtitutions, but that you mitigate it as far as poſſible, by refraining from all bitter reproaches, more capable of irritating than moving to repentance.

Let your reprimands be thoſe of a friend; let your correction be ſuch as is given by a Father; let your firſt meeting with him, inſtead of being auſtere, be gracious, that you may not frighten the poor criminal.

Remember that it is Charity, which ever is to act, that charity is to puniſh, and charity is to pardon.

I embrace you moſt ſincerely as my ancient brother, and I hope to hear by the very perſon I recommend to you, that he has found in you a Father, rather than a Master. No one loves you or honours you more than

CARDINAL GANGANELLI.

Convent of the H. Apostles, Nov. 18, 1764.

LETTER CXV.

To the Rev. Father COLLOZ, *Prior of* GRAFFEN-
THAL *and Superior-General of the Order of the*
Guillelmites.

REV. FATHER,

YOUR Letter shewed me both the share you took in my promotion to the Cardinalate, and in the choice the Holy Father has made of my person, among all the members of the Sacred College, to intrust with the protection of your Order. I never doubted of your real sentiments; but it was a satisfaction to me to see, stamped on your letter, the joy which is in your hearts, and to find in it certain marks of the confidence with which you honour me. Your Order has assuredly suffered a loss in Cardinal GUADAGNI, who was a great and powerful support. May the hopes you have conceived of me, make calm and peace arise again in your hearts! I will at least use my utmost endeavours, Rev. Father, that you, and all yours, may find in me a tender friend, a vigilant protector, a zealous defender of your privileges. I often, with pleasure, hear the Procurator-General of the *Capuchins* make the

encomium

encomium of your Reverence, and of your Order.

I have only one thing, Rev. Father, to desire of you, which is to excuse me, if this answer come too late, as I have been overpowered with business, which has scarce left me time to breathe, in so new a change of my condition, and so little looked for on my part. I beg also that you will put me to the trial, and see if I can be of any service to you. I have spoken to our Holy Father about you. I will speak to him on your affairs, as often as you commission me. I recommend myself strongly to the prayers of your Order: and I hope to fulfil the intentions of your Reverence, so as to convince you, that your whole Order have in me a truly affectionate Protector.

I am with my whole heart, Rev. Father, &c.
Rome, Convent of the H. Apostles, May 20, 1760.

LETTER CXVI.

To the Abbè F***.

YOU do not read, my dear Abbè the Fathers of the Church as much as you ought to do; this is easily discovered both in your Discourses and in your Writings. Know you not that they are the soul of Christian Eloquence, and like those fruitful trees, which, at once the ornament and riches of a garden, yield both flowers and fruit.

The

The Church glories in producing their works, as so many monuments of the victories she has gained over her enemies; and every Christian of learning ought to make the reading of them his delight. The more a person dips into them, the more extensive he finds their learning: and each Father of the Church has a genius that characterizes him. That of TERTULLIAN resembles iron, which breaks the hardest substances, and will not bend: that of St. ATHANASIUS may be compared to the diamond, which can neither be deprived of its lustre nor hardness. St. CYPRIAN is like the sharpened steel, which cuts to the quick; St. CHRYSOSTOME like gold, whose intrinsic value corresponds to its beauty; St. LEO like those decorations which exhibit grandeur; St. JEROME like brass, which fears neither arrows nor swords; St. AMBROSE like silver, which is both solid and beautiful; St. GREGORY like a mirror, where every one sees himself: St. AUGUSTINE can be compared to nothing but himself, as being singular in his kind, though universal.

As to St. BERNARD, the last of the Fathers in the order of Chronology, I compare him to those flowers, which are cloathed in the velvet of nature, and which spread around an exquisite perfume.

If the *French* reckon Monsf BOSSUET, Bishop of *Meaux*, among the *Fathers* of the Church, their judgment in this is a little too hasty, and to which one cannot subscribe, till the uni-
                                                                versal

versal Church has pronounced; as she alone has a right to assign to her Writers the rank due to them. St. Thomas of *Aquino* himself has not been able to obtain the title of a *Father* of the Church; and it is not to be presumed, that the Doctors who have come after him, should enjoy that prerogative—But every nation is enthusiastically fond of its own Writers, though we are forced to acknowledge that the CELEBRATED BISHOP of MEAUX was a burning and bright lamp, whose light will never be extinguished.

I confess to you, my dear Abbè, that if I know any thing, I owe it entirely to the reading of the Fathers, and, above all, to reading the works of St. AUGUSTINE. Nothing escapes his sagacity, nothing is beyond his depth, there is nothing above his sublimity. He is concise, he is copious; he is single and alone, or he is many, according to the subject in hand, which he ever treats in the same interesting manner; ever elevates the soul to the very bosom of God, a sanctuary of which he seems to have had the key, and into which he insensibly introduces those who feed on his noble ideas. I admire him above all on the subject of GRACE. Ah! I wish to heaven that his Doctrine, on that point, had fixed all the schools and the minds of men! Some audacious Writers would not then have attempted to sound impenetrable depths, and the GRACE of JESUS CHRIST would have preserved all its rights, and Man his LIBERTY.

What gives me the greatest concern is, that the writings of the Fathers are but little read, and that even those who have occasion to consult them, rely on extracts, often unfaithful, and always too short. A Priest or a Bishop formerly used to make it as much a part of his duty to read the Fathers of the Church, as to say his Breviary; and now-a-days, few know any thing more about them, than their names; except it be in the Cloisters, where this excellent custom is not entirely laid aside. Hence, in many countries we find Theologians who are mere Skeletons, without soul or life; Students who know nothing but to syllogize; Instructions, which contain nothing but words, and are void of all substance.

I ought to declare however, to the praise of the sacred College (without meaning to compliment it) that it has at all times had members, who studied the Fathers with perseverance, and even at this day some might be mentioned, who prefer this kind of reading to every other occupation: and our schools feel the influence of their practice, where no other doctrine is taught, but that of St. Augustine and St. Thomas: the sure means of avoiding every thing that breathes Novelty.

I conjure you then to lay yourself under an obligation of every day reading the works of the Fathers. You need only to begin, for you never will be able to quit them. They are always with God, and they will place you where they are, if you daily feed on their writings. To read them, is to read the Holy Scripture itself, for they explain it like Masters, and cite it on every occasion.

It would be tearing from me three-fourths of my existence, to deprive me of the consolation I enjoy in conversing with the Fathers. The more they are present to my mind, the more I am comforted, the more I rejoice, and the more I think myself immense.

Improve by my lessons, if you love me, or if you love yourself; for by reading the Fathers you will gain acquisitions a thousand times more valuable than estates and titles. An *Ecclesiastic* has nothing to do with the world, but to instruct and edify it. I am with all my heart, and with the most ardent desire of seeing your mind fructify to advantage, your most affectionate

CARDINAL GANGANELLI.

Rome, December 13, 1768.

LETTER CXVII.

*To the Rev. Father *** his Friend.*

YOU have done me a pleasure in not mentioning that I had written to you. Without making a mystery of every thing, I would have a person to be discreet. Though I have now been in the Convent *of the Holy Apostles* eight and twenty years, I have never mentioned to my brethren any correspondence I had;

I had: they may guess if they will, or if they can; but they know nothing for certain—*My secret is my own.**

I have lately seen the Cardinals of YORK, CORSINI, and JOHN FRANCIS ALBANI, whose rare qualities I infinitely esteem, but I learned nothing from them of what I wanted to know.

I subscribe with pleasure to every thing obliging you say of the Prelate DURINI; he joins to the pleasing manner of the French, the sagacity of the Italians; and he deserves to arrive at the highest dignities.

I have learned nothing of the late resolutions of the great Personage whom you mention; I see him but rarely; he is very reserved, and does not believe me to be one of his friends. Is he right? Is he wrong? This is what he himself surely cannot decide, notwithstanding all the *finesse* of which he is supposed to be possessed: but most certainly God knows that I wish him no harm, because I never wished harm to any man.

I will recommend the good work you mention to their Eminences the Cardinals FANTUZZI and BORROMÆO, who breathe nothing but charity. You will deliver the inclosed, with your own hand, to M*** and you will charge yourself with the care of returning me his answer by the flying post, which will be the quickest and surest way. For some time past my correspondencies almost kill me; and yet I cannot get rid of them. Do not henceforth

---
* Secretum meum mihi.

forth lose half a page to shew me more respect: I like you would write to me as to *Brother Ganganelli*. I am still the same Individual, let people take what pains they please to make me believe the contrary: for alas! Were I to mind *Etiquettes* and flattery, I should be intoxicated with the most fulsome praises.

I like to be simply myself, and not to be surrounded with all the concomitants of Grandeur; they are generally very great meannesses, which put me out of patience, and of which a man can never be jealous, unless he have a mean way of thinking indeed.

There is no appearance that our common friend can recover: he has a complication of disorders, each of which would be singly enough to kill the most robust man. I am soliciting a place for your nephew, which will suit him, provided he can bear confinement and scolding: for the great man, whose Secretary I design him to be, labours under the unfortunate madness of flying into a passion for a mere nothing; but his heart is not the less excellent on that account. It is a fault which must be overlooked, in consideration of his goodness of heart. He is like BENEDICT XIV, who always concluded his scolding by bestowing some favour on the object of it. You see I am in the mood for chatting, and that I have not the air of a man of much business. When I have said my Breviary, and have done what I have to do, I talk more than some people like; for I then stand in need of it.

I leave

I leave you now with yourself, that is to say, in the best company I know; and am, as usual, and for all my life, your affectionate servant.

CARDINAL GANGANELLL.
Rome, *Dec.* 6, 1768.

LETTER CXVIII.

To Mr D***.

IT is not sufficient to give alms in order to please God, for charity extends to every thing. You must therefore neither oppress your farmers, nor plague your Vassals. Those men have not the true spirit of Religion, who exact, with the utmost severity, trifles which they ought to despise. Christianity knows not that sordid interest, which is taken up with things of the least consequence: and that man has no more than the outer bark or external appearance of Religion, who is ever upon the watch, for fear of being cheated by his tenants. The heart cannot but be wordly-minded, when it is too eagerly bent on worldly concerns.

Ah! Sir, how can you torment yourself so much about perishable goods? The Kingdom of JESUS CHRIST demands Worshipers *in spirit and truth**, whose hearts are not to be contracted by an interested conduct, and views merely carnal.

* John iv. 23.

I am

I am excessively grieved, when I see people of worth afraid lest the Earth should slip from under them; and who often, though very rich, are more attached to a vile bit of money, than would be the most wretched mechanic.

I am bold to add, Sir, that all your practices of Devotion will be absolutely of no advantage to you, if you are not entirely detached from the good things of this world, and if you continue to be the scourge of your Debtors by a too eager desire of riches. A man ought rather to know how to suffer loss, than to put others to trouble. The spirit of justice which you plead in excuse, has no connection with perpetual mistrusts, and disquiets about what may happen, and with endless bustle and hurry.

If there be any disputes between you and your tenants, accommodate matters more to their advantage, than to your own: to do so is agreeable to the counsels of JESUS CHRIST, who tells us to give also our *coat* to him who demands our *cloak*. Every thing superfluous (and, in cases of urgent want, even a part of the necessaries of life) belong to the poor: you will therefore contract guilt, if you heap up riches—These are hard truths; but it was not I who made the law.

The business you mention to me, could no where be better than in the hands of Monsignor BRASCHI: his uprightness is equal to his understanding, and there is no fear that he will suffer himself to be prejudiced: I will however,

however, if you please, speak to him a word or two. I am, Sir, with the sentiments due to you, &c.

CARDINAL GANGANELLI.

Rome, 21 Inst.

LETTER CXIX.

To My Lord ***.

I Can never think of seeing a genius like yours become the dupe of the modern Philosophy. Your learning and good sense ought to secure you against the sophisms it brings forth, and which reduce us to the melancholy condition of brute beasts.

If there be a GOD, as nature every where proclaims a loud, there is; then is there also a RELIGION. If there be a RELIGION; it must necessarily be incomprehensible, sublime, and co-eval with the world, since it emanated from an Infinite and Eternal Being: and if such be the character of RELIGION, it is certainly CHRISTIANITY, and no other. If it be CHRISTIANITY, we must necessarily acknowledge CHRISTIANITY to be divine, and acquiesce thereto with heart and understanding.

Can any one then believe, that God has displayed the Universe in so bright a manner for no other end, than to feed the eyes of a herd of men and animals (between whom we are to make no distinction, as they have the same destination) and that the Intelligence, which resides in us; that Intelligence which combines, which calculates,

calculates, which extends itself beyond the bounds of the Earth, which raises itself above the Firmament, which recals to its remembrance all past ages, which penetrates into ages to come, which, in a word, has an idea of what is to laſt for ever; can this radiate and ſhine only for a moment, to be afterwards diſperſed like a fleeting vapour?

What is that voice, which, every inſtant, is crying out within you, that you were born for ſomething great? What are thoſe deſires, perpetually renewed, and which make you feel that there is nothing in this world, that can fill your heart?

Man is a ſick perſon, toſſing and tumbling in his pains, while at a diſtance from God: and the light of reaſon, which he ſtifles, leaves him in the midſt of a horrid night.

The ſame truth that aſſures you of your own *Exiſtence* (I. mean your own inward teſtimony) aſſures you alſo of the *Exiſtence* of GOD; and it cannot give you a lively idea of *his Exiſtence*, without impreſſing you with that of the *Exiſtence* of a RELIGION. The worſhip we pay to the ſupreme Being, is ſo connected with him, that our heart is never ſatisfied, but when it pays him homage, and when we conform to the order which he has eſtabliſhed.

If there be a GOD, he muſt neceſſarily be *beneficent:* if he be *beneficent*, you ought, by a juſt conſequence, to thank him for his *benefits*. Neither that of your Exiſtence, nor that of the Health you enjoy, really come from yourself. Seven and twenty years ago you were not: and, all at once, you became an organized body, enriched with a mind that commands that body like a master, and leads it at its pleasure.

This reflection engages you to seek after the Author of life, and when you are disposed to sound yourself, you will find him within you, and in every thing that surrounds you: but not one of these objects can boast of being a part of his substance: for God is *simple*, *indivisible*, and absolutely incapable of being the same with the Elements.

If the RELIGION, which he established, has assumed different forms: if it has been perfected since the coming of the MESSIAH, it was because God treated it, as he does our reason, which at first is only a weak light; but unfolding itself by degrees, appears at last in a meridian brightness.

Besides, is Man to interrogate God with regard to his conduct? Is he to regulate the ways of God, and to prescribe to him, how he is to proceed? God communicates himself to us, reserving still to himself the right of acting like a Master, because there is nothing, but what is really subject to him. Were he clearly to manifest to us his designs here below: were the mysteries, which astonish and confound, unfolded to us, there would then be that intuitive vision here, which he reserves for us after this life; and to die would be useless. Evi-

dence

dence is reserved for heaven: *Then shall I know God, as I myself shall be known* by him*. And we want to anticipate that moment, without reflecting, that every thing is regulated by an infinite wisdom, and that we have nothing to do, but to submit and adore. The Unbeliever alters nothing in the designs of God, when he dares to rise up against him: he even then enters into his plan, that vast plan, where evil concurs with good, for the harmony of this world, and the happiness of the next.

NATURE and RELIGION derive equally from God, and each, though in a very different manner, have their mysteries, and incomprehensibilities: and for the same reason that we do not deny the *Existence* of NATURE, though its operations be often concealed, we neither can, nor ought we to deny the *Existence* of RELIGION, notwithstanding its obscurities.

There is nothing here below, that has not a dark side, because our soul, while rendered heavy and dull by a body which darkens it, and which is a burden to it, would not be capable of seeing all. It is here below in a sort of Infantine State, and the light of the days must be proportionate to the weakness of its sight, until death disengage it from the weight which presses it down. It is like a little bird, that flutters and chirps in its nest, till it is able to spring forward into the air and fly.

[* Cognoscam, sicut et cognitus sum. 1 *Cor.* xiii. 12.

The progress of Religion is wonderful in the eyes of a real Philosopher. He sees it first like a twilight arising from the bosom of *Chaos*; then like the Aurora, the harbinger of day; he at last sees the day itself appear, but clouded on every side, and he is sensible it will not be perfectly serene in its meridian brightness, till the moment in which the heavens will be opened to us.

Has then the Unbeliever, who, without a principle to go on, explodes Revelation, any particular one made to him, which assures him that the Revelation we believe, is absolutely chimerical? But at what time, and in what place did this secret light come and shine upon him? Was it at the moment his passions got the mastery over him, and he was totally taken up with the gratification of them? Was it in the midst of the public shews and pleasures, where he spends the greatest part of his life?

It is astonishing, My Lord, to think how men abandon all the authority of Tradition, elude all the force of the strongest testimonies, to blindly give themselves up to two or three men, who give them lessons of Infidelity! They will not hear of any Inspiration, and yet they consider these two or three men as inspired: from whence the conclusion is easily drawn, that they are the passions alone which draw people over to Infidelity. A Religion that lays its followers under any restraint, is abhorred by men who are for following the torrent of
their

their vices, and fwimming down the tide of a world covered with waves and foam.

CHRISTIANITY is a magnificent piece of painting fketched by the hand of God himfelf, which he prefented to mankind, when only the out-lines were drawn, and was to remain in that ftate till the time JESUS CHRIST fhould come and finifh it; and we are to wait until he give it all the luftre and colouring it is to have in Eternity—Then will RELIGION be the only object that will fix our fight, becaufe it will be in the effence of God himfelf, making *A whole with him*, according to the expreffion of St. *Auguftine*.

This progrefs is conformable to the time which conftitutes the fpace of this life, and which exifts only by fucceffion. God has therefore varied the forms of Religion, becaufe we are in a world that varies; and he will fix it in an unchangeable manner in heaven, becaufe there no change is known. Thefe combinations and proportions difplay the wifdom of the fupreme Being. As Religion is only for man, it was his pleafure that it fhould follow the progrefs of man according to his different ways of exifting.

Nothing of all this is feen by the Earthlyminded; and you would judge as I do, were you difengaged from all thofe pleafures and riches, which materialize you in fpite of yourfelf. Chriftianity is *fpirit* and *life*; and that man withdraws to a prodigious diftance from it, who is entirely taken up with what
concerns

concerns the body alone. Souls become luminous at death, only becaufe they have no longer a body to inclofe and darken them. True Philofophy does now, what death will do hereafter, by difengaging a man from whatever is carnal:—but fuch is not the modern Philofophy, which knows no other Exiftence than that of matter, and confiders Metaphyfics as a fcience merely chimerical, although it be more certain than Phyfiology or natural Philofophy, which is grounded only on the fenfes.

I enter not on the proofs of Religion, becaufe they have been fo often and fo well explained in fome immortal works, that I fhould only repeat what others have faid. JESUS CHRIST is the beginning and end of all things, the key of all the myfteries of grace and of nature; fo that it is no wonder, that men bewilder themfelves with a thoufand abfurd fyftems, when they have not that fublime compafs to direct them. "I can account for nothing either in the phyfical or moral world," faid the celebrated Cardinal BEMBO to a Philofopher of his time, "if you admit not JESUS CHRIST." The Creation of the world itfelf is inexplicable, incomprehenfible, nay impoffible, if it were not made for the WORD INCARNATE: for God can have no other object in whatever he does, but what is infinite. It is for this reafon that JESUS CHRIST is called by St. *John*, *Alpha* and *Omega*, and St. *Paul* tells us, that the *ages* were made by him.*

* Per quem fecit & fæcula. *Heb.* i. 2.

Study

Study thoroughly this MAN-GOD, as far as a Creature is capable of doing it, and you will find in him all the treasures of Wisdom and Knowledge, and discover him to be, as it were, the first link of the chain, which joins all things visible and invisible, and acknowledge him to be that divine breath, which makes righteousness and sanctity germinate in the hearts of men.

The Unbeliever can give no satisfactory answer, if he be asked what JESUS CHRIST is, that man at once so simple and so divine, so sublime and so abject, so pure during the whole course of his life, so great at the time of his passion, so magnanimous at his death. Here however an explicit answer must be given. If he be no more than a *man*, he is a mere Impostor; for he said he was God. In that case what becomes of those sublime virtues? What becomes of his Gospel, which forbids the use of the least Equivocation? How can we account for his victories, and those of his Disciples in every part of the world? If he be GOD, what must we think of his Religion? What must we think of those, who dare oppose it?

Ah! my Lord, this is what you ought to know, this is what you ought to search to the bottom, rather than all the profane sciences, to which you give yourself up. The sciences will have an end: *tongues will cease, sciences will be destroyed**; the knowledge of JESUS

---

* Linguæ cessabunt, scientia destructur. 1 *Cor*. xiii. 8.

CHRIST

Christ alone will flote on the furface of that Abyfs, wherein all ages and the elements will be fwallowed up.

Confider yourfelf, and that fight will neceffarily lead you to the truth. The leaft motion of your finger points out to you the Agency of God on your perfon; this Agency declares to you a Providence; this Providence tells you that you are dear to the Creator; and the telling you that, will lead you from truth to truth, till it bring you to thofe which are revealed.

If you be neither your own Creator, nor your own laft end, you ought neceffarily to feek out him, who includes thefe two qualities: Ah! if it be not God, what can it be?

Religion will be ever fure to gain its caufe in the eyes of all who proceed on principles. To know the truth of what it teaches, nothing more is required, than to go up to its fource, to analyfe it, to follow it to where it is to terminate; but is disfigured, it is dishonoured; and it is no more than a fkeleton, that wicked men fubftitute in its place. I am therefore no longer furprifed, that thofe who have never received any inftructions, fhould fwear on the reputation of our modifh wits, and be afraid of it.

The uprightnefs of your foul, and the extent of your underftanding make me hope, my Lord, that you will form a more folid judgment on Chriftianity than you have hitherto done. Lay afide the fyftems and opinions
with

with which you have unhappily filled your head: enter, like a new man, on the road which Tradition will open for you, and you will judge very differently. Appeal from your prejudices to your own heart, for it is not you, who have hitherto pronounced. But I really act as my heart and mind dictate to me, when I assure you of all that affection, with which I shall continue, during my whole life, your servant, &c.

CARDINAL GANGANELLI.
Rome, Nov. 29, 1768.

LETTER CXX.

To Count ***.

YOUR reflections, Count, on the present state of the different Courts of *Europe*, are extremely judicious. You shew that you are intimately acquainted with them, and that, though you are not admitted into the cabinet of Princes, you perfectly know what passes there.

It is a fine thing to be on a level with the age we live in, in order to know it well, and to discover the secret springs, which actuate the personages who shine on the theatre of the world.

The person you mention to me is insignificant, unsteady, irresolute, and consequently not to be depended upon. There is another person, whom you know, zealous, as any one ought to be, for the auguſt houſe of Bourbon; and he ſets out from his palace with a moſt determined reſolution to ſpeak, in the ſtrongeſt manner, to the Holy Father relatively to the affair of *Parma*; but ſcarce does he appear in his preſence, when he dares not ſay a word. As to the little Prelate, who was to have acted and become a mediator on his own accord, he is an undetermined ſoul, who is always for putting things off till to-morrow, and from whom you can never get any other anſwer but: *we will ſee**.

One may even ſpeak a word to the General of the ***; but he muſt not be too far intruſted, eſpecially at preſent, when even the ſecret enjoined by the Holy Office, is not kept. As to his Aſſiſtant, he is good ſort of man enough.

FRANCE and SPAIN have here many of the firſt rank juſtly attached to them; but they are ſo much harraſſed by a multitude of people who ſurround them, and who make heaven ſpeak in their favour, that they dare not explain their ſentiments.

An ignorant Devotion, and which unhappily is but too much in vogue, is continually whiſpering, that every thing is to be ſacrificed to maintain the intereſts of God; as if God required of his prime Miniſter on Earth, that he ſhould quarrel with all the Catholic powers, to maintain a few territorial rights, and to keep up, whether they would or not, a body

* Vederemo.

of men, who no longer can do any good, when the Catholic Powers are once set against them. For let us suppose for a moment, that these Powers are merely influenced by prejudice, it is still true that this body of men can no longer be of any service, when it is become an object of dislike to powerful Princes: but it is impossible to make people hearken to reason, when they have once adopted a manner of thinking agreeable to the opinions they have before imbibed.

All this forms a Labyrinth, to get out of which there is no way seen: and the best thing a man can do, is to be silent, and to wait God's time. He can, whenever he pleases, enlighten the minds of men, and let them know his designs.

The misfortune is, that the more delay is used, the more the minds of people are exasperated. I am convinced, Count (though I know your great talents) that you do not see any easy means of extricating us from our present difficulty. We have to deal with people who cry out, when an accommodation is mentioned; and there is no possibility of reasoning with them, because they look upon themselves as inspired.

This, however, does hinder my indignation from rising, when I hear what is said against CLEMENT XIII. and the more so, as it is never lawful to speak against the High-priest, and as we read in St. JUDE's Epistle, that St. *Michael* durst not curse even the Devil, but that

that he contented himself with saying: May God *controul you*.*

Hence I conlude that, whatever way of thinking men may have, they generally make Religion bend to their prejudices. Some are excessively fond of the Religious body, which is the present subject of contestation; others carry their enmity against them to an excess: and hence it is, that neither the one nor the other see things, as they ought to be seen; and that truth is no longer hearkened to, but passion alone. As to my part, as I have all along kept the medium between two extremes of each party, and have ever detested all cabals and prejudices: my opinion is, that a Pope can do nothing better, than to examine whatever has been written *pro* and *con*, in the presence of God; as also the inconveniences, which may arise from his determination one way or other; and then, and only then he either can, or ought to pronounce a definitive sentence: for he is the Judge, nor did I ever consider him, as the simple Executor of the will of the Potentates. The power that established a Religious Order, is the only power that can destroy it; and the right is so indisputable, that it would be madness to contest it.

But my comfort in the midst of these evils is, that although St. PETER's bark is to be forever tossed, the Lord is likewise ever to support it, even in the midst of the greatest storms.

* Non est ausus judicium inferre blasphemiæ, sed dixit: imperet tibi Dominus. *Jude* 9.

You,

You, Sir, are more perfuaded of this, than any one elfe, as you have always applied yourfelf to meditate on the eternal truths, and to fee, whatever relates to Religion, with the eyes of Faith. Thofe are eyes, quite different from the eyes of Philofophy, and raifing us above this world, fpread us in the immenfity of God himfelf. Nothing is therefore fo abfurd, as to affert with our modern Philofophers, that the views of a Chriftian are exceffively limited. A foul that expands itfelf even into Eternity, and rifes above the Univerfe to reach to God himfelf (who is a fpirit purely immaterial) can this foul be contracted in its ideas?

Whenever a man fhall be difpofed to draw a parallel between Religion and Philofophy, it will not be long before he perceive that the one enlarges, to an immenfe degree, all the faculties of the foul, while the other contracts them into a circle extremely narrow. This world is the *ne plus ultra* to a modern Philofopher; but to a Chriftian it is no more than an atom. The one makes it his happinefs and laft end; the other confiders it only as a figure that paffes away, and gives only a fimple glance at it. The one adores it, becaufe it is his God, and his all; the other fees it only as a vapour, that will foon difappear.

· Rely not on the Prelate ***, he has too much to do.

If any alteration happen here, I will fpeedily let you know it: but there muft be a terrible fhock shock before that can take place. I have the honour to be, Count, &c.

My Compliments to the Abbé.

LETTER CXXI.

To a Prelate.

YOU have layed me under a very sensible obligation by the service you have rendered Father *Amatus de Lamballe*. He is a *Capuchin-Friar*, for whom I have a particular affection on account of his good qualities. He has the virtues of his profession, that is to say, he is humble, meek, zealous; and very attentive to see the Rule observed in its full vigour.

I wait your return with impatience, and the more so, as we have to discourse on people saying a great deal and, doing nothing. Each day brings us the most extraordinary news, and each day contradicts it. When the minds of men are in a ferment, and affairs of importance are in agitation, every one sets up for a Politician, and a Newsmonger, especially in *Rome*, where we have a world of speculators and idle people.

As this life is nothing but a succession of inquietudes and desires, some fear, others hope. It was yesterday reported that the King of *Naples* was making some troops file off towards us.

St. IGNATIUS, who was inflamed with a desire of promoting the glory of God, did not
foresee

foresee the disturbances, that one day were to happen on account of his Children. It is however said of him, that he begged of God, that they might ever be in a state of suffering; if that be true, his prayer was certainly heard; for it must be owned, that, for some time past, their calamities have been very great. I have really felt for their sufferings; they are doubly my brethren, both as men, and as Religious; and if the green wood be treated thus, what will become of the dry*.

You will find your Director here no more —he is buried. Death, which always comes without being sent for, gives us no respite. It makes its round night and day, and men live in as much security, as if they were sure that it would never come near them.

I hope you will bring me the little picture I begged of you. Continue to depend on my esteem and friendship; I can give you nothing else; but these I give in a plentiful manner, being &c. *Rome, April 23, 1768.*

* Si in viridi ligno hæc faciunt, quid in arido fiet. Luke xxiii. 31.

LETTER CXXII.
To the Marquis CARACCIOLI.

I Return you, Sir, a thousand thanks for the work you sent me, entitled: *The last Farewell of the Marechal's Lady to her Children:** it

* Les derniers Adieux de la Marechale à ses Infans.

is a book of sentiment, and affects the heart in so strong a manner, that I was sensibly moved with it: you ought to give it us in *Italian*, and the rather, as I consider it in the light of a most complete Treatise on Education.

I am sorry you were not in time supplied with all the interesting Anecdotes relating to the life of BENEDICT XIV; you were too late in endeavouring to procure them. When a person designs to publish the History of a Sovereign Pontiff, the memoirs must be collected during his life-time; every one is then eager to give them; whereas after his death, he is soon forgotten, and very often by those who owe to him all they are.

I exhort you, Sir, to continue your literary labours, which are so advantageous to the public; provided it be not at the expence of your health; and believe me more than I can express, your most affectionate servant,

    CARDINAL GANGANELLI.
Rome, Sept. 13, 1768.

LETTER CXXIII.

To the Embassador of ***.

IF the affair of *Parma*, or that of the *Jesuits*, interested Faith, then indeed there could be neither any temporizing, accommodation, or capitulation; for the answer of the Sovereign Pontiffs to him, who was for altering the Faith, ought to be; "put me to death."

          Certain

Certain it is, that I fear very much, left the Potentates end in doing just what they please, and that we at last shall be obliged to submit, when all submission will be rejected.

Those times are no more, when men of every rank came to bring their offerings to Rome, and to lay their vows before her. But were that still the case, could she, with any conscience, violate the rights of crowned Heads? A Pope, no doubt, ought to maintain his immunities, but not when the maintaining of them might cause a schism; especially as Rome is the centre of Unity, and she cannot, for points that concern neither Faith nor Morals, expose those who live in her bosom, to the danger of a separation from her.

If, when the Potentates first began to complain of the *Jesuits*, the *General* himself had written to the Monarchs, in order to appease their wrath, and to beg of them to punish, in a severe manner, those who might have offended them: if the Holy Father himself had followed this plan, the Monarchs might have been appeased: and I really believe it would have been so, provided always, that an offer of a Reformation had been made: but some people were then obstinately bent, and are so still, on supporting the Society; and this it is that has set all against them.

Father *Pontalti*, the General of the Carmelite Friars, acted like an excellent Politician, when he wrote to the King of Portugal, to beseech him to hinder the Religious of his Order

Order from trading in the *Brasils*. He advised the Rev. Father *Ricci*, the General of the Jesuits, to take the same step; but he would not hear of it.

Where is the Sovereign, who is not the Master to keep in his territories, or to expel from them such as displease him? I am bold to say, that the present Minister of his Holiness has not laid hold of that affair properly, nor has he foreseen all the consequences of it: *There are some fine eyes, that see nothing.**

Avignon, Benevento, Porto-Corvo tell us, that unless matters be soon made up, other places will be seized on: and thus it is, that territories are insensibly lost, a long enjoyment of which had rendered the possession of them very lawful.

Benedict XIV, though of a timid disposition, would have satisfied the Sovereign Princes at this Crisis; and it is a pity that Clement XIII, whose piety we all respect, as well as that of his Nephew, should see things in a different light. I took the liberty to speak to him on this subject, and he appeared struck with what I said; but immediately after, some, whose interest it is to keep him in the way of thinking which they have suggested to him, present themselves, and by specious reasoning, persuade him to persist in his former sentiments. They tell him, " that a Religious body of men, who have rendered such services both in the old and new world, who make an ex-

* An Italian proverb.

press vow of obedience to the Holy See, must absolutely be preserved, and that the attempts made to destroy them, proceed entirely from a hatred to Religion." But they do not tell him, "that the common Father of the Faithful ought not to provoke Princes the most religious and most obedient to the HOLY SEE: they tell him not that his behaviour may cause a schism between the HOLY SEE and PORTUGAL, and that a Head of the Church ought to tremble, when there is danger of a separation, which may have the most fatal consequences."

The loss of a few territories is nothing in comparison to the loss of so many souls by a schism. What a picture would *England* be to CLEMENT VII, were he now alive! The thought makes one tremble. The Sovereigns now reigning, one may be pretty sure, will never think of a separation; but can any one answer for their successors? What presents itself under an appearance of piety, is not always the most expedient. A Pope is appointed Head of the Church to *pluck up*, as well as *to plant :* the good books written by the *Jesuits*, will subsist, when they are no more. Neither Infallibility nor indefectibility have fallen to the share of Religious Orders. Were they all to be extinguished at this time, the loss, no doubt, would be great; but the Church of Christ would neither be less *Holy*, less *Apostolic*, nor less respectable. The Religious Societies are on the footing of auxiliary troops; and it belongs to the supreme Pastor to judge when they are of use, and when they are no longer so.

The *Humiliati*, or *Humble Brethren*, even the *Knights-Templars* did good for some time; for there is no Order but what gives edification, and especially at its first Institution: nevertheless they were extinguished, when the Kings and the Popes judged it proper.

I shall certainly regret the loss of the good the Jesuits might do; but I should still more regret the loss of those Kingdoms which may separate from us. These Fathers must themselves feel the justness of my reasons; and I have the presumption to think, that I could make them own they did, had I a conference with them, and would they divest themselves of the prejudices attached to every condition of life.—If my Friend, Father *Timone*, had been their General, they would not have met with the storms to which they have been exposed.

These are my real sentiments, though a Religious man myself: and I would say the same of my own Order, if (which God forbid) it ever should become an object of displeasure to the Catholic Powers.

There are certain devotional impressions, which happily never dazzled my eyes. I weigh events according to Religion and Equity; and as these are two sure lights, by their judgment I determine myself.

Were there no other party in the Church, but that of J<small>ESUS</small> C<small>HRIST</small>, all the Faithful would

would wait in peace for the event marked out by divine Providence, without being furious partifans for *Cephas* or *Apollo*. But people now fuffer themfelves to be led only by fenfible affections, and becaufe they know one Religious man, whofe conduct has been edifying, and whofe doctrine has been very found, a conclufion is drawn from hence, that the Order, of which he is a member, neither can, nor ought to be extinguifhed— But there is neither found judgment nor good reafoning in fuch a conclufion.

When a perfon has not feen the cafe drawn up, nor the reafons on which judgment is to proceed, it is abfurd to attempt pronouncing. Here is a great difpute between the fovereign Princes and a body of Religious men, famous for their talents and credit; and unlefs a perfon knows what has occafioned the difpute, he neither can, nor ought to fpeak of it. Once more, I do not mean that the *Jefuits* ought to be deftroyed; but I think that the complaints of the Potentates ought to be heard; and that thefe Religious ought to be fuppreffed, if there be ftrong reafons for doing it.

It is not exactly known to this day, why the *Templars were* deftroyed, and people want already to know why the *Jefuits may* be deftroyed. I wifh with my whole foul they may clear themfelves, and that there may be neither divifion amongft us, nor deftruction of them; for my foul loves peace, and is incapable of
hating

hating any individual, much less a Religious Order. I have the honour to be, &c.

Rome, *Oct.* 29, 1768.

LETTER CXXIV.

To the Marquis of ***.

WE are now, behold at the greatest Crisis that ever happened. All Europe is thundring against us, and unhappily we have nothing to oppose to this roaring tempest. The Pope relies on Providence; but God does not perform miracles every time he is asked to do it. Besides, is he to perform one, that ROME may enjoy a right of seignory over the Dutchy of PARMA?

ROME has no more than an administration purely spiritual in Catholic Kingdoms, and her temporal authority exists no where, but in the Ecclesiastical State; and even her temporal authority there is from the grant of the Sovereigns, whom some are for having us oppose.

The Court of ROME cannot forget that she is indebted to FRANCE for almost all her riches and splendour; and if she remember it, how can she hesitate about yielding to the will of LEWIS XV: especially as he asks no more than he has a right to demand.

I compare the four principal Kingdoms, which support the Holy See, to the cardinal virtues; France to *fortitude*, Spain to *prudence*, &c.

Surrounded

Surrounded and defended by these the Holy See is formidable to its enemies; and then may we say to it: *a thousand shall fall on thy left, and ten thousand on thy right, but to thee evil shall not approach.**

I sigh, my dear Sir, I own, at the sight of the misfortunes, which, what we are now doing, prepares for us, and could willingly say: *let this bitter cup pass from us*, not because *our cloak is taken from us*, and *our coat*† may be also taken, but because I fear a rupture: and what misfortunes will not that drag after it, though Religion can never be destroyed?

Would the Holy Father, whose heart is purity itself, only order the acts of beneficence, which the Holy See has received from the French Monarchs, to be laid before him, he could never hesitate to comply with the desires of Lewis XV. respecting the Dutchy of Parma: but you know that every thing may be seen two ways, and the aspect under which this affair is presented to the Holy Father, is directly opposite to the views of the Sovereigns.

There will be found a necessity of retreating; and unless this Pope do it, his successor must: a thing the more disagreeable, as Clement XIII is a Pontiff worthy of the primitive ages of the Church, and deserves to be blessed

---

* Cadent à latere tuo mille, & decem millia à dextris tuis; ad te autem non appropinquabit. *Ps.* xc. *Vulg.*
† *Matt.* v. 40.

by

by all the Kingdoms, which acknowledge his Authority.

The Sacred College might remonstrate to him: but besides the difference of sentiments, which is found among its members, relating to the affair of *Parma* and that of the *Jesuits*, the Pope will always act as his Council directs him.

I am not surprised that Cardinal *** interests himself so warmly in favour of the Society and its General; his attachment arises from very natural reasons: but what surprises me is, that he, whose way of thinking is known to every body, should be consulted preferably to others. In critical circumstances, the advice only of such, as are perfectly disinterested, ought to be taken: otherwise a person becomes a party-man without design, or even without mistrusting it.

It is a fine thing to be in love with truth alone, and to know it, as it is in self: but there are so many illusions which assume its appearance, that we are often misled by them. When a person would see clearly in any affair that comes before him, he must divest himself of all he hitherto knows, he must inform himself, as if he knew nothing; in a word, he must take advice of those, who see and judge without prepossession.

An upright intention moreover is required, and such as may draw down upon us supernatural lights; for the *Lord founds our hearts and reins,** and if the love of justice animate us

Rom. viii. 27.   not

not in our researches, he abandons us to our own darkness.

I am, with all the fulness of my heart, &c.
Rome, Jan. 7, 1769.

LETTER CXXV.

To a Religious man of his own Order.

WHEN Providence raised me to the dignity of a Cardinal, it did not make me lose sight of the place from whence I came: the view of that is always before my eyes, and wonderfully serves to keep off self-love and vanity. The dignity I enjoy, and to which I was not born, has more thorns than roses, and in that respect, it is like all other eminent stations.

I am often obliged to be of a contrary way of thinking to the person, whom I respect above all others, and who, above all others, demands my gratitude—'Tis the most cruel struggle my heart can feel.

Charity, which is inseparable from truth, has not always the most agreeable things to say: but many people are deceived in this point, because they fancy that charity is ever meek and complaisant: in that case it would resemble flattery. There are occasions, on which charity takes fire, blazes out and thunders. The Fathers of the Church, who were filled with it, spoke only by its organ, even when they expressed their zeal in the strongest manner.

When you write to the Bishop of ***, you will make my sincere compliments, and let him know, that every thing has been done to pacify matters, but to no purpose. God will sooner or later manifest his will: for we ought ever to have him in sight.

You restore me to life, by telling me that our common friend will not die. His extensive learning is of important service to those who consult him. He has, in an eminent degree, the talent of directing souls, without any of those trifling silly ways, too commonly found among the generality of Directors: for it must be owned, that many men direct others, who stand in need of being directed themselves: and the women are almost ever their ruin, by shewing them an attention and respect, which is due only to God. When they see the man, in whom they have placed their confidence, they consider him at least, as the *Arch-Angel Gabriel*. It is fit, no doubt, that a person should have a real esteem for those he consults, and whom he hearkens to as the oracles of the law; but that must not be carried to an excess.

They who are ever enthusiastically fond of their Director, may assure themselves that there are many human motives in such an attachment.

What a surprise will it be to many devout ones of the sex, (who sincerely thought their affections fixed on God, but were in reality fixed only on their Directors) when, at the moment of of their death, they shall hear from that supreme mouth, which is to pronounce the last sentence: " It was not I whom you loved; *begone therefore from me; I know you not.*"*

This thought has long made me tremble for Directors. I could wish, that he who was formerly mine at *Rome*, and who died *in the odour of sanctity*, had made public his manner of directing. He was a heavenly man, who raised people above humanity, and absolutely insisted, that they should forget him, to attach themselves to God alone.

We want in *Italy* a good book on the subject of *Direction*. We have many that contain nothing but common-place stuff. But to compose such a book, a man must, first of all, have the spirit of God. Secondly, he must have a great knowledge of the human heart: for it is incredible with what address self-love and a thousand sensible affections come and reside there, while we persuade ourselves, that they are so many sublime sentiments, and worthy the eyes of the Eternal.—'Tis this, that renders it so difficult a thing to form a right judgment of ourselves.

I wish you whatever you can desire, because I know you will desire nothing but what is excellent; and I am your most dear and affectionate servant,

CARDINAL GANGANELLI.
Convent of the Holy Apostles.

---

* Discedite, nescio vos. *Matt.* xxv. 13.

LETTER CXXVI.

To the Count de ***.

WE are at laſt ſummoned to a Confiſtory, which is to determine great things. We have to confider of the unhappy affairs, which, for ſome time paſt, have embroiled us with the Potentates. It ſeems now, that the Holy Father, finding himſelf unable to ſtand out any longer, will acquieſce in the defires of the Houſe of BOURBON. He will at leaſt lay before us, for the ſubject of our deliberation, his prefent uneafineſs, and every one will give his opinion.

Would to God this plan had been followed from the beginning! But, unhappily, the diſagreeable confequences of an affair are often not feen, till a perſon is entangled in them.

I advife you to confer with ****: ROME, though famed for its policy, is not always— You underſtand me.

The Miniſters continue to make the moſt bitter complaints; and the parties intereſted, in order to prevent any thing being concluded, form circumvallations, contravallations, &c.— Your own mind will tell you the reſt.

There is great room to think that FRANCE, SPAIN, and PORTUGAL will ———.

I ſhall let you know nothing, if filence be enjoined; and in that you will moſt ſurely approve my conduct. I ſhall not expofe myſelf to the fame reproaches the little man in queſtion did, for betraying a fecret.

Befides

Besides the probity of a Cardinal, I have a natural probity, which constitutes the essence of an honest man; and this is a double engagement to secrecy: but it will not be so well kept, as to hinder the thing from being immediately divulged: nor should I be surprised, were the Gazetteers of HOLLAND to receive intelligence of it.

I can know nothing before hand, because nothing is said. The life I lead here is as obscure as my habit; and consequently I shall not be found in those brilliant circles, where people hear and tell great news. I learn nothing, but by means of our dear Abbè... But does he know every thing, or does he always tell the truth? Not that he designs to impose on people; but his imagination, his lively temper, &c.

I have again seen the flying-post.... He brought me the letters I looked for, and they contain nothing but wise reflections on what I wanted to know. Adieu without ceremony, as you ordered me.

Rome, Jan. 31, 1769.

LETTER CXXVII.

To the same.

HERE is a Revolution quite different from that expected in the Consistory I mentioned to you in my last. The Holy Father, getting into bed last night, was seized with a dreadful

dreadful convulsion—screamed out—and expired. This was the day appointed to have drawn from the Alembic, what keeps all the Catholic courts in suspence, and has embroiled us with them. People will reason differently on this so extraordinary a death in the present circumstances.

I most sincerely regret the loss of the late Pope, on account of his excellent qualities, and the gratitude I owe him—Religion must make his Elogium, and mourn for him. He rendered it truly respectable, to all who were near him, by the purity of his morals equal to the uprightness of his intentions, and a zeal proof against every thing: but I shall continue to say, that it was a pity he did not see things in the light in which he ought to have seen them.

He has left behind him Nephews recommendable for their excellent qualities, and especially the Cardinal, who has the best soul that can be met with.

The great difficulty now is, to know who will be chosen in his place: I pity him beforehand whoever he be. I shall not pretend to tell you, it is such a one, or such a one; for it is always some one, who was never thought on. This is certain, that I will not give my vote to any, who unites not learning with piety. A Pope, as the Vicar of JESUS CHRIST, ought to have true devotion; and, as a temporal Prince, a deal of knowledge and sagacity. Happily the sacred College offers us an

easy

easy choice from among its members. Pray that the Lord may inspire us, and give us a Head according to his own heart, and according to that of the sovereign Princes.

I have lately seen *Monsignor Marefoschi*: he is a wonderful Prelate for his knowledge and candour.

The Conclave will be more supportable than in summer, and will make little alteration in my manner of life. I am only going to exchange one Cell for another; and if there be any intrigues, I protest to you I will be a stranger to them, as I am a man who meddle the least of any thing with forming parties.

You know my heart, and I need not tell you, that I am, &c. *Rome, Feb.* 3, 1769.

LETTER CXXVIII.

To a Religious man, a Friend of his.

I AM going to the Conclave; pray to the Lord that he may bless our intentions, and send a calm after so long a storm.

I am almost engaged to take a *Frenchman* for my *Conclavist**. Besides my great fondness for his nation, he has some excellent qualities: but after all I shall trust nobody but myself, that I may have nothing to fear from his indiscretion, should he be disposed to blab: *my secret is my own*†.

* A Cardinal's Secretary, while in the Conclave.
† Secretum meum mihi.

You will tell our Prelate, that I could not answer his letter, but that I expect to see him at the Convent of the Holy Apostles the very day the Conclave ends. The minds of men are divided, but God is the sovereign Master of hearts, and it is his work about which we are going.

Endeavour to procure me the book I mentioned, the moment I shall be at liberty again. Adieu. I am ever your servant and friend.

CARDINAL GANGANELLI.

Six o'clock in the morning.

LETTER CXXIX.

To Monsignor *****.

FOR these four months past I have neither belonged to myself, nor to my friends, but to all the different Churches of the world (of which, by divine permission, I am become the Head) and to all the Catholic Courts, several of which, as you know, have great matters to settle with ROME.

It was impossible to become Pope in times of greater strife and contention; and it is precisely on me that divine Providence has appointed so oppressive a burden to be laid. I hope the same Providence will support me, and bestow on me that prudence and fortitude, both of which are so necessary in order to govern according to the rules of justice and equity.

I take pains to acquire the moſt exact knowledge of what my Predeceſſor left me to do; and which cannot be concluded till after a long examination.

You will do me a real pleaſure in bringing me what you have written relative to this object, and in truſting nobody with it, but myſelf alone.

You will find me, ſuch as you ever have known me, as much a ſtranger to all the Grandeur that ſurrounds me, as if I knew not the very name; and you may ſpeak to me as freely as you formerly did, ſince the Papacy has given me a ſtill greater love for truth, and a freſh conviction of my own nothingneſs.

Rome, Sept. 21, 1769.

LETTER CXXX.

To a Portuguese *Nobleman.*

YOU ought not to doubt, Sir, of my moſt earneſt deſire to unite more than ever thoſe ties, which ſome have attempted to break, between the Court of Rome and that of Portugal. I am no ſtranger to the intimate union, which at all times has reigned between thoſe two Powers, and it will afford me the greateſt pleaſure to put things on their ancient footing: but as the Common Father of all the Faithful, as the Head of all the Religious Orders, I will not proceed to act, till I have examined, weighed, and judged of every thing

thing according to the rules of juſtice and truth.

God forbid that any human confideration whatever ſhould determine me! I ſhall already have an account fufficiently rigorous to give to God, without loading my confcience with any new fin; and it would truly be an enormous one to profcribe a whole Religious Order on rumours, prejudices, or even fufpicions. I will never forget, that while I give to *Cæſar* what belongs to *Cæſar*, I am to give to GOD what belongs to God.

I have already employed fome perfons to examine the Archives of the *Propaganda*, and to procure for me the correfpondence of SIXTUS-QUINTUS, my illuſtrious Brother-Friar and Predeceſſor, with PHILIP II. I require, moreover, that the heads of the accuſation, fupported by fuch teſtimonies as cannot be rejected, be laid before me. I will be in private the Advocate of thoſe whofe deſtruction is demanded of me, to the end that I may feek, in my own breaſt, every means of juſtifying them, before I pronounce ſentence.

The King of PORTUGAL is too religious a Prince, as alfo are thofe of FRANCE, SPAIN, and NAPLES, not to approve of my manner of proceeding.

If Religion require a ſacrifice, the whole Church ſhall hear me, and *****.

I heartily wiſh that Providence had not referved me for fuch calamitous times; for let me act as I will, I ſhall make male-contents, occaſion

a deal

a deal of grumbling, and render myself odious to a multitude of people, whose esteem and friendship I could wish to enjoy.

I consider myself as one of those Prophets, whom God raised up in the midst of tempests, and one of those men, whose rank exposes them in battle, though they have no other views but those of peace; but who, from the nature of their post, are obliged to act.

All is in the hands of God—May he direct my pen, my tongue, and my heart; I will submit to every thing—I will do whatever ought to be done—without apprehending the consequences, &c.

LETTER CXXXI.

To a Religious, a Friend of his.

IF you think me happy, you are deceived. After having been hurried the whole day, I often awake in the night, and sigh after my Cloister, my Cell, and my books: and I can truly say, that I envy your situation. What encourages me is, that Heaven itself placed me in St. PETER's Chair, to the great astonishment of the whole world; and that, if it design me for any great work, it will support me.

I would shed all the blood in my veins (God knows it) that every thing was quiet, that all people would return to their duty, that those, who have given offence, would reform, and that there be neither Division nor Suppression.

I will not proceed to extremities, till urged to it from the most powerful motives, that Posterity at least may do me justice, in case my own age refuse it me. But this is not what employs my thoughts; it is an eternity so dreadful to all, but especially to Popes.

I will send you my answer to what you asked me about. You shall find that I do not forget my friends, and if I see them not so often as formerly, it is because business and cares are my centinels: they may be found at my gates—in my chamber—in my heart.

Mention me to my old acquaintances: I sometimes think how great their astonishment must be, when they heard of my Elevation.

Particularly tell my old school-fellow, that he did not prophesy truly, when he used to tell our companions, that I should go and end my days in *France*. There is no appearance of that coming to pass; or else I must be destined to very extraordinary things indeed. I am ever your most effectionate,

CLEMENT.

Castel-Gandolfo.

LETTER CXXXII.

To the Rev. Father AMATUS DE LAMBALLE, GENERAL *of the* CAPUCHINS.

I AM sincerely obliged to you for the prayers you address to heaven for my safety. I stand doubly in need of them, both as a particular, and as Head of the Church. I unite myself to all your sufferings, and to all your labours, being persuaded that you bear all in a spirit of penance, and in a manner pleasing to God.

If you make any long stay at *Paris*, as I fear you will on account of your disorder, you will have an opportunity of seeing MONSIGNOR DORIA, whom I love with all the plenitude of my heart, as a Prelate, who will one day be the joy and honour of the Church. I see you among a set of people, where there are great vices and great virtues; and where, by a particular Providence, the zeal of the most Christian King, and of the whole Royal Family, and the great Piety of the Prelate, who fills the See of PARIS, stop the progress of Infidelity.

Bring back with you one of the *French Cordeliers*, who, by his learning, may here do honour to his Nation. The *Dominicans* acted wisely, when they called Father FABRICI, your worthy Countryman, to the *Minerva*; he perpetuates the glory of his Order by his Erudition.

If

If your disorder hinder you not from going to pay your homage to Madame Louisa, I commission you to tell her, that I continue to admire the sacrifice she has made. Assure all your brethren, that I sincerely love them in the Lord; and that I exhort them to continue to live in a manner worthy of our Founder.

What you desire, I will mention to Cardinal de Bernis. He will be often enquired after in *France*; for I know he is as dear to the *French*, as he is to the *Italians*.

I wish to see you again in good health; and am, as heretofore, entirely yours.

Signed, Clement XIV.

Rome, April 2, 1773.

APPENDIX:

CONTAINING

An ENCYCLICAL,

OR

CIRCULAR LETTER,

ADDRESSED TO ALL THE

Patriarchs, Primates, Archbishops, and Bishops,

On his Exaltation to the Pontificate.

Other LETTERS

To LEWIS XV of FRANCE, MADAME LOUISA, the DUKE of PARMA, &c.

BRIEFS and DISCOURSES,

TOGETHER WITH

The BULL

For the UNIVERSAL JUBILEE of the YEAR 1775.

AN ENCYCLICAL LETTER

OF

CLEMENT XIV,

To all the PATRIARCHS, PRIMATES, ARCHBISHOPS, and BISHOPS, on his EXALTATION.

CLEMENT XIV

To our Venerable Brethren, Health and Apostolic Benediction.

WHEN we consider the duties of the supreme Apostolate, with which we are invested, the weight of so great a burden bears us down; and, after being dragged from the repose of a life of tranquillity, we seem to be thrown into the depth of the sea, where we are ready to sink under the violence of the waves.

But it is the *work of the Lord, and our eyes see it with admiration*[*]. The unsearchable judgments of God, and not human Counsels, loaded us with the most awful functions of the Apostolate, when we were far from entertaining any thoughts of it. This Conviction fills us with a confidence, that he who has called us to the laborious cares of the supreme Ministry, will come and allay our fears, aid our weakness, and graciously hear our prayers. PETER, who ought to be our model, was encouraged by the Lord, who reproached him with his want of faith, when he thought he was drowning in the sea. There is no doubt, but that our Divine Head, who, in the person of the Prince of the Apostles, has entrusted us with the *keys of the*

[*] *Ps.* cxvii. 23. *Vulg.*

*kingdom of Heaven**, and has commanded us to *feed his sheep*†, designed that we should lay aside all uncertainty of obtaining assistance. We submit therefore without reserve to him, who is our strength and support‡, abandoning ourselves entirely to his might and to his fidelity. He, through his own goodness, will finish in us the work he has begun; and our own lowliness will serve to make his mercy shine the brighter in the eyes of all men. For if he be resolved to accomplish, in these unhappy times, any thing for the advantage of his Church, by the ministry of so unprofitable a servant as we are, all men will evidently see, that he alone is the *Author and Finisher* thereof, and that all the glory is to be given to him alone. But the more mighty the aid is on which we rely, the more efforts will we use to co-operate with it: the more sublime the honour, to which we have been raised, the more care ought we to take to worthily fulfil the functions thereof.

While we cast our eyes over the different countries of Christendom, we perceive you, our Venerable Brethren, sharing with us our glorious labours, and this sight fills us with consolation. We acknowledge in you, with the greatest joy, worthy Co-operators, faithful Pastors, and Evangelical Labourers. It is for this reason that we are eager to address ourselves to you at the commencement of our Apostolate. It is in your bosom, that we will pour forth the most inward sentiments of our soul; and if we seem to exhort you, or give you any advice, attribute it only to the distrust we have of ourselves; and reflect that it is the effect of that confidence, which your virtues, and your filial love towards us inspire.

In the first place, we pray and beseech you, Our Venerable Brethren, to continually beg of God, that he would strengthen our weakness: it is a return of kindness which we have a right to claim from you. Pray for our wants, as we do for yours, to the end that mu-

---

* Matt. xvi. 19.   † John xxi. 17.   ‡ Heb. xii. 2.

tually supporting one another, we may be the stronger, and the more watchful. We will prove by the unity of hearts, that Unity by which all of us together make only one and the same body; for the whole Church is one Edifice, the foundations of which were laid by the Prince of the Apostles. Many stones are joined together to construct it; but all rest upon a single one, which is Jesus Christ himself.

Intrusted, as his Vicar, with the administration of his power, we are, by his will, raised to the most eminent place.; but you, united with us, as with the visible Head of the Church, are the principal parts of this same body. Nothing can happen to any of us, but the others must be affected by it; as there is nothing which can concern you, but what is an object of our solicitude. Wherefore, in perfect concord, animated with the same spirit, which flowing from the supreme Head, and spreading through all the members gives them life, we ought principally to labour, that the whole body of them may be found and entire, and that, without *wrinckles or spots*,* it may flourish by the practice of all Christian virtues. This we may attain by the divine assistance, if each, according to his power, be inflamed with zeal for the defence of the flock entrusted to him, if each apply with care to secure them from all seduction, and to procure them solid instructions, and the proper means of sanctifying themselves.

There never was a time, wherein it was more necessary to watch over the salvation of souls. Each day sees opinions, the most capable of overthrowing all Religion, spread every where, and crouds of people suffer themselves to be seduced by the bait of Novelty. It is a mortal poison, which pervades all ranks, and causes the most cruel havock.

A fresh motive this, our venerable Brethren, to labour with more ardour than ever, in repressing that madness, which audaciously attacks the most sacred laws, and insults even the Divinity himself.

You will succeed in this glorious enterprize, not by the aids of human wisdom, but by the simplicity of the

* *Eph.* v. 27.

word of God, *sharper than a two-edged sword.** You will repel without difficulty, all the attacks of the enemy; you will easily blunt all his darts, when you present in your discourses nothing but JESUS CHRIST *and him crucified.*† He built his Church, that Holy City, and has strengthened it with his laws and ordinances. He has entrusted to it the Faith he came to establish on Earth, as a *depositum*, which it is religiously to preserve in its utmost purity. It was his will that she should be the inexpugnable rampart of his doctrine, and of his truth, and that the *gates of hell should never prevail against her*‡. As we are appointed to govern and guard this holy City, let us, Venerable Brethren, carefully preserve the precious inheritance of the Faith of our holy Founder, and divine Master, which our Fathers have transmitted down to us entire, that we in the same manner may transmit it to our descendants. If our actions and counsels be agreeable to the rule consigned in the sacred books, if we walk in the steps of our Forefathers, which cannot mislead us, let us be assured that we shall have strength enough to avoid every false step capable of weakening the faith of the Christian people, or of hurting in any point the Unity of the Church. Let us draw only from scripture and tradition, what it concerns us to know and observe; they are the sacred sources of divine wisdom, and in them is found whatever we are obliged to believe and practise: whatever concerns the worship of God, the discipline of the Church, the rules of a good life, are found in that two-fold depository. We shall there see the depth of our sublime Mysteries, the duties of piety, the rules of justice and humanity. We shall there learn what we owe to God, to the Church, to our country, to our neighbour, and be sensible that there are no laws which better establish the rights of Nations and of Society, than true Religion. And in fact never was the doctrine of JESUS CHRIST attacked without disturbing the public tranquillity of nations, infringing on the obedience

* *Heb.* iv. 12.   † 1 *Cor.* ii. 2.   ‡ *Matt.* xvi. 18.

due

due to sovereigns, and spreading every where trouble and confusion.

Such is the connection between the rights of the divine Majesty, and those of Earthly Princes, that, when the laws of Christianity are observed, the sovereign is obeyed without reserve, his power is respected, and his person beloved.

We therefore exhort you, Venerable Brethren, as far as in us lies, to frequently inculcate into the minds of the people entrusted to you, obedience and submission towards the sovereigns; for, among other commandments of God, this is specially necessary for the maintenance of Order and Peace. Kings were raised to the eminent rank they enjoy, for no other end, but to watch over the safety and security of the public, and to keep men within the bounds of wisdom and equity. They are the Ministers of God to see justice observed, and they bear the sword only to execute the vengeance of God, by punishing every one, who swerves from his duty.* They are moreover the dearest sons of the Church, and its Protectors; and it belongs to them to maintain its rights, and defend its interests. Take care, therefore, that the very children be taught, as soon as they are susceptible of reason, that fidelity to the sovereigns is to be inviolably observed, that their authority is to be submitted to, their laws obeyed, not only through fear of punishment, but from an obligation of conscience.†

When you have by your application and zeal thus disposed the minds of subjects to obey the Kings, to respect and love them with their whole hearts, then will you have laboured efficaciously in promoting the tranquility of the Citizens and the interest of the Church; for the one is inseparable from the other. But to acquit yourselves of this duty, so as to insure an infallible success, you will join to the prayers which you daily say for your people, particular prayers for the Kings, to obtain from God their preservation, their prosperity, and the grace necessary to govern with justice and equity.

By thus labouring for the happiness of all men, you will worthily fulfil the functions of your holy Ministry;

* *Rom.* xiii. 4. † *D.* xiii. 5.

for it is meet and just, that *Pontiffs established for men in what concerns the worship of God,** should present to God the vows of all the Faithful, beseeching the Lord without intermission, that he would support and strengthen him who watches over the public tranquility, and safety of all the Citizens.

It would undoubtedly be superfluous to recall here to your memories, all the other obligations, which the Pastoral dignity imposes on you. You perfectly know all the duties which the Christian Religion exacts, as you live in the practice of every virtue: for you fail not continually to have before your eyes, JESUS CHRIST himself our Head, the Prince of all Pastors, and to exhibit in your own persons a perfect model of charity, sanctity and humility. Our labours, our thoughts, cannot have a more glorious and excellent object than him, who being the *brightness of the glory of his Father, and the figure of his substance,*† has vouchsafed to raise us to the quality of children of God by adoption, and to make us his co-heirs. It is the way to preserve the union and alliance of men with JESUS CHRIST, and to imitate that divine model of patience, meekness, and charity. Hence it is said: *Get thee up upon a high mountain, thou that bringest good tidings to Sion.*‡

If you have an ardent desire to comply with these duties, it is impossible but that holy ardour must pass from your hearts into those of the faithful, and that they be vehemently inflamed: for the example of a Pastor has an astonishing efficacy and force to move the hearts of the faithful, intrusted to his care. When they observe all his actions regulated by the model of true virtue; when they see him avoid whatever has the appearance of cruelty, pride or haughtiness; that he is quite taken up with works inspired by a motive of charity, mildness, humility; they will then find themselves strongly animated to follow such wonderful and edifying examples.

When people are convinced that a Pastor forgets himself, in order to become useful to others, that he

* *Heb.* v. 1. † *Ib.* i. 3. ‡ *If.* xl. 9.

takes a pleasure in assisting the indigent, in comforting the afflicted, in teaching the ignorant; that he delights in helping them by his good offices and by his counsels; in a word, when ever he shews himself perfectly disposed to lay down his life for the salvation of his people: then every one, struck with his virtues, and moved by his example, enters into himself, and amends his faults. But if on the other hand a Pastor, attached solely to his own interest, prefer the goods of this world to those of heaven, how can he persuade his flock to love God alone, and render mutual aid and assistance to one another? If he sigh after riches, pleasures and honours, how can he inspire others with a contempt for them? If he love pomp, if he be puffed up with pride, how can he persuade others to the practice of meekness and humility?

Since therefore, Venerable Brethren, you are under an obligation of forming the people according to the maxims of JESUS CHRIST, your first duty is to live in that holiness, that meekness, that innocence of manners, of which he has given us an example. Be assured that you will never make a worthy use of your authority, but by choosing rather to give proofs of your modesty and charity, than in displaying the marks of your dignity. Lay it down as a first principle, that if you scrupulously acquit yourselves of the duties imposed on you, glory and happiness will be heaped upon you; and on the contrary if you neglect them, you will be covered with shame, and will lay up for yourselves the greatest evils. Desire therefore no other riches, than to gain to God the souls he has redeemed with his own blood: seek no other glory, than that of consecrating yourselves entirely to the Lord, that you may incessantly labour to extend his worship, increase the beauty of his house, extirpate vices, and cultivate virtues. Such ought to be the only object of your thoughts, your desires, your actions, your ambition. And think not, Venerable Brethren, that after having spent a long time in painful labours, there will nothing more remain to exercise your virtue. Such is the nature of our Ministry, such the

condition

condition of a Bishop, that he is never to see the term of his solicitude and cares; he never can allow himself any rest; for they, whose charity ought to know no bounds, ought not to set any to their activity. The expectation of an eternal recompense is very capable of sweetening all our pains.

Ah! What can appear hard to those, who never lose sight of that ineffable happiness, which the Lord will bestow on such as have faithfully guarded and increased his flock, when he comes to demand an account of their administration? Besides this so precious and so pleasing a hope, you will experience in the midst of the very toil of an Episcopal life, such joys and comforts, as cannot be expressed. When God seconds our endeavours, we see the people, intimately united by the bands of a reciprocal charity, distinguish themselves by their innocence, candour and piety: we see a quantity of excellent fruit which our watchings, our fatigues, our sweat have produced in the field of the Church.

Oh that we could, by an unanimous concert of will, zeal, application, Oh that we could, our most dear and Venerable Brethren, revive in the time of our Apostolate, this flourishing state of Religion, and restore it to the full beauty of its first age! Oh, that we could felicitate you, and rejoice with you in the Lord on that occasion! May he, that God of Mercy, vouchsafe to support us by the assistance of his grace, and fill our hearts with whatever is well-pleasing to him!

As a pledge of our love, we give to you, with all possible affection, and to all the faithful of your Churches, our Apostolic benediction.

Rome, at St. Mary-Major's, the 12th of December, in the year of Christ 1769, and the first of our Pontificate.

A LETTER

To Lewis XV, the Most Christian King, on Irreligion.

WE know nothing more proper to inflame your zeal, than the motive which engages us to write to you. This letter regards not our perfonal Intereſt, but the intereſt of Religion. If we be ſure of your Royal protection for ourſelves, we have much more room to believe that you will grant it to our earneſt entreaties, which have no other object, than the advantage of the Church.

It is the common cauſe of God, and of Chriſtianity, which we lay before you, our moſt beloved Son in Jesus Christ. We ſee, not without the deepeſt ſorrow, the public worſhip eſtabliſhed by the ſupreme Legiſlator, attacked, for a long time paſt, by impious men, who ceaſe not aiming at it the ſacrilegious darts of their perverſe wit. One would ſay, that they had formed a general conſpiracy to entirely overthrow, by the moſt audacious attempts, whatever is moſt venerable and moſt ſacred. They bluſh not daily to publiſh heaps of writings (eternal monuments of their folly) in order to deſtroy the firſt principles of Morality, to break aſunder the bands of all ſociety, to ſeduce ſimple ſouls, by the baneful talent they have of ſpreading abroad and propagating their perverſe opinions.

The aſtoniſhing rapidity of their progreſs perſuades us, that there is not a concern of greater importance, or more preſſing, than to oppoſe a mound againſt this torrent.

It is not enough to take out of the hands of the Readers the poiſonous works which iſſue every day from that horrible ſchool; it is moreover neceſſary that the zeal of our Venerable Brethren, the Biſhops, ſhould come to our aſſiſtance; ſo that uniting our forces, we may, with common conſent, engage the different enemies of Religion, and defend it from the inſults daily offered it.

We see, on this occasion, with an inexpressible joy, that the Prelates of your Majesty's vast and flourishing Empire (who are now assembled at *Paris* for the affairs of the Clergy) enter perfectly into our views, and that their pastoral solicitude engages them to use every means of stopping the ravages of Infidelity. We have a firm confidence, that by labouring, as they are going to do, for the cause of God, they will receive abundantly the spirit of *Counsel* and *Fortitude*. It is no small comfort to us to see them, of their own accord, apply themselves, with so much ardour, to the fulfiling so important a duty.

But if they stand in need of the protection of the Most High, they have also a right to expect from you, our most dear son, the necessary succours for seconding their labours, and crowning them with success. We therefore, to the utmost of our power, beseech you to favour them in whatever they do for the good of Religion, and to support them with vigour. They will then give effectual proofs of the zeal that animates them, not only for the salvation of the faithful, but also for the temporal advantage of their country, and your Majesty's sacred person: for as RELIGION is the strongest support of Thrones, the nations who obey God, are most easily kept within the bounds of that obedience which is due to Kings.

Hence it easily appears, that our cares and solicitude tend no less to the strengthening of your Majesty's royal Authority, than to the maintaining the interests of God. Human Societies are more indebted for their preservation and security to the exercise of the true worship of God, and to the stability of the revealed Doctrines, than to the force of arms and abundance of riches.

The true means of drawing down on your sacred Person, on the Princes and Princesses of your blood, the most precious effects of the divine mercy, is publicly to maintain Faith and Piety in their purity. Thus will you possess, in an eminent degree, the art of reigning, that art by which your Ancestors ever shewed themselves MOST CHRISTIAN KINGS; and you will support

port your own glory and their's, by inceffantly adding thereto, after their example, the brighteft marks of your own Religion.

This fubject, no doubt, would require to be treated by us more at large; but the high opinion we have of your truly Royal Piety makes us confider any longer difcourfe on this fubject as fuperfluous.

In a firm confidence, that your Majefty will grant what we afk with equal zeal and juftice, We beg of the Almighty, by whom you reign, long to preferve you, as well as your Auguft family, and we impart to you, with all the tendernefs of which we are capable, our Apoftolic Benediction. May it be a happy prefage of the grace and happinefs we wifh you!

Roma, March 21, 1770.

A LETTER

To Madame Louisa of France.

CLEMENT XIV

To our dearly beloved Daughter in Jesus Christ, health.

THE moft painful labours of the Apoftolate, with which we are invefted, appear to be fweet and light, fince we were informed of your holy and generous refolution. You could not have undertaken any thing more grand, any thing more fublime, than to exchange the pomp of a Royal Court for the low and abject ftate of living in a Nunnery. Whether we confider the pious condefcenfion of our moft dear Son in Jesus Christ, Lewis, your Auguft Father, the Moft Chriftian King, who allows you to accomplifh fuch a facrifice; or whether we confider the precious advantages which muft hence accrue for the good of the Church, we cannot contain our joy and admiration.

May forever thanks be rendered to God, the Author of all good, for having vouchfafed to fet, in your perfon, fo ftriking an example to all Princes and Nations;

tions; for having been pleased to consecrate our Pontificate by so glorious an æra: It is a subject of felicitation both for us and you. Ah! How could we help being in raptures at the sight of those abundant riches, which the Lord has just heaped on you, and of that divine fortitude, which, after the most mature deliberation, has engaged you to embrace a kind of life, which may be called a sketch of heaven? No other but God himself could inspire you with so generous a design. You learned, by the favour of his light, that all the grandeur of the world is no more than a thin vapour; that all its pleasures are only illusions; that all its promises are only lies; in a word, that the soul can find its peace only in the sweet exercise of the love of God, and that it is by serving him alone, that you can reign.

It is now, in the port you are in, that, removed from all danger of rocks or shipwreck, you are going to enjoy the most delightful tranquility, to taste more than ever those holy and divine pleasures, which are the lot of the servants of God. When we know how to triumph over the world, we possess the greatest riches in the midst of want. We find true liberty, by renouncing ourselves, true grandeur and glory in the abasing practices of the most profound humility. Nothing is comparable to the happiness of concentering all our thoughts, all our desires in the bosom of God; of living with him alone; of being inflamed with his love; of having no other hope than of possessing him for ever.

Let your courage encrease, our most dear Daughter, in proportion to the graces which the Lord so abundantly pours out upon you. Persevere, with all your might, in the noble design which you have formed, of aiming and arriving at sanctity. Think continually on him, whom you have proposed to yourself, as the object of your love, and whom you have taken the resolution to serve all the days of your life: reflect with yourself, that the object of your desires is infinite, and that the fruits you look for, are incorruptible. Thus will you change your labours into delight, and enjoy a foretaste of our heavenly country.

The more we reflect on the generous step you have just taken, the more we rejoice in hope that this glorious example may excite in many others a desire of following it. You will not fail calling to mind, that as the King, your affectionate Father, has sacrificed even the pleasure he had of living with you, that he might not oppose your vocation, you also must do every thing to testify a just return. The only way to acquit yourself of this obligation, is continually to beg of God his happiness both in this life and the next.

Your zeal for the Church, which is well known to us, as also your respectful attachment to the Holy See, are fresh motives of joy and consolation: for we are persuaded that you will uninterruptedly represent to God both our particular wants, and those of Religion. We offer you in return for these good offices, every advantage you can expect from our paternal kindness. Nothing can come up to the extreme desire we have of seconding your pious intentions, and favouring the fervour with which you march on in the paths of virtue. Wherefore, although we are thoroughly convinced of your zeal and perseverance, we grant to your Confessor, both present and future, a power to mitigate your Rule, or even to dispense with you from it, in every case, where the weakness of your constitution is not correspondent to your courage. We grant you moreover, in virtue of our Apostolic authority, a plenary and complete Indulgence* every time you approach the

---

* " Whenever God remits the guilt of sin, he remits at the same time the eternal punishment due to sin, but he requires some temporal punishment, in order to keep us to our duty. This temporal punishment consists in those penitential and laborious practices which we perform in a spirit of sorrow and humility, and the performing of them is called *satisfaction* or *Canonical penances*. When in consideration of the fervour of the Penitents, and of other good works prescribed, the Church remits any of these penitential works, this remittance is called an *Indulgence*." Bossuet's *Exposition of the Cath. Doctrine*, §. 98. *of Satisfaction, Purgatory, and Indulgences*. Here is nothing in all this that has the least appearance of giving leave to commit sin, or of purchasing the remission of sin by money—A truly uncharitable suggestion!

Holy Table; and the further to teftify to you our affection, we grant the fame to all our holy Daughters in Jesus Christ, your worthy companions, and we render them partakers with you of our Apoftolic Benediction.

Given at Rome, May 9, 1770, the firft year of our Pontificate.

A Second LETTER

To Lewis XV. *the moft Chriftian King, on occafion of* Madame Louisa's *taking the Habit.*

To our moft dear Son in Jesus Christ, health.

IT is juft that at the fame time when we write to our dearly beloved Daughter in Jesus Christ, the Princefs Louisa-Maria, to congratulate her on her great facrifice, we fhould alfo pour forth our joy into your Majefty's paternal bofom. You caufe in us the greateft tranfports of joy, in as much as you have the greateft fhare in an action fo glorious and fo wonderful; but what fills our heart with infinite fatisfaction is, that after having applauded the generous determination of your auguft Daughter, you fhould moreover fhew an extraordinary courage and refolution in parting with her, notwithftanding the valuable qualifications, which made her fo dear to you. When you heard the voice of Religion, you ftifled the cry of nature, and you no longer faw any other in her, who was your beloved Daughter, than a future fpoufe of Jesus Christ. Thus did you yourfelf open the way of heaven to a pious Princefs, who earneftly defired to enter thereon, and, by your generous confent, you contributed to the placing her, where fhe will be fheltered from the dangers which furround human life, and the boifterous waves which agitate it.

I fee her, from that facred retreat fhe has chofen, teaching the whole world, that there is nothing more frail

frail and more vain than all the delights, and all the grandeurs of this life: that it is necessary to consider them only as so many rocks and shelves, and the more so, as they become the lamentable causes of a multitude of evils, by hindering the acquisition of an eternal happiness.

The share you have in so glorious an action, ought to afford you the greatest confidence in the prayers of your Illustrious Daughter. She will not cease recommending to the Lord your august person, your Royal family, your whole Kingdom, and what must interest your Majesty the most of all, the salvation of your soul. It is a powerful intercession, which you have procured for yourself with the Almighty. It is therefore of the greatest concern for you to reap all possible fruit from an event, which providence has permitted for your good.

We wish, with all the fulness of our heart, that you would receive these testimonies of our attachment, as the sweet overflowings of the affection of a Father, who tenderly loves you, and who is no less zealous for your glory and happiness, than he is for his own. To convince you of this, we give you with all possible affection, Most dearly beloved son, our Apostolic Benediction, as an indubitable proof of the singular love, &c.

Given at Rome, May 9, 1770, the first year of our Pontificate.

A THIRD LETTER

To Lewis XV, on the same subject.

AFTER felicitating your Majesty by our letter of the 9th of May, on the heroic courage with which your august Daughter was going to embrace the Religious state of life; after having testified to her the whole fulness of our joy on that occasion, we could not help expressing again to you our raptures and transports at the approach of such a sacrifice. Her zeal is so ardent, that it can bear no delay, and she finds herself
inflamed

LETTER II. *to* MADAME LOUISA.

inflamed with a defire of feeing herfelf cloathed in the holy habit of the Carmelite Nuns, by the hands of our Venerable Brother, BERNARDIN, Archbifhop of *Damafcus*, our *Nuncio* in Ordinary with your Majefty. As foon as ever we were informed of her generous defign, we were fenfible that the fpirit of God acted in a moft wonderful manner on the foul of that auguft Princefs; and we felt ourfelves preffed with the greateft defire to go and perform in perfon, the ceremony of giving the habit, which our *Nuncio* is to perform, to add thereby to the glory and celebrity of fo great a day. As the diftance of places rendered the thing impoffible; we, in part, accomplifh our defire, by charging the *Nuncio*, our aforefaid dear Brother, with that auguft function: We fhall feem, in fome fort, to affift thereat ourfelves, and to lead our moft dear Daughter in JESUS CHRIST to the nuptials of her divine fpoufe. We entreat you to allow of the letters which we have fent for that purpofe to the *Nuncio*, who is to reprefent us; and we perfuade ourfelves that you will acquiefce thereto the more eafily, as thefe difpofitions arife folely from our zeal and affection for your Majefty.

Receive, as an undoubted pledge of thefe fentiments, and as a happy prefage of divine bleffings, our Apoftolic Benediction. We give it you with all the tendernefs of a Father, as well as to all your Auguft Children, and efpecially to the Auguft Princefs, who is the memorable fubject of our common joy.

Given at Rome, July 18, 1770, *the fecond year of our Pontificate.*

A SECOND LETTER

To MADAME LOUISA *of* FRANCE.

To our moft dear Daughter, health.

THE moft glorious and moft fortunate day of your life at laft approaches; the day on which, by the tighteft and moft facred bands, you are going to become the spouse of Jesus Christ himself, and to consecrate to him all your actions, all your desires, and all your thoughts.

We were transported with joy, and applauded your magnanimity from the time, when, trampling under foot the vanities of the world, you renounced all the delights of the most brilliant Court, to confine yourself to the obscurity of a Cloister, and there serve an apprenticeship to a life the most humble and most mortified; but your public profession, by which you are going to render heaven and earth witnesses of your generous sacrifice, compleats our joy. Never forget that the Lord, when he called you from the bosom of Grandeur to live in the shade of the cross, marked you with the zeal of the predestinate. The higher the rank you occupied in the world, the more signalized is this mercy, and the more ought your soul to be penetrated with love and gratitude.

All the days set apart for the public rejoicings of the world have nothing in them comparable to this great day, on which, docile to the inspirations of grace, you are going to abandon yourself entirely to the conduct of God, and take him in a solemn manner for your inheritance.

Oh! Had it pleased heaven, our most dear Daughter, that it had been possible for us to have assisted in person at that ceremony, and to have been, not only a witness, but the Minister also of so heroic a sacrifice! But though that honour be denied us, we will nevertheless enjoy it, as much as possible, by ordering our *Nuncio* in ordinary, our Venerable Brother, the Archbishop of *Damascus*, to represent our person. It was by his hands we gave you the sacred habit; and by his hands we will also receive your vows; and, that nothing may be wanting to the solemnity of so great a day, we charge him to impart to you all the treasures of the Church.

We doubt not but you will answer all the marks of our paternal tenderness, by advancing more and more in the career you have entered, by the constant practice of all the virtues, especially that of humility. That virtue will teach you, that you have nothing of your own in which you can glory; that you have received all from God; that you are continually to distrust your own strength, not to rely on your own merits, but only on his almighty grace, and to think yourself, at the same time, capable of every thing, through him, who strengthens you, having recourse without ceasing to his infinite mercy.

These sentiments, deeply engraved on your soul, will spread a Christian modesty over your whole exterior; and, in the shade of this humility, the divine love will take root in your heart, and send forth the most useful and abundant fruits.

It is not by way of advice that we speak to you in this manner, thinking as we do, that you stand not in need of any; but to enhance to you the value of that state of life to which God has called you.

You will most undoubtedly make it a capital duty to testify, on every occasion, the most lively gratitude to your August Father, that Father who loves you so tenderly, and has done every thing for you. You will never cease begging of God that he would preserve him, prosper his Kingdom and his August family, and above all, that he grant him eternal happiness.

As to us, if we may be allowed to claim the rights which our paternal tenderness gives us, we conjure you to draw down on our person (as being your Father in Jesus Christ) the favourable looks of the Lord, and to pray continually for the Church intrusted to our solicitude and care. Now that you are more intimately united to him, you ought to interest yourself more than ever, in what concerns its advantage and glory. Be you persuaded on your part that we will continually pray to God that he may bless your pious resolutions, and that he may make you advance more and more in his love.

Receive, as a pledge of our paternal affection, our Apostolic Benediction; we give it you with our whole

heart,

heart, as also to the whole Order of the *Carmelites*, to which you are going to be for ever associated.

> Given at Rome, at St. Mary-Major's, under the Fisherman's ring, Aug. 14, 1771, the third year of our Pontificate.

A LETTER

To Monseigneur BERNARDIN GIRAULT, *Archbishop of Damascus, and Nuncio at the Court of the Most Christian King.*

Venerable Brother, Health and Apostolic Benediction.

WE are informed that the Princess LOUISA-MARIA of FRANCE, our dearly beloved Daughter in JESUS CHRIST, who has retired to the Monastery of the discalceated *Carmelites* of St. *Denis*, most ardently desires to embrace their holy Institute, and the more completely to satisfy her devotion, she is to receive the habit from your hands, you being the superior of the Order.

When I represent to myself that Princess, born in the midst of pleasures and Grandeur, in a word, born in the most brilliant Court of the whole Universe, consecrating herself to a most austere and retired life, I cannot but at once admire and acknowledge the impression of the Holy Spirit, which may be called a miracle *of the most High*. We are penetrated thereby in so lively a manner, that, to answer the inexpressible sentiments of the zeal which animates us, and the joy which transports us, we charge you to perform that Ceremony in our name.

Therefore to give that sacred and celebrious function all the splendor it deserves, and all the solemnity it is susceptible of, we, in an especial manner, depute you, our Venerable Brother, and commission you to perform it in our name.

We shall be the more interested in this, as we shall imagine ourselves to be present, and to see with our own eyes those holy transports, with which our most beloved Daughter in Jesus Christ will confecrate herself with her whole heart to her heavenly spouse.

Desiring moreover to encrease the common joy of the Order, and to render it more complete, by imparting to all the Nuns who compose that Order, the spiritual treasures of the Church, by an effect of our benevolence, we grant plenary Indulgences to all the *discalceated Carmelite* Nuns of the Kingdom of *France*, who on the day that she takes the habit, shall receive the sacraments of penance and of the Eucharist, and implore the clemency of the Almighty for the exaltation of the Holy Catholic Church, for our most dearly beloved Son in Jesus Christ, Lewis the Most Christian King of France, for the Royal family, and particularly for the Princess, who is this day the subject of our joy, and who is going to enter on the noviciate of a state of life the most austere, and the most holy, to the end that being enriched, day by day, with new graces, she may become more the ornament of her Order by the regularity of her life, than by the splendour of her name; and we charge you, our Venerable Brother, speedily to inform all who may be concerned, of the salutary favour we kindly grant them; and as a mark of our Pontifical benevolence, we give you, &c.

Rome, July 18, 1770, *the second year of our Pontificate.*

To the Most Christian King.

To our most dearly beloved Son in Jesus Christ, Health.

WHenever we think of your Illustrious Daughter, Louisa-Maria of France, who is also our Daughter in Jesus Christ, we bless God for having inspired her with so holy a resolution: we have constantly

stantly before our eyes, the great example she sets to the whole world; an example, which is an honour to the present age, and will be the admiration of Posterity. The more the moment of the sacrifice draws nigh, the more we redouble our prayers, and the more we desire to pour forth into your heart the sentiments which attach us to your person, in paying you the tribute of praise justly due to you for the share you have in the great event, of which the Church is going to be witness.

You could undoubtedly have done nothing better, than to secure to yourself a support in the prayers and vows of her, who is totally devoted to your person, and so well-pleasing to God. In that your wisdom and religion equally shine forth; and we are thereby persuaded, that the divine Goodness will enable you to reap the greatest advantage from so favourable an event. We fecilitate you thereon with our whole heart, and we congratulate ourselves that our connection with our most dearly beloved Daughter in Jesus Christ is soon to become stricter than ever. It would be our most ardent wish to tighten these knots still faster by presiding ourselves at the Ceremony which we see drawing near, and receiving in our hands the solemn vows which the most tender and affecting piety is going to pronounce.

This wish penetrates us the more, as that would be the happiest opportunity for us of discoursing with you, of embracing you, and of shewing in our countenance and in our eyes the sentiments with which you inspire us. Then our paternal tenderness, and our pastoral charity fully displayed, would assure you, in the strongest manner, of the whole extent of our affection. But alas! We are unhappily reduced to enjoy this satisfaction only in idea.

As to every other advantage, we have endeavoured to procure them for ourselves, in spite of our absence, by making choice of our Venerable Brother the Archbishop of *Damascus*, to supply our place, having given him, for that effect, the most special and ample powers, as we did before, when we charged him with the representation of our person at the taking of the habit.

Informed

Informed as we are, that your Majesty was then satisfied with the manner in which we ordered our August Princess's taking the habit, we flatter ourselves, that you will equally approve of the same orders and dispositions on this occasion.

We therefore earnestly intreat you to second our views with your usual goodness, by allowing us the consolation of seeing our place again supplied by him who represents us. Receive, as the best proof we can give you of our attachment, our Apostolic Benediction, which, like a pledge of the blessings of heaven, will extend to all your August Race, and your whole Kingdom, if our vows are heard.

Given at Rome, at St. Mary-Major's, under the Fisherman's ring, Aug. 14, 1771, the third year of our Pontificate.

A LETTER
To the DUKE of PARMA.

IT would be very difficult for us to express all the joy your letter gave us, as in it we found the sentiments of the most tender affection. We are the more pleased with receiving at this time the marks of your friendship, as we always were sincerely attached to you, and ever uninterruptedly interested ourselves in whatever concerned you.

We felicitate ourselves at the same time, for your having received, with all possible kindness, the testimony of our friendship, with regard to the illustrious young shoot, who will one day inherit your virtues, and the marks of our gratitude, for the ardour with which you laboured to reconcile us with the most Christian King. By that you crowned your piety towards the Holy See, and took a step equally glorious and meritorious. The mediation which you are to employ with our dearly beloved Sons in JESUS CHRIST, those most virtuous Kings, your Grandfather,[*] Uncle[†] and Cousin,[‡]

[*] Lewis XV.   [†] King of Spain.   [‡] King of Naples.

to engage them to efface the smallest traces of all past misunderstandings, and to restore to us the territories of *Avignon, Benevento* and *Porto-Corvo*, cannot fail being very efficacious. You did us justice, when you appeared convinced of our extreme love for peace and concord, particularly with the August Sovereigns of the house of Bourbon, who have always deserved so well of us, of the Chair of St. *Peter*, and of the Church in general. We never doubted but that the religion and piety of those Princes, would inspire them with the pacific dispositions, we ourselves had. We conceive the greater hopes from your mediation, on account of your royal virtues, and the love your August Relations justly bear you. They will be the more earnest to second your good designs, as they will be pleased to see peace and harmony arise from the very source, from whence had proceeded the subject of misunderstanding and disunion. We will, by way of return, take every opportunity of proving in the most conspicuous manner, our gratitude and affection. We give to you, with all the tenderness of a paternal heart, our Apostolic Benediction, as we also give it to your virtuous spouse, and to your dear new-born son; and we pray Almighty God to encrease from day to day your virtues, and to bring you to that glory which he reserves for his Elect.

A Second LETTER *to the same.*

AS soon as we were informed of the care and pains you had taken to reconcile us with the Monarchs, our dearly beloved sons in Jesus Christ, and to reinstate the Apostolic See in its ancient possessions, we resolved to return you our most sincere thanks. Since, by your wisdom, you have accomplished that great work, we will make our joy and gratitude break forth: We assure you that we never will forget that generous step, which procured us the most signal benefits, and that the paternal tenderness we bear you, is equal to your rare virtues. We therefore wish you, with all the fulness of

our

our foul, whatever can contribute to your glory and happiness. The Marquis of Laso, for whom we have a tender affection on account of his merit, and the services he has rendered us, must have informed you of our sentiments with regard to you. To cement these sentiments still more and more, we continually pray to the Lord to second, by the abundance of his heavenly gifts, the Apostolic Benediction with which we gratify you, as the most certain pledge of our affection, &c.

A BRIEF

To our beloved Son Peter-Francis Boudier, *Superior General* [*] *of the Benedictine Monks of the Congregation of St. Maurus.*

CLEMENT XIV.

Our dear Son, Health and Apostolic Benediction.

YOUR Letter, which was dictated by respect, attachment, and the most tender love, shews the extent of the joy which you and your Congregation felt at our Exaltation to the Sovereign Pontificate. But we knew before that time your sentiments with regard to the Apostolic See, and the fresh testimony you have given us, serves less to prove those sentiments, than to assure us of them more and more.

We were therefore sensibly affected by these demonstrations of your zeal, the value of which you and your Congregation have enhanced, by beseeching, as you do, the Father of Mercies to support and strengthen our weakness by his powerful assistance, in the discharge of so important an employ.

As to the judgment you form respecting our person, we only see it in your indulgence, your filial love, and the ardent zeal which animates you towards us. On our side, we earnestly wish for an opportunity of testifying

[*] This Gentleman is now Grand-Prior of the Royal Abbey of St. Denis.

in an obliging manner the kindness we bear you and those who are in subjection to you. In the mean time, we give, as a pledge of our paternal tenderness, to you and to all yours, with all the effusion of our heart, our Apostolic Benediction.

> *Given at Rome, at St. Mary-Major's, under the Fisherman's ring, Aug. 11, 1769, and the first year of our Pontificate.*

BENEDICT STAY.

A BRIEF

To our dear Son BODDAERT, *Prior-General of the Order of the Guillelmites.*

CLEMENT XIV.

Our dear Son, Health and Apostolic Benediction.

THE joy you testify to us on our coming to the Sovereign Pontificate, corresponds with the attachment your Order has had for us now this long time. We doubt not, but that, to these exterior marks of your zeal, you join the succour of your prayers to Almighty God, that he would vouchsafe to support our weakness; and in consequence of this persuasion, we earnestly beg the continuation of them, as an effect of your charity towards us. As to our sentiments with regard to you, the proofs we have heretofore given of our kindness, shew sufficiently what you may expect hereafter. Be assured that our new dignity, so far from weakening this kindness, only encreases and augments it; especially after the testimony you give us, that, having visited with care the Monasteries of your Order, you found them faithful to the rules of their Institute. This assurance coming from you afforded us the greatest pleasure, and redoubles the tenderness we had for you: and, as a pledge of it, we grant to you, our dear Son, and to the whole Order entrusted to your care, with all the effusion of our heart, our Apostolic Benediction.

> Given at Rome, at St. Mary-Major's, under the Fisherman's ring, July 9, 1769, and the first year of our Pontificate.
>
> BENEDICT STAY.

A DISCOURSE

Pronounced by CLEMENT XIV, *in a secret Consistory held Sept. 24, 1770, on occasion of the reconciliation of* PORTUGAL *with the Court of* ROME.

IT looks, Venerable Brethren, as if Providence had made choice particularly of the 24th of this month, for me to notify to you the great event, which has brought us together in this place. This same day, the anniversary of my coming to *Rome*, of my elevation to the purple (however unworthy I were of that honour) is also that, on which I announce to you a full and entire reconciliation with PORTUGAL.

We have just received the most sincere and most glorious proofs of the submission and zeal of his MOST FAITHFUL MAJESTY towards us: they have even surpassed our expectations. Not only the ancient customs, and the ancient mutual respect, which have ever subsisted between us and that Court, are renewed, but confirmed in such a manner, as to acquire new strength.

When we foretold what is come to pass, we grounded our hopes on the faith and piety of our most beloved Son in JESUS CHRIST, who at all times has given the most assured marks of his zeal for the true Religion. The day on which we were informed of his reconciliation, has augmented the glory and advantages of the Holy See, filling us at the same time with consolation and joy. There is nothing therefore, which we ought not to do, in order to testify the full extent of our gratitude to his MOST FAITHFUL MAJESTY; nor is there a wish which we ought not to form for his preservation, that of his August and dear Spouse, MARIA-ANNA-VICTORIA, who emulated him in labouring herself with the greatest zeal in bringing about this accommodation. The COUNT d'OYERAS, Secretary of State, is likewise deserving of our gratitude and elogiums, without forgetting the COMMANDER of ALMADA, Plenipotentiary Minister at our Court, and whom we have often heard, with the greatest joy, declare to us the pious and magnanimous sentiments of the MOST FAITHFUL KING. As there are no means more proper to testify our gratitude towards a Prince so worthy of our elogiums, than to pray God that he would pour down his blessings on him; let us entreat him continually to grant us that great favour, &c.

A DISCOURSE
Of CLEMENT XIV, *in a private Consistory held June* 6, 1774, *on the death of* LEWIS XV.

VENERABLE BRETHREN,

IF any thing could afford us comfort in the midst of our painful labours, it was to learn that LEWIS the MOST CHRISTIAN KING had the best intentions, and the greatest attachment to Religion and our Person: But Alas! That comfort is this day become the subject of the most piercing grief. Our life is filled with bitterness ever since the melancholy event of his death, which happened in consequence of a most cruel distemper. Our consternation is the greater, as we have lost him at the moment he just had given us the most shining proofs of his justice, his greatness of soul, and his most tender affection towards us and the Apostolic See. What adds to our affliction is, that we can now discharge, only by our tears and grief, what we owe to him.

Let us however adore the decrees of divine Providence, and while we submit to the orders of the Almighty, on whom absolutely depends the destiny of Kings, let us also acknowledge that every thing is directed by his wisdom, and for his greater glory.

Nothing but thus refigning to the divine will can alleviate our grief. Scarce had we learned the danger which threatened the King's life, but we addreffed our moft fervent prayers to heaven for obtaining his recovery. All *France* then weeping joined with us, and the whole Royal Family, with torrents of tears, performed the fame duty; but above all our deareft beloved Daughter in Jesus Christ, Maria-Louisa of *France*, who from her holy retirement raifed her hands to heaven, and fent forth the deepeft groans.

Though our vows were not heard, we have at leaft a firm hope that our prayers may be of advantage towards the repofe of his foul, and procure him an eternal glory.

Our hopes are grounded on the love he ever had for the Catholic Religion, his attachment to the Holy See, his kind difpofitions towards us, of which he gave us marks to his laft breath; finally on the fincere repentance he teftified in the prefence of the whole Court, begging pardon of God, and of his Kingdom for the errors of his life, and defiring to live for no other end, but to repair them.

The fame prayers which we offered in private for the repofe of his foul, we will perform alfo in public; nor fhall that hinder us from remembering him before God to the laft hour of our own life.

We are to declare to you on this occafion, Our Venerable Brethren, that Lewis-Augustus, our moft dearly beloved Son in Jesus Christ, Grand-fon of the late King, fucceeds to the territories and kingdom of his Grand-father, inheriting at the fame time all the heroic virtues of the auguft houfe of Bourbon.

We are already perfectly acquainted with his zeal and attachment to Religion, as alfo with his filial love towards us. His moving and affectionate letters joined to what fame already every where publifhes of his rare virtues, are the moft convincing proof. Nor have we any thing more at heart, than to correfpond, as far as lies in our power, with fentiments fo commendable.

We are in like manner to inform you, that our Venerable Brother, FRANCIS-JOACHIM, Cardinal de BERNIS, heretofore Minister of the late King in our Court, is confirmed in that post by credentials which he has presented to us. While we shew our entire satisfaction on that account, we see your joy break out, knowing that you are persuaded equally with us, that he is a most faithful Interpreter of both the King's intentions and of our's, in order to maintain the most happy harmony.

Let us, with the most fervent prayers, conjure the Almighty, from whom Kings hold their crown and Empire, to shower down his most abundant blessings on our most dearly beloved Son in JESUS CHRIST, LEWIS-AUGUSTUS King of FRANCE, that he may, during the course of his reign, enjoy every kind of prosperity, and that he may live in a manner equally useful to Religion and advantageous to the illustrious *French* nation.

The BULL
FOR
The UNIVERSAL JUBILEE
of the Year 1775.

CLEMENT, Bishop, servant of the servants of God, to all the Faithful in JESUS CHRIST, who these present shall see, health and Apostolic Benediction.

THE Author of our salvation, JESUS CHRIST our Lord, contented not himself with procuring for mankind, by his passion and death, a deliverance from the ancient slavery of sin, a return to life and liberty, and elevating them to the sublime title of

co-heirs

co-heirs of his glory, and of children of God; but to all these favours he added one of infinite value, designed for those, who dragged away by human weakness, and their own wicked dispositions, should have the misfortune of losing all right to that divine inheritance. By the power which he gave to the Prince of the Apostles of remitting sin, when he committed to him the keys of the Kingdom of heaven*, he procured for sinners the means of expatiating their crimes, of recovering their first righteousness, and of receiving the fruits of their redemption. As this is the only thing they can do, who have departed from the law of the Lord, in order to be admitted again to the friendship of God, and arrive at eternal salvation, the successors of St. Peter, the heirs of his power, never had any thing more at heart, than to invite all sinners to these divine sources of mercy, to offer and promise pardon to true penitents, and lastly to invite to the hopes of remission even those who should be chained down under the most heavy load of their crimes.

Although in the exercise of so important a function, and so necessary for the salvation of mankind, they never interrupted the solicitude of their Apostolic Ministry; they however thought proper to choose and pitch upon, in the succession of ages, certain remarkable *Epochas*, wherein to engage sinners to appease the divine wrath, embrace repentance as the only plank after shipwreck, and this from hopes of a more ample harvest of graces and pardon, and from the public and general liberty of partaking of the treasures of the Indulgences, of which they are the depositaries. And to the end that no generation might be deprived of the precious advantages annexed to this time of releasement, they appointed the renewal of the *Jubilee*, every five and twenty years; which year is the holy year, a year, above others, of grace and pardon, the opening of which they appointed in the City, which is looked upon as the Centre and seat of Religion.

* *Matt.* xvi. 19.

In conformity therefore, to so salutary a custom, and being very near one of those privileged years, we are eager to announce to you all, our Children, who are united in the profession of the same faith with us, and the Catholic, Apostolic and Roman Church; and we exhort you to labour for the salvation of your souls, and to profit by the means of salvation, which may turn out the most efficacious for you. We will make you sharers and partakers of all the riches of the divine goodness and mercy; and in the first place, of those which have their source in the blood of JESUS CHRIST. We will then open to you all the doors of the rich Magazine of satisfactory works, which derive merit from the most Holy Mother of God, the Holy Apostles, the blood of the Martyrs, and the good works of all the saints; so lively and so sincere is our desire to facilitate for you the recovery of peace and reconciliation.

Now nothing can contribute more to this end, than the multitude of succours, which may be expected from the *Communion of Saints.* United to their August company, we altogether compose the body of the Church, which is one indivisible body, and that of JESUS CHRIST himself, whose blood purifies us, restores us to life, and enables us to be of use one to another. For to shew, in a more glorious manner, the immensity of his love and mercy, to render more sensible the infinite force and efficacy of his passion, and of his merits, the Redeemer of mankind has been pleased to make the effects thereof flow on all the members of his mystical body; to the end that they may have every easy means of mutually aiding one another by a communication of succours, and reciprocal advantages. His intention was in this wisely contrived association (the principle of which, is his precious blood, and the union of hearts all the strength) to prevail on the tenderness of the Eternal Father to shew us mercy, by offering him motives the most capable of determining him thereto, viz. the ineffable price of the blood of his son, the merits of his Saints, and the power of their sufferages.

We

We invite you, therefore, to come and drink of this immense canal of indulgence, to enrich yourselves from the inexhaustible treasures of the Church; and according to the practice and institution of our ancestors, with the consent of our Venerable Brethren the Cardinals, &c.

O all ye, who are children of the Church, let not pass this so valuable an opportunity, these days of salvation, without employing them in appeasing the justice of God, and in obtaining pardon. Alledge not in excuse of your delay, either the fatigues of the journey, or the difficulty of the passage. When you are to be enriched with the Largesses of heavenly grace, and to be introduced into the tabernacle of the Lord, would it be fit that you should suffer yourselves to be disheartened by inconveniencies and obstacles, which never frighten those, whom curiosity, or a desire of riches lead every day to the most distant regions? The very labour and difficulties, which you may apprehend, undertaken on so noble a motive, may be of infinite service towards reaping the most abundant fruits from your repentance. And, indeed, the Church has all along regarded, as of singular use, the practice of *Pilgrimages*, being persuaded, that the trouble and inconveniences necessarily attending them, are so many compensations for past sins, and convincing proofs of a sincere repentance. Should the activity of your zeal, the ardour of your love for God inflame you to such a degree, as to make you entirely forget your fatigues, or to diminish them, be not alarmed on that account: that holy joy and alacrity will accelerate your reconciliation, and will even be a principal part of the satisfaction due for your sins, since *much shall be forgiven him, who hath loved much*.[*]

Come, run therefore, to the city of *Sion*; come and feed of the abundance, which reigns in the house of the Lord. Every thing here will draw you to repentance; even the sight of this City, the ordinary abode of Faith and Piety, the sepulcher of the Apostles, the tombs of the Martyrs. When you shall see that ground, which was watered with their blood, when

[*] *Luke* vii. 47.

the numberless vestiges of their sanctity shall on every side present themselves to your sight, it will be impossible for you to hold out against that bitter grief, which you will feel for having gone so far from the rules and laws they followed, and which you had promised to follow as well as they. You will find in the dignity of the divine worship, and in the majesty of the Temples a powerful voice, which will recall to your mind, that you yourselves are the Temple of the living God; and which will encourage you to embellish it with the more ardour, as you had formerly an inclination to profane it, and make sorrowful the Holy Ghost. Lastly, the tears and groans of a great number of Christians, whom you will see deploring their past errors, and begging pardon for them of God, will support your good resolutions. The sentiments of grief and piety, of which you will be witnesses, will slide into your hearts with a facility, that will surprise you.

But the most affecting of all consolations will not fail speedily to follow that holy sorrow, and religious mourning, when you see a multitude of people and nations running in crouds to practise works of repentance and righteousness. In fact, can you ever hope to see a spectacle more pleasing, more enravishing, than that which a moving representation of the glorious triumph of the cross and of Religion presents to the whole earth ? We at least, on our part, shall be at the height of our joy, when there will be an almost general meeting of all the children of the Church ; being persuaded that we shall find for ourselves a superabundance of aid and resources in the mutual efforts of your charity and piety. For we have an entire confidence, that when you join with us, in intreating the supreme distributor of graces to preserve the Faith, to bring back those nations who are separated from its Unity, to bestow tranquillity on the Church, and happiness on the Christian Princes, you will also remember, in your prayers to God, your common Father, who has you all in his heart, and procure, by vows and earnest entreaties, the strength

strength our weakness stands in need of to bear the immense load laid upon it.

As to you, our VENERABLE BRETHREN, PATRIARCHS, ARCHBISHOPS and BISHOPS, share with us in our solicitude; take on yourselves, at one and the same time our functions and your own; publish to the people entrusted to your care this time of repentance and reconciliation. Employ all your care and authority, that this favourable opportunity of obtaining pardon, which our paternal love has offered to the whole Christian world, in conformity with the ancient practice of the Church, may produce the most ample fruit in the salvation of souls. Let them hear you explain what works of humility and Christian charity they are to perform, in order that they may be the better disposed to receive the fruits of that heavenly grace, which is offered to their wants. Let them learn, by your precepts and examples, that they ought particularly to have recourse to fasts, prayers, and almsdeeds.

If there be any among you, our Venerable Brethren, who are willing, over and above their other Pastoral toils, to add that of leading themselves a part of their flock towards the City, which is, as it were, the Fortress of Religion, and from whence will flow the springs of Indulgences, they may promise themselves, that we shall receive them with all the feeling tenderness of a Father. Independant of the lustre they will add to our solemnity, they themselves will be able, after such noble fatigues, and meritorious toils to reap a most ample harvest of the largesses of the divine mercy; and at their return with their flock, they will have the consolation of distributing this precious harvest among them.

Neither can we doubt, but that our dearly beloved Sons, the Emperor, the Kings and all Christian Princes, will aid us by their authority, in the vows we form for the salvation of souls, that they may be crowned with the happy success we expect from them. We therefore exhort them with our whole soul, to concur, in a manner answerable to their love for Religion, with the zeal

of

of our Venerable Brethren the Bishops, to favour their undertakings, and to procure the Pilgrims all safety and convenience on the road. They are not ignorant that such cares cannot fail of contributing much to the tranquillity of their reign; and that God will be the more favourable and propitious to them, in proportion as they shew themselves more attentive to augment his glory among the people.

But to the end that these presents may come to hand, &c.

Given at Rome, at St. Mary-Major's, &c. May 12, the year of Lord 1774, and the fifth of our Pontificate.

CONCLUSION.

THIS Bull, with which I conclude this Collection, may be considered as the last Will and Testament of CLEMENT XIV. Death, which was then working within him, told him his end was drawing near, that he was then speaking to all the Faithful for the last time, and that God demanded of him the sacrifice of his life.

Every one took a share in this misfortune; and all the different Communions, however divided in their belief, united to beg of the Lord the preservation of a Pontiff so agreeable to all the crowned Heads, and dear to the whole world. Some called to mind the kindness with which he had received them; others his prudence and pacific disposition, while, a stranger himself, to the greatness of his sufferings, he employed his intercepted breath in sending up sighs to heaven to obtain on earth the reign of Concord and Truth, and to leave behind him marks of his love for juſtice and peace.

I wiſhed to have ſome of his letters, which he wrote during the ſix laſt months of his life, which were a time of trial and ſufferings, but I could not procure any. We have however enow to convince us, that this great Pontiff was ſincerely attached to what is eſſential in Religion, without being tied down to any ſcholaſtic opinion, and without any ſpirit of party: and certain it is, that no one can refuſe becoming his Panegyriſt but from prejudice, and that Poſterity, which will appreciate him according to his merits, will be ſincerely afflicted for not having known him. There will be then neither paſſions, nor cabals, nor prejudices capable of tarniſhing his glory, and truth alone will draw his portrait.

F I N I S.

A

GENERAL INDEX.

A

	Page.
ADAM and *Eve*, their state before the fall	39
Ages, all cannot be alike	201
Albani (Card.) Ganganelli esteems him	324
Algarotti (Count) Author of the Newtonianism of the Ladies 222. Letters to him 44, 141, 222	
Almada, Commander d', commended by Clement XIV	405
Alpes and *Apennins*, what those mountains are	7
America, a Climate dangerous to the Passions	125
Ancients (The) it is beautiful to come near them in our manner of writing	198
Anthony (St.) why he quitted his desert	3
Antonio (Signor) Card. Ganganelli applies to the Cardinal Datary in his behalf	297
Arcadians (the Academy of) the object of their studies frivolous	184
Augustine (St.) and St. Thomas, lead to the purest sources of Theology 168. The former has never been praised enough 197. How to make his Panegyric ib. The admirable qualities of that Father 321	
Aymaldi (Monsignor) Letters to him	118—226

B

Banchieri (Card.) a Letter to him — 203
Bayle, the mists raised by him and other unbelievers against the Christian Religion long since dispersed — 27
Bazardi (Signora) a Letter to her — 29
Bembo (Card.) what he said to a Philosopher of his time — 334
Benedict (St.) institutes a Seminary for young Gentlemen — 6
——— XIII (Pope) the cause of his uneasiness. See *Coscia*
——— XIV why he enjoyed so good a state of health 22. Gives a lustre to Rome 158. His Elogium 209. Advantages of his treaty with Spain ib. An instance of his cheerful temper 242. His funeral Oration a fine subject to treat 280. Directions for making it ib. Preserves his cheerfulness to the last 284. His work on the Canonization of Saints 285. Always did some kindness to those he had scolded 325
Benedictins (of St. Maur) how they gained so great a reputation 4
Benedictins, importance of their learned works 23. For what most commendable 24. The great men they have produced ib.
Bentivoglio (Card.) what he said of the English — 137
Berkley, an illustrious mad-man — 26
Bernard (St.) in what he rendered himself truly useful — 4
Bernardin Girault (Archbishop of Damascus) a Letter to him 395. Clement XIV's Nuncio at the Court of France 397
Bernis (Card.) the action that immortalizes him 227. As dear to the French as to the Italians 376

Bielk (Count) a Letter to him — — — 170
Birds, those of America, seldom brought alive to our climates 216
Bishops, their studies 153. Their dignity to be dreaded 177. The qualifications they ought to have ib. Their obligations 181
Boddaert (Superior-General of the Guillelmites) a Brief to him 403
Bologna (city of) the sciences cultivated there — — 9
Book, a good one the patrimony of the whole world — 30
Books (French) difference between the last and present age 184
——The sacred, how to be read — — — 113
Borromæo (Card.) breaths charity — — — 324
Bossuet (Mons.) has reduced to powder all the objections of the Protestants in two learned works 211. Is not to be ranked among the Fathers of the Church 320. His Elogium 321
Botari (Monsignor) his character — — 136
Boudier (Superior-General of the Monks of St. Maur) a Brief to him — — — — — 402
Bouget (M.) Chamberlain to Ben. XIV. his amiable qualities 21
Bourbon (House of) its alliance with Austria 216. The happy effects of that alliance ib. Has done great kindnesses to the Holy See 351
Bruere (la) Letter to him — — — 157
Bourdaloue (Father, a Jesuit) a pattern for Preachers 108. His Sermons translated into Italian ib.
Boxadors (Father) chosen General of the Dominicans 241. His character ib.
Braschi (Monsignor, now Pius VI.) his character — 327
Bremond (Father) General of the Dominicans, his character 119
Buffon (Monf.) His natural History praised and blamed by Father Ganganelli — — — — 216
Buona-Fede (the Abbé) his Elogium — — 87
Buonamici, Author of the Compagnes of Don Carlos 114

.C

Cabane (the Chevalier de) Letters to him — — 1, 94
Canillac, a Letter to him — — — — 128
Canonisation of Saints, the severe precautions used in that business at Rome 285. What two English Gentlemen thought of it 286
Capitol, the Metamorphosis there — — — 32
Capuchins, the good they have done 104. Never did any harm ib.
Caraccioli (Monseigneur) Letter to him — — 130
——— (Marquis) Letter to him — — — 343
Cardinals (The Roman) their great affability 297. The design of their institution 304. What ought to regulate their steps 305 Apply to the reading of the Fathers 322
Carrachio, his peculiar talent — — — 225
Carthusians, their institute not to be multiplied 2. The fault of their Priors 122
Celsus, his impotent attack on the Christian religion — 27
Caserta (city of) its beauties — — — 15
Cerati (The Prelate) full of curious Anecdotes 30. Letters to him 30, 52, 127, 136, 196, 241
Charities, the manner of bestowing them — — 133
Charity, (Christian) its first rule — — — 167
Cheerfulness, the balm of life — — — 259

Chris-

GENERAL INDEX.

Christianity, the Ancient Philosophers, who attacked it 27. The only true Religion 328
Church (The) on what its infallibility is grounded 212. No innovations of Faith possible in it ib. Alone has a right to assign a rank to its Writers 321. One only Edifice, of which the Prince of the Apostles laid the foundation 381
———— of Rome, her favourable dispositions with regard to the Protestant Communions — — 299
Clement VII. too precipitate in excommunicating Henry VIII. 306
———— XIII. saw not things in a right light, in his dispute with the Potentates 346. Reasons presented to him, in favour of the Jesuits ib. Those that were not represented to him 347. He ought to have complied with the desires of Lewis XV. respecting Parma 351. A Pontiff worthy of the primitive Ages ib. Guided by his Council 362. His sudden death 367. His excellent qualities 368. Those he wanted ib.
Clerici (the Marquis) a Letter to him — — 31
Cloisters, their value 69. Emulation necessary in them ib. The Fathers of the Church read in them 322
Collius attacks Christianity — — 27
Colloz (Father) a Letter to him — — — 318
Colombini (Father) his Elogium — — 279
Concina (Father) a Letter to him — — 173
Conclave, (The) state of Rome during one — 288
Confessor (The) of a Sovereign Prince, an employment to be dreaded. See Letter 21 — — — 334
Coffee prejudicial to health — — — 298
Corsini (Card.) his character — 297—324
Coscia (Card.) the cause of Benedict XIII. uneasiness 289
Counsel, of whom to be taken — — — 352
Count ***, Letters to him 54, 56, 77, 111, 171, 258, 301
Crescenci (Card.) a Letter to him — — 299

D

Death makes its round night and day — — 343
Dæmonomania, its causes — — 63
Descartes, his system ridiculed — — — — 217
Devotion (True) in what it does not consist 32. In what it does consist 34. Its practices useless without a detachment from the things of this world 327
Direction of souls, a good book on that subject, wanted in Italy — — — 365
Directors generally ruined by the women 364. Some devout one of the sex more attached to them than to God ib. The excellent qualities of him who directed Ganganelli in his youth 365
Disputes in the Church, how they might have been avoided in teaching Theology 168
Doria (Monsignor) Clement XIV. opinion of him — 375
Durini (The Prelate) his character — — 324
D* (Mr.) a Letter to him — — — 316

E

Education of children, Letters on that subject 139, 185
Eloquence, that which is called puerile 191. True, consists neither in wit nor words 197. What it is ib. A defect in Orators, when

when they aim at it ib. Its qualities, and how it differs from
Elegance 198

English (The) travel to advantage 137. Are Enthusiasts of their country 247. Why likely to preserve their liberty 227. Their Philosophers have advanced some extravagant notions 270. Letters to some of that nation 243, 328

Errors that creep into morals to be opposed — — 173
Eternity, reflections on it — — — 201
Evidence in matters of faith, not to be found till after death 166
    Reserved for heaven — — 330

F

Fabrici (Father) a Dominican, his Elogium — — 375
Fantuzzi (Card.) breathes nothing but charity — — 324
Fathers, their fault with regard to the Preceptors of their children
     188
——— (The) of the Church, their writings, models, of Christian Eloquence 319. Their Elogium 320. Speaks only by the organ of Charity 363
Ferghen (Abbè) a Letter to him — — — 7
Ferrara (city of) what is to be seen there 9. Celebrated for great events — — — 203
Firmiani (Bp. of Perugia) a Letter to him — — 135
Fleury (Abbé) passes too slightly over some great events 66. Modestly censured by F. Ganganelli 67. Blamed by the Italians for being too zealous for the Gallican privileges ib. Ganganelli's remark on that censure ib.
Florence (city of) its Elogium 15. Famous for literature 208
Founders of Religious Orders, their designs in their different institutes — — — 95
French (The) have communicated an agreeable elegance to the Italians 200. Are fonder of Literature than of deep learning 253. Given to Literary squabbles ib.
Frescati (city of) a delightful abode — — 46
Friends (True) their resource, when the mind cannot make a return of friendship — — — 156
Friendship, what St. Augustine said of it 138. The greatest Saints have cultivated it — — — ib.

G

Gaillard (Dom.) Letters to him — — — 120, 123
Ganganelli (Father) his letter to one of his sisters 19. Loves the English nation 25. His thoughts on Religion 27. Why unwilling to advise a religious state of life 29. His disinterestedness, as a Religious man 36. Composes a Discourse for a friend 37. Interests himself in the military success of the French 38. His laborious studies and relaxation 39, &c. How he would have a work on Religion written 41. Where he desires to die 45. His favourite science ib. His reflections on the rapidity of time 48. Is overpowered with work 52. Complains of the superficial manner in which people study 54. His Letter to an Abbess 71. Blames puns 106. Desires the reformation of the Breviary 110 Recommends the reading of the Gospel and St. Paul's Epistles 112. His advice to a Religious man setting off for America 114.
    His

His sentiments of humility 136. His advice to a Lady on the Education of her Daughters 139. To a Religious, chosen Bishop 176. To a Father on the Education of his sons 185. Reflections on French Elegance 200. Condemns all hasty censures of a Pope's proceedings 210. Discusses the contested points of Religion with a Protestant Gentleman 212. Refutes the various systems on the formation of the world 218. The plan he would follow in writing Natural History 220. His pleasure in speaking of God 221. His reflections on the destination of our souls 222. His reflections while walking on the banks of the Tiber 228. The object of his labours in his Cell ib. Is visited by the French, and why 229. Justifies the Ecclesiastical Government 244. His advice to a Physician, to live at peace with his wife 248. Prefers his Cell to all the pleasures of the world 250. Describes his way of life 252, 263. How he treats writers 252. What qualities a work ought to have in order to please him 254. His reflections on the Papal dignity 289 : and on Sovereigns 290. His sentiments on being raised to the purple 292 & seq. Desires the reunion of the Protestants 300. Jokes with a friend, on his being made a Cardinal 302. Is not fond of the honours paid him 303. His fears on account of a dispute between Rome and the house of Bourbon 305. His sentiments on the affair of the Jesuits 309. His remonstrances to a Religious man, who had quitted his Convent, &c. 315. His Letter to a Guardian in favour of a Lay-brother 316. Exhorts an Abbé to read the Fathers, 319. Loves discretion 323. Blames a Gentleman for oppressing his tenants 326. His reasoning on Religion 328. His Letter to an English Nobleman on Religion 328. Complains of those who dare not speak to the Pope, on the affair of the Jesuits 338. Other reflections on the affair of Parma, and that of the Jesuits in a letter to an Embassador 344. Speaks to the Pope on those affairs, but to no purpose 346. Fears a schism 348. His thoughts on the complaints of the Sovereigns and the fate of the Jesuits 349. Hopes the Pope will acquiesce in the desires of the house of Bourbon 366. Enters the Conclave 369. Is chosen Pope 370. His sentiments on his Exaltation ib. Informs himself of affairs 371. Labours to bring about a reconciliation with Portugal in a Letter to a Nobleman of that country ib. Declares his impartiality with regard to the affair of the Jesuits 372. His Encyclical letter 399. His Discourse in a secret Consistory on the reconciliation with Portugal 404. His Bull for the Jubilee 407. His Elogium 413.

Genesis (the book of) whatever departs from it, grounded only on paradoxes or suppositions — — — 217
Genoa, its Port, Churches, and Doge — — 17
Gerdil (Father) a learned Bernabite — — 114
Genori (Count) a Letter to him — — 263
Gentili (Card.) a Letter to him — — 17
Georgi (F.) an Eminent Augustinian — 296
Germans have the proper qualities for friendship — — 157
Gersen, Abbot of Vercelli, Author of the *Imitation of Christ* 114
God, how always to be spoken of 166. What to be avoided in the schools in speaking of him ib. His Agency on us points out a providence 336. Does not perform miracles every time he is asked

asked 350. Government (The Ecclesiastical) his judgment on it 143. Too mild a government, dangerous to the state 272.
Gospel, the rule of a Christian 2. An Elogium on it 112
Grace and Freewill, moderation to be observed on that subject 165
Great ones, the greatest part lost by prepossession — 266
Gregorio Leti censured — — — — 272
Guadagni (Card.) — — — — 218
Gustavus, a Conqueror — — — — 227

H

Happiness, in what it consists — — 171
Heart (The) what tends to the reformation of it not generally liked — — — — 153
Henriquez (Monseigneur) a Letter to him — 70
Herculaneum swallowed up — — 14
History, the only good friend of Kings 145. What it may be compared ib. How to be studied 191. Its advantages 256
——— Natural less studied than Antiquity — 264
Humanity, a fine word substituted by our modern Philosophers in lieu of Charity — — — 145
Humility, what it teaches — — — 396

I

Ignatius (St.) did not foresee the disturbances to be raised one day about his Children 343. What he begged of God for them ib.
Imagination, the mother of dreams — — 270
Imitation of Christ. See Gersen. The Elogium of that book 114
Jerome (St.) his character — — 320
Jesuits (The) what sciences they have cultivated with success 218
——— (Their General) what ought to have been his Behaviour, in order to save the society 345. Would not follow the advice given him by the General of the Carmelite Friars 346
Jesus Christ, the key of all the Mysteries of Grace and Nature 334 Men bewilder themselves in a thousand absurd systems, when they have not him for their compass ib. Why called Alpha and Omega ib.
Innocent XI. (Pope) what he said of the Benedictin Monks 23
Inspiration, pretenders to it will not yield to circumstances 310
Job, the beauty of his reflections — — 109
Journal (A) of all the publications of Europe, what is learned by one — — — — 208
Journalist (A) the qualities required in one 183. Ought not to criticize with too much severity ib.
Islands (The Borromean) the beauties of them — 17
Italians, their manners 18. Their love for the sciences ib. The stamp of their Genius lightness 200. Do not write History well 256.
Italy, every man of learning owes homage to it 7. A short description of it ib. What the Government there is most taken up with 8. Presents whatever can exercise the curiosity of the naturalists 264.

K

Kronech (Baron) a letter to him — — 156

L

L⁎⁎⁎ (Abbé) a letter to him — — — 167
Lamballe (Father) a letter to him — — 375

GENERAL INDEX.

Lami (Abbé) Letters to him 46, 75, 154, 183, 206, 255, 284, 288
Lances (Card. des) his Elogy — — — 184
Lano (Marquis of) praised by Clement XIV. — 402
Law (The ancient) only a figure of Jesus Christ — 41
Lay-brother, a letter to one — — — 315
Le Dante, a saying of his — — — 47
Learned (The) ought to set an Example of moderation 252
Leghorn, its port — — — 16
Leibnitz, a Mathematician. See *Theodicea*
Lewis XIV. or the Great. A Conqueror — 227
——— XV. Letters to him 387, 392, 393. Discourse on his death 398
——— XVI. his piety and zeal for Religion — 406
Lewis of *Cremona* (Father) a letter to him — 108
Libels and Satires affect only weak brains — — 266
Literature more exposed to squabbles than the Sciences 253. Difference between it and profound Learning ib.
Lock transl. by a Venetian Lady 104. A passage in him censured 105
Lord***, a letter to, — — — 328
Loretto a famous Pilgrimage — — — 9
Louisa (Madame of France) Letters to her — 389, 394
Luciardi (Father) a letter to him — — — 260
Lucretius, believes matter eternal — — 217
Luxury corrupts writings as well as manners — 128

M

Mabillon (Father) had the advantage of Abbé *Rancé* in the dispute about Monastic Studies — — — 4
Madame ***, a letter to — — — 32
Malta (The Order of) how a man may sanctify himself in that state of life — — — 2
Man, every one in office has his enemies — — 266
Martinelli (Father) commended — — 279
Marzoni (Father) commended — — ib.
Massoleni (Father) an Author — — 137
Mathematics (The) Advantages of those Sciences — 148
Maupertuis, a man of abilities — — 46
Medicis (The family of the) what they did for the Arts and Sciences, an interesting part of the History of Tuscany — 258
Mekner (M.) A Protestant Gentleman, a letter to him 211
Melancholy, why we are subject to it at certain times 134. How to free ourselves from it 135
Metaphysics (The) of the last century more useful than the ancient — — — 106
Milan, its Church 16. The Company found there ib. Its Library ib. Letter to a Prebendary of 203
Miracles (The testimony of) necessary for the canonization of Saints 287. Why they continue only for a time ib.
Modena (The city of) for what famed — — 16
Monasteries, from whence the relaxation in them is thought to proceed 3. Reflections on the occupations of those who live in them 4.
Monastery, A letter to an Abbess of a — — 72
Moses, his account of the creation overthrows all systems 217
Mountains, God's apparent predilection for them — 48
Monte-Cassino, a regular, tho' rich monastery 15. A letter to the Abbot 23.

Mont-

Mont-faucon (Father) the ornament of the Congregation of St.
    Maur — — — — — — 4
Muratori, his treatise on true devotion recommended 83. Author
    of the Annals of Italy 114. His relaxation after study 39. A Say-
    ing of his 153.

N

Naples, the Churches of 14. Its Environs ib. The character of
    its inhabitants, ib.
Nature, is nothing without God — — 210
Newton, what he said of an Astronomer and an Anatomist 47.
    Read and admired by Ganganelli 26. His character ib.
Nicolini (Abbè) Letters to him — — 59—228
Nivernois (Duke of) his fine qualities — — 159
Nocetti (Father) a Jesuit, his work on the Rain-bow commended 118

O

Opinions capable of overthrowing Religion every where spread 381
Orator, the medium he ought to follow in his Discourses 268
Orders (The Religious) neither indefectible nor infallible 347. Are
    auxiliary troops in the Church ib. Can be suppressed by the
    Pope alone 340. None in the fine ages of the Church 313. Not
    to be kept up in opposition to the Catholic Powers 348. Jus-
    tified against false imputations 96. All considered by Ganga-
    nelli as one family 136
Orsi (Father) Letter to him — — — 66
Oyeras (Count) commended — — 405
Osimo, a Letter to a Prebend of — — 39

P

Painter (A Letter to a) — — — 225
Panegyric, what that species of writing ought to be — 204
Papacy, the obligations of the — — — 288
Papi (Abbè) Letter to him — — — 223
Parma, the Theatre of that city 16. Letters of Clem. XIV to the
    Duke of, 400, 401
Paschal' Thoughts commended — — — — 114
Passionei (Card.) a Letter to him 117. His surprising Memory 65
Passions, to what they may be compared — — 27
Patriarchs (The ancient) observed the Law of Nature — 40
Paul (St.) the difficulty of making his Panegyric 103. His cha-
    racter 105, &c.
Petrarch, the Italians want him to shew the true way to Par-
    nassus 184
Pharisees, how found in all ages — — — 153
Philosophers (the modern) why they reject Revelation 146. Are
    not what they pretend to be ib. Impose on the public ib. See
    Letters 82 and 119
Philosophy, its inconveniences 116. Ought to be joined with
    Geometry 150. Feels the impressions of the imagination 169
——— (scholastic), the ancient, its Ergotisms seem to render the
    most certain truths problematical — — 161
Physician, Letters to a — — 248, 252
Pigliani (Lady) a Letter to her — — 139
Pisa (The City of) why famous — — 16
Plato, his Elogy — — — 106
Pliny, M. *Aurelius*, and *Seneca* commended — 115

Poets,

GENERAL INDEX.

Poets, the difference between the Italian, English, German and French 154. The fault of our modern ones ib. What they ought to observe in their poems ib. In what the danger of being too fond of the Poets consists 190
Poetry, perfects languages — — — 190
Poland, the great men it has produced 175. The wars have made their Authors miscarry ib.
Poles, (The) insensibly loose their national spirit — 227
Policy, the different effects of a worldly, and Christian 230. In what found Policy consists ib, &c. That of Rome 233
Politician (A) what he ought to know 231. How he is to behave towards people — — — — 232
Pontalti, his advice to the General of the Jesuits — . 345
Portici what found there — — — 14
Porte-Corvo restored to the Holy See — 401
Porto-Carrero, what he said of the Prelate Cerati — 31
Prayers (vocal) constitute not the merit of Prayer — 2
Preacher (A) the qualities he ought to have 108. What he ought to avoid ib.
Preachers (Italian) their fault — — — 108
Preceptor, the necessary qualities of one 188. How treated by some Fathers ib.
Prince (A sovereign) the weaker he is, the more despotic his government, and why — — — 290
——— (A at the head of a great kingdom) the snares which surround him — — — — — 144
Protestant (Minister) a Letter to one — 299
Protestants, in what they went too far 213. What they falsely object to the Church of Rome 213, &c. Stopped by worldly interest 214. Have broken the chain which united them to the Centre of Unity ib. Are as many Sects as different Communions ib.
Provincial, Letter to a one — — — 87
Prussia (the King of) what will be the History of his reign — 44
Psalms (The) surpass in sublimity all other pieces of Poetry 113

Q

Querini (Card) Letters to him 63, 101, 160, 200. His death and Elogium 223

R

Rancé (Abbé) See Mabillon.
Raphael and Michel-Angelo, their Master-pieces of workmanship in the Vatican — — — — 10
Ravenna, a Letter to a Gentleman of — — — 63
Reason (without faith) digs precipices for itself — — 219
Relicks (of Saints,) two shelves to be avoided with regard to them — — — — — 98
Religion, why people suffer themselves to be dazzled with the sophisms brought against it by modern Philosophers 27. The false judgments of men respecting it 28. Its first temple on earth 39. Alone forms adorers in spirit and truth 40. It changed the face of the world, and how, ib. The best way for young Theologians to study it 169. The advantage young people reap from the study of it by principles 187 The proofs of it perfectly laid open in some immortal works 334. Will persuade all those, who have principles to go on 330. Most men make it bend to their prejudices 340.

Rhetoric,

Rhetoric, to be taught more by examples, than precepts — 191
Rimini, a Letter to a Parish of the Diocese of — — 209
Revelation puts us in the right road — — — — 26
Rezzonico (Card.) chosen Pope, and takes the name of Clement XIII 188. The character of his Nephews 368.
Romans (the modern) their character 13. Are not the majestic people they formerly were 200
Rome, a description of it 9. The Basilic of St. Peter there 10. Supports a number of Beggars 12. Difference between ancient and modern 191
——— (Court of) owes all its riches to France — — 350
Rota (Monsignor) Letter to him ——— ——— ——— 142
R***, the Marchioness, a Letter to her ——— ——— 91

S

Sagri, Ganganelli's reflections on occasion of that young man 199
San-Marino, Letter to the Gonfalonier of ——— ——— 143
San-Severo (Prince) Letters to him — — — 86—168
Schism, fatal to souls — — — — — 347
Sciences (The) are to the mind, what food is to the body 190
Scipio Maffei (Marquis) Letter to him ——— ——— 119
Sienna (City of) for what remarkable ——— ——— 16
Sigismond (Father) General of the Capuchins, a letter to him 103
Sextus-Quintus, vindicated ——— ——— — 271
Sobieski, see Poland
Somascha, a Letter to a Religious of that congregation 280
Sovereign (A) many reasons requisite to condemn one 209
Sovereign (Princes) can keep in, or expel their territories whom they please
Spinelli (Card) a letter to him ——— ——— ——— 152
Spoletta, a Letter to the Bishop of ——— ——— 98
Stuart (Mr.) Letters to him ——— ——— 25—230
Superior (A) of Religious Communities, his duties 121. The necessary qualities he ought to have 120
Superfluous (What is) belongs to the poor — — 327

T

Teresa (St.) her Elogium — . — — — — 49
Theodices (the) of Leibnitz could not have been written by him unless he had been a Mathematician 148
Theology, on the study of, Letter 66
Thierry (Mr.) Physician to the late Chevalier de St. George, his opinion of Coffee — — — — — 298
Tissot (Monsf.) Superior of the Priests of the Mission — 296
Tivoli, the beauty of its cascade ——— .— — 7
Trappe (la) a house of that order in Italy, as regular as that in France — ——— ——— ——— — 1
Travelling, enlarges the soul — — — — 202
Truth, the Book entitled *A Search after*; could not be written but by a Mathematician 148. How a person is to act, who wants to see it clearly 362
———The one Catholic, by what alone solidly proved 161
Tuscany, the Restauratrix of sciences 127. The history of it a fine subject to treat of — — — — 255

Valenti

V

Valenti (Card.) a Letter to him 50. Secretary to Benedict XIV 289
Vatican, what to be seen there — — — 10
Venice (City of) a description of it — — — 8
Vesuvius (Mount) its eruptions — — — 24
Virgil, his tomb 13. No less eloquent than Cicero 190
Voltaire, one of the great men at Potsdam 46. Must lament the death of Card. *Querini*, if Poets be susceptible of friendship 214
Universe (The) a Riddle without Religion — — 28

W

Wesler (Mr.) kindly entertained by P. San-Severo — 86

Y

York (Card. of) commended — — — — 324

Z

Zaluski ——— A Letter to him — — — 74

ERRATA.

Page 157 line 27 For BUYERE read BAUERE.
175 — For Referendary read Referendary.
201 21 For Char. read Car.
212 23 For interrupted read uninterrupted.
331 note For Cognoscam read Cognoscam.

www.ingramcontent.com/pod-product-compliance
Lightning Source LLC
Chambersburg PA
CBHW030543300426
44111CB00009B/838